Praise for
BORN TO KILL

Aquiles Jacas

ABOUT THE AUTHOR

T. J. ENGLISH is a noted journalist and screenwriter, and is the author of *Havana Nocturne*, *Paddy Whacked*, and *The Westies*, all national best-sellers. He has written for *Esquire*, *Playboy*, and *New York* magazine, among other publications. His screenwriting credits include episodes for the television crime dramas *NYPD Blue* and *Homicide*, for which he was awarded the Humanitas Prize. He lives in New York City.

Born to Kill

Also by T. J. English

Havana Nocturne
Paddy Whacked
The Westies

HARPER

NEW YORK . LONDON . TORONTO . SYDNEY

Born to Kill

The Rise
and Fall of America's
Bloodiest
Asian Gang

T. J. English

HARPER

A hardcover edition of this book was published in 1995 by William Morrow and Company, Inc.

HarperCollins books may be purchased for educational, business, or sales promotional use. For information please write: Special Markets Department, HarperCollins Publishers, 10 East 53rd Street, New York, NY 10022.

FIRST HARPER PAPERBACK PUBLISHED 2009.

Designed by Cheryl L. Cipriani

The Library of Congress has catalogued the hardcover edition as follows:
English, T. J., 1957–
    Born to kill : America's most notorious Vietnamese gang, and the changing face of organized crime / T. J. English.
        p. cm.
    Includes bibliographical references.
    ISBN 0-688-12238-8
    1. Born to Kill (Gang) 2. Gangs—United States. 3. Gangs—
New York (N.Y.) 4. Vietnamese American criminals. I. Title
HV6439.U5E54   1995
364.1'06'0899592073–dc20   94-21474

ISBN 978-0-06-178238-1 (pbk.)

09 10 11 12 13   JPS/RRD   10 9 8 7 6 5 4 3 2 1

For Steven Wong,

my *dai low*

Acknowledgments

One of the great myths about Chinatown is that it is a "closed society" where an attitude of insularity makes it impossible for the truth to be told. In fact, this book could not have been written were it not for the generous cooperation of numerous Asian and Asian American citizens, both within Chinatown and beyond. For opening doors and offering insights into their respective communities, I owe a special debt of gratitude to Shiauh-Wei Lin, Alex Peng, Cambao de Duong, Virgo Lee, Ying Jing Gan, Odum Lim, Kim Lee Lim, and many others who, unfortunately, cannot be identified by name due to the very real threat of gang retribution.

To Tinh Ngo, I offer a heartfelt *cam on* for agreeing to share painful memories and observations at great length in various far-flung locations. This book, in many ways, is a testament to Tinh Ngo's efforts to turn his unusually tumultuous life around.

Many people at differing levels of law enforcement were unselfish with their time and expertise. Special thanks to Detective Sergeant Vincent Klebaur of the Linden Police Department, Linden, New Jersey; Lieutenant George Damanski of the Hudson County prosecutor's office, Jersey City, New Jersey; Mark Peterkin, formerly with the Hudson County prosecutor's office, now with the Bureau of Alcohol, Tobacco and Firearms; Sergeant Aida Remele of the Bridgeport Police Department, Bridgeport, Connecticut; Captain Cliff Edwards of the Doraville Police Department, Doraville, Georgia; Lieutenant Joseph Pollini, Detective Sergeant Douglas Lee, and Detective Alex Sabo of the New York Police Department's Major Case Squad; special agents John O'Brien, Joe Greco, John DiAngelo, Don Tisdale, Dan Kumor, and Albert Trinh from the U.S. Treasury's Bureau of Alcohol, Tobacco and Firearms.

Assistant U.S. Attorney Alan Vinegrad from the Eastern District of New York was a great help, as was Luke Rettler, head of the Manhattan District Attorney's Asian Gang Unit, formerly known as the "Jade Squad."

Others to whom I am grateful for their assistance include Phil Hannum of the International Association of Asian Crime Investigators in Falls Church, Virginia; Virgo Lee, the former Director of Asian Affairs for the City of New York; attorney James Meyerson; Lisa Wager; Peg Tyre of *Newsday;* attorney Dave Secular; and, most especially, attorneys Michael Grossman and Thomas White.

Michael McNickle, a friend and associate, helped with the investigative work and spent long hours mulling over the difficulties involved in telling the story. Frank Kuznik, a friend and mentor ever since he first taught me journalism in high school, read an early draft of the manuscript and, as always, offered invaluable suggestions.

I am also indebted to Barbara Lowenstein, my agent, to my editor, Paul Bresnick, who guided the manuscript through troubled waters, and to Suzanne English, my mother, for reasons too numerous to mention.

CONTENTS

By the time young Tinh Ngo arrived for the funeral of his fallen gang brother, the mourners had already spilled out into the street. In front of the Wah Wing Sang Funeral Home, six pallbearers hoisted a sleek beige casket to their shoulders, while nearby a handful of elderly musicians played a lethargic funeral dirge. Tinh adjusted his wraparound sunglasses and surveyed the crowd. It looked as if the entire gang had assembled. Blackeyes was there. So was Shadow Boy, Little Cobra, Monkey Man, and Teardrop.

On the morning of July 28, 1990, in the sweltering midday heat, Tinh and his fellow gang members were not hard to spot. To show their respect for the deceased, many wore white gloves, signifying purity and eternal life. Dressed in identical black linen suits, black shoes, black sunglasses, and sporting an assortment of spiked hairstyles typical of young Asian gangsters on the make, they were a sprawling mass of solemnity on an otherwise bright day.

Known to the others as "Tim" or "Timmy"—the anglicized version of his name—Tinh waded into the crowd, nodding to friends and acquaintances. At eighteen, Tinh was one of the gang's younger soldiers, and he always seemed to be lagging behind.

Tinh's appearance—barely five feet five inches tall, with soft features and jet-black hair sculpted into a stylish ducktail—made him nearly indistinguishable from the others. He had adopted the gang's patented look as an expression of kinship. In the five years since his arrival in the United States, Tinh had lived a lonely, rootless existence until he fell in with this wayward collection of youths whose long journey to America was similar to his.

As gangsters, theirs was a demanding life fraught with innumerable dangers. Even today, as they mourned the death of their fallen brother, Tinh and the others were engaged in a bloody turf war with rival criminals in New York City's Chinatown. In recent months, the sound of gunfire and wailing sirens had become an all-too-familiar neighborhood refrain. Young gangsters were gunned down in gambling parlors, restaurants, and on crowded street corners. Although the gunplay undoubtedly hurt the local tourist trade, business was booming at Wah Wing Sang and the other funeral parlors clustered among the old tenements, tailor shops, and warehouses along lower Mulberry Street.

Oblivious to traffic, Tinh and the others began their procession down the middle of the street toward the heart of Chinatown. With faces ranging from the innocent and angelic to those hardened well beyond their years, the mourners trailed behind the six pallbearers, who held the casket aloft with unwavering steadiness. The entourage walked past bustling seafood and produce stands, noodle factories, tea shops, video stores, and dozens of restaurants with large, sometimes garish signs.

The store owners and street merchants along Mulberry Street halted their morning duties and watched from stoops and shop windows. Normally, these citizens of Chinatown might have greeted the funeral procession with a well-rehearsed indifference. Over the decades they had seen the lives of far too many young males cut short because of their criminal affiliations. The gang funerals, with their showy air of importance and strutting displays of macho bravado, had become numbingly familiar.

But today's ceremony was different. For one thing, the deceased and most of the mourners were Vietnamese, relative newcomers to the community. These Vietnamese gangsters did not seem to respect the old ways. In recent months, they had violated Chinatown's arcane, honor-bound codes of behavior time and time again, and they had done so with a level of brazenness that was especially offensive to the community's more established residents.

As if to illustrate their youthful audacity, the gang members halted in the middle of Mulberry Street and unfurled a neatly lettered cloth banner. Emblazoned across the banner, in white lettering set against a black background, were the words: STAND BY BTK/CANAL BOYS. BTK stood for Born to Kill, the name of the gang. Canal Street was their main base of operation.

As the procession continued on, the mourners soon came under the watchful eye of a smattering of police detectives and uniformed cops. In recent months, the gangsters known as Born to Kill had achieved a special level of enmity among local lawmen. In the past, a tacit understanding had always existed between the cops and the community. Local leaders were allowed to handle local problems free of interference from the police, as long as the criminal activity was kept behind doors and out of the newspapers. Lately, the BTK had obliterated this understanding. The gang's criminal activities were getting out of hand, and their exploits had begun to get clamorous attention in the city's tabloid press.

At the corner of Mulberry and Bayard streets, an officer shook his head contemptuously and stepped forward, trying to pull the banner from one of the mourner's hands. There was a brief tussle; the cops and gangsters squared off in the middle of the intersection. Only after one of the gangsters folded up the banner did the policemen retreat.

"Fuck you!" a few of the gang members shouted at the cops in heavily accented English. Some used a gesture easily understood in any language: the extended middle finger. The older residents watched in dismay, shook their heads, and cursed this new breed of gangster who knew nothing of civility or respect.

Having wound their way through seven or eight of the most densely populated blocks in Chinatown, the pallbearers stopped at Canal Street, the neighborhood's main commercial thoroughfare. The casket was loaded into a waiting hearse, and the mourners piled into nearly two dozen nearby limousines. Once again, onlookers took notice as the gangsters made a grand display, driving slowly along Canal Street in a long caravan. The entourage continued west through the Holland Tunnel into New Jersey, where they eventually arrived at the Rosedale Memorial Park Cemetery in the town of Linden.

A mere thirty minutes by car from lower Manhattan, the Rosedale cemetery was a sprawling, immaculately landscaped burial ground. The roughly ninety acres that comprised the grounds were separated from a nearby highway by a chain-link fence. Inside, gently pitched green hills were layered with oak and sycamore trees, giving the cemetery an air of suburban grandeur. In recent years, Rosedale had become a popular resting place for prematurely deceased gang members, mostly of Chinese extraction.

Once inside the cemetery's cast-iron gates, the mourners were each given a single white carnation and a good-luck penny, which they were to toss into the open grave of their fallen gang brother. A metal garbage can next to the grave had been loaded with some of the deceased's personal belongings—including clothing—and set afire. When Tinh Ngo arrived and saw the flaming garbage can with gray smoke billowing toward the sky, he asked a fellow gang member, "Why the fire?"

"Timmy," answered the gang member, "don't you know anything? They burn our brother's clothes. This way, when he go to heaven or hell—wherever—he got something to wear."

Tinh nodded gravely. "Ahhhhh, yes. Of course," he replied.

Surveying the crowd from near the back, Tinh estimated the entourage had doubled in size since this morning. Now, roughly two hundred people had gathered, and they were assembled around a grave festooned with dozens of bouquets and wreaths. Nearby, incense burned in an urn in front of the casket, which was adorned with the same black-and-white BTK/CANAL BOYS banner that had earlier been paraded through Chinatown.

Tinh took in the scene with a sense of wonder. He knew one reason so many mourners had gathered was the popularity of the deceased, Vinh Vu, known to the gang as Amigo. At twenty-one, Amigo had been the gang's *dai low*, or "big brother," on Canal Street. Everyone knew and liked Amigo, who controlled his minions through guile and kindness rather than brute force. When Born to Kill angered rival gang factions in Chinatown, as they had often in recent months, Amigo's high esteem within the gang made him an attractive target.

Just three days earlier, Amigo had come out of a Canal Street massage parlor around 1:00 A.M. He was with another gang member and four female employees of the parlor at the time. A cab was flagged down. Seeing as there were too many people for one cab, Amigo let the girls go on ahead. While he and the fellow gang member waited for a second taxi, a car drove up. From the backseat, rival Chinese hitmen opened fire, their gun barrels spitting blue flames. Amigo's companion was shot twice but survived. Amigo tried to run; he was struck twice in the leg and twice in the chest, with one bullet piercing his heart, killing him instantly.

Amigo's death had stunned his gang brothers. Certainly, today's huge cemetery gathering was a manifestation of the grief they felt at his passing, but Tinh knew it was also more than that.

Since joining the gang thirteen months ago, Tinh had been impressed to hear more established members brag of criminal affiliations in the underworld that reached far beyond New York City. Many Born to Kill gangsters were outlaws on the run, and their far-flung exploits had led them to establish a national network of sorts.

For today's burial, gang members had traveled south from Canada and Massachusetts, north from Virginia and Georgia. Dozens came from the New York–New Jersey–Connecticut area. Tinh heard that the gang had received letters of condolence from as far west as Colorado and California.

Nearly everyone who made the pilgrimage to Rosedale Memorial Park Cemetery did so with at least one thing in common: their Vietnamese heritage. Born and reared in villages and hamlets in a country ravaged by war, they had survived refugee boats and border camps. Some were Amerasian, the half-American, half-Vietnamese children of American GIs who abandoned them during and after the war. Violently uprooted from their battered homeland, they now found themselves adrift in America, unwelcome reminders of an infamous conflict that had scarred the national soul. Those assembled today were representatives of this lost generation of Vietnamese youth. And the size of the gathering was a show of fellowship unlike anything most of them had ever experienced in America.

Tinh Ngo, for one, could not help but feel a near overwhelming sense of pride. And he knew they owed it all to one man: David Thai, known to the gathering as *Anh hai*. Literally, *anh hai* meant "number two brother." In Vietnamese families, *anh hai* was second only to the father; he was the wisest and most esteemed brother of all.

Standing at the head of the crowd, directly in front of Amigo's grave, David Thai exuded authority. At thirty-four, he was ten to fifteen years older than most of the gang's rank-and-file *sai lows*, or "little brothers." Where many young Vietnamese were awkward and unpolished in public, David was regal. His handsomeness and smooth demeanor were exceeded only by his seemingly genuine concern for the welfare of his gang brothers.

To Tinh, *Anh hai* was a prince. He and the others willingly entrusted their futures to David Thai. And they would continue to do so, no matter how many home invasions, bombings, cold-blooded killings, and other outrageous acts of mayhem he asked them to commit.

A soothing summer breeze rustled the treetops, sending the aroma of incense wafting through the cemetery. A crew of grounds keepers siphoned water from the open grave with a gas-powered pump, then readied the casket to be lowered into the earth.

"Who those people?" whispered Tinh, to no one in particular.

A number of nearby gang members looked to see what Tinh was talking about. In the distance, three young males approached, bearing flowers. They wore black sunglasses, just like everyone else, and long black overcoats that fluttered gracefully in the wind. Although they were not readily familiar to Tinh or the others, they were definitely Asian, perhaps Chinese-Vietnamese. Many of the mourners were themselves *Viet-Ching*—ethnic Chinese born in Vietnam—so this was no great cause for alarm.

These strangers, however, were unusually purposeful as they neared the crowd, walking in unison. When they got to within twenty feet of the mourners, they abruptly came to a halt.

Tinh was one of the first to dive for cover. He saw the lead stranger toss his bouquet of flowers aside. The other two seemed to throw theirs in the air. All three produced guns that glistened in the midday sun.

The harsh, staccato rhythms of automatic gunfire rang out, decimating the afternoon calm. At first, many in the crowd seemed to think it was fireworks, a common sound at Vietnamese and Chinese ceremonies. Then a couple of the mourners went down, struck by bullets. "Where's the gun!?" a gang member shouted. "Who fire!?" shouted another.

Utter pandemonium ensued, with people screaming and scurrying for cover. The leader of the grounds crew, a beefy African American, dove headfirst into Amigo's open grave. Many of the mourners crawled behind tombstones for protection. The gunmen used an Uzi submachine gun and a .12-gauge pump-action shotgun, spraying the gathering with no specific target in mind.

Tinh saw one of the mourners take a bullet in the hand; another was hit in the leg. A lone gang member pulled out a handgun and returned fire while fleeing through the cemetery, toppling tombstones. Later, the gang members would curse themselves for not having been properly armed, but who could have guessed rival gangsters would dare to seek retribution on such hallowed ground? Earlier, perhaps, on the already bloodstained streets of Chinatown, but not here, where even your worst enemies are supposed to have the right to peacefully bury their dead.

The sound of gunfire echoed sporadically through the cemetery. Peering from behind a small tombstone, Tinh saw one of the gunmen getting closer and closer. He knew he had to make a run for it.

Tinh fled past dozens of mourners lying on the ground, some who had been hit, some pretending they were dead, hoping the gunmen would pass them by. He snaked his way through rows of tombstones until he arrived at the chain-link fence, where more gang members were frantically trying to escape. Both male and female mourners clawed at the fence, tearing their clothes and lacerating their flesh on the sharp metal.

A few made it over, running along the shoulder of the highway to safety. Dozens more collapsed in the excitement and exhaustion of the moment. It seemed as if a good half hour had passed, but it was more like sixty seconds when the gunfire finally subsided, to be replaced by the sound of approaching sirens. In all the confusion, the gunmen vanished as mysteriously as they had arrived.

When Al Kroboth got there, the cops had already begun rounding up what was left of the mourners. A strapping six feet five inches tall,

Kroboth was the cemetery's head grounds keeper and director of security. He was also a veteran of the Vietnam War. For nearly three years Kroboth had traversed the jungles and rice fields of Indochina. He'd seen plenty of combat and eventually spent fifteen months in a cage as a prisoner of the North Vietnamese.

Kroboth surveyed the damage: A medevac helicopter had landed in the middle of the cemetery, and the injured were being loaded on stretchers to be taken to a nearby hospital in Newark that specialized in gunshot wounds. Seven people had been hit, dozens more trampled while fleeing the barrage of gunfire or badly cut while attempting to scale the metal fence. Medical personnel and local police tended to the others—one hundred or so young Vietnamese still traumatized by the sudden fury of the attack. As the chopper drifted skyward and the remaining wounded moaned in pain, Kroboth couldn't help but be reminded of battlefields he'd seen a long time ago, in a country most of these mourners called home.

At the Linden police station, New Jersey cops struggled to understand what were, to them, nearly indecipherable accents and names, though most of the names were probably fictitious anyway. Of the nearly one hundred mourners brought in for questioning—including Tinh Ngo—only two carried identification. The cops scratched their heads and made phone calls, trying to find out whatever they could about a group of gangsters they hadn't even known existed until today.

In the days that followed, the cemetery shootout would become a popular news item, receiving fervid coverage locally and in the national media. Since the perpetrators were not yet known, accounts tended to focus on the targets of the shooting: the Vietnamese. Few journalists could resist the angle that these gangsters, born in a country brutalized by a shameful war, appeared to respect no one—not even the dead. Forevermore, the shooting at Rosedale Memorial Park Cemetery would be remembered as a defining event, the moment at which the idea of Vietnamese gangsters in America entered the national consciousness.

Truth was, the problem had been brewing for some time. Across America, the face of organized crime was changing, and the old-world courtesies of the past no longer applied. The underworld was now an ethnic polyglot, with a new generation of gangsters taking over where the Irish, the Jews, and the Italians left off. Only now, a new ingredient had been added to the melting pot: a nihilistic, unconscionable type of violence that harked back to a dark, troubling era in American history. An era when U.S. soldiers stormed hamlets and bamboo huts in places like Danang, Khe San, and Nha Trang while terrified, wide-eyed children cowered in dark corners.

To those throughout mainstream America who took the time to acknowledge what was happening, it was as if their worst fears were being realized. U.S. foreign policy had come home to roost, and the untidy residue of the Vietnam War had taken on yet another ugly, unexpected permutation.

For Tinh Ngo and the others who had become identified with the gang known as Born to Kill, the consequences were even more immediate. For years, they had struggled to survive, to find their place within a society that did not seem to want them. For a time they drifted aimlessly, like small sampans on a large, turbulent ocean. Eventually, they banded together in cities and small towns throughout the United States, and they had begun to pursue their own unique version of the American dream.

Theirs was a brotherhood born of trauma, sealed in bloodshed. A brotherhood that had first begun to coalesce many months earlier in the bustling restaurants, pool halls, and back alleys of New York City's Chinatown.

PART ONE

The Gang

When men lack a sense of awe,
there will be disaster.

—LAO-TZU
The Tao-te Ching
(sixth century B.C.)

Chapter 1

The group of five young males stood in the dingy second-floor hallway of an old industrial building, banging on a door.

"Who's there?" asked a middle-aged woman on the other side.

"It's me, Tommy. Tommy Vu," answered one of them. Behind him, the others waited anxiously, puffing on cigarettes, staring at the floor.

The woman looked through a peephole, then slid back the latch on the door's cast-iron, dead-bolt lock. When she opened the door, a pale golden light from the hallway streamed into the front room of her small, unadorned massage parlor.

Tommy Vu entered, followed by the other youths. All were in their late teens or early twenties. Dressed mostly in black, with assorted punk hairstyles and glaring tattoos, they swaggered and blew streams of cigarette smoke in the air, exhibiting the general demeanor of bad boys on the prowl. Normally, the woman—an experienced madam—would have been worried at opening the door to a handful of such raffish youths. It *was* one o'clock in the morning, and it wouldn't have been the first time her establishment—located at 59 Chrystie Street on the outskirts of Chinatown—was robbed by gangsters. But the woman recognized Tommy. Many times he had come to her massage parlor as a customer and enjoyed the ministrations of her stable of young females.

Seated around the room on an upholstered sofa and matching chair, a half dozen smooth-skinned Korean and Malaysian ladies looked expectantly toward the young men. A few of the women straightened their tight-fitting dresses and sought to catch the boys' attention with shy smiles and coquettish glances. Tommy and his companions seemed preoccupied, and they avoided eye contact.

A security person stepped forward—a Chinese male in his thirties. "Hey, these guys look kind of young." Turning to Tommy, he asked, "You got some ID?"

Tommy sniffled. "Yeah. This my ID." He pulled a 9mm from inside his jacket and stuck it in the guy's face.

With that, all hell broke loose.

"Get down! Everybody! On the floor!" shouted Blackeyes, the tallest of the group, immediately assuming the role of leader.

"Cooperate!" commanded Kenny Vu, Tommy Vu's brother. "Cooperate or we will kill you." All five of the young hoodlums waved handguns in the air.

The girls immediately dropped to the floor. The security guy also lay flat on his belly. Blackeyes instructed Tommy Vu, Kenny Vu, and a member of the crew named Andy to check the back rooms. Then he turned to Tinh Ngo, who seemed to be almost cowering in the background. "Timmy, you check basement. See who down there," he ordered.

Holding a .22-caliber pistol, his face moist with perspiration, Tinh didn't even try to hide his nervousness. This was his first armed robbery, and as the others began rounding up the employees and customers, he froze in his tracks.

"*Go!*" barked Blackeyes.

Tinh headed out the front door and down the hallway to the rear of the building. He descended a set of steep, rickety stairs, not knowing what to expect, his gun pointed straight ahead.

He had already convinced himself that if the occasion arose, he would try not to shoot anybody. Tinh hadn't had much experience with guns. In recent months, he had carried a weapon during numerous muggings of people in subway stations, but mostly just for show. Often the gun wasn't even loaded. In his apartment, he would stand in front of a mirror, whip out a gun, and pull the trigger, just like in the old movie Westerns. But he had never actually fired a loaded weapon, much less into the body of a living human being.

He was told not to worry. Blackeyes and the others had robbed many massage parlors before. "We just go in, take the money, say bye-bye," Blackeyes explained.

Robbing a massage parlor wasn't like robbing a legitimate establishment. Thinly veiled houses of prostitution, the parlors were big juicy chickens just waiting to be plucked. There was always plenty of loose cash on the premises. And since it was an illegal business, the owners weren't likely to call the police and file a report. About the only thing you needed to worry about was the possibility that the parlor was under the protection of a rival gang, in which case there were likely to be armed security guys hidden somewhere on the premises.

Tinh crept slowly down the dank basement hallway. From somewhere, he could hear the sound of a television playing a Chinese-language program. He came to an open doorway and peered inside. A man stood facing the TV. At roughly six feet tall, he looked like a giant to Tinh, who was short and small-boned and had a blank, wide-eyed face that made him look about fourteen, though he was actually three years older than that.

Sensing trouble, the man's head turned; his and Tinh's eyes met.

Without hesitation, Tinh ran, darting down the hallway, up the stairs, and back into the massage parlor. "Blackeyes," he gasped, still winded from the run, "somebody down there. Big Chinese guy."

"Yeah?" said Blackeyes. "Okay, I take care of it. You help the others."

Tommy, Kenny, and Andy had already gathered the employees and patrons in the front room. With Tinh's assistance, they began taking the girls one by one to the small massage rooms that lined a back hallway, forcing them to produce cash, jewelry, and other hidden valuables. Tinh noticed his companions were waving their guns around, cursing and treating the girls roughly.

"Move, bitch!" Tinh shouted, imitating the others. "Give us the money!" He saw the fear in the girls' faces and felt the pure adrenaline rush of doing something dangerous, something he knew was wrong. It reminded him of the terror that had been wrought by robbers and rapists on the refugee boats during his long, horrific voyage out of Vietnam. Tinh's heart beat fast and the hair on the back of his neck tingled. For a change, he knew what it felt like to be the one instilling fear rather than recoiling in its wake.

Blackeyes brought the Chinese guy up from the basement and made him lie down with the others. The money and jewelry had been dumped on a coffee table in the front room. Kenny Vu stashed the loot into a pillow case and shouted, "Let's go!"

Abruptly, Tommy Vu ripped the telephone off the wall; chips of paint and plaster rained down on the terrified employees spread out on the floor.

The boys scurried down the stairs and out into the night, where a car and driver were waiting—not a getaway car or even a driver they knew. These young gangsters had merely called a car service. The driver, an oblivious Hispanic male, had driven them to the massage parlor and waited, just like they requested.

Blackeyes directed the driver to a hotel far in the outer reaches of Brooklyn, where the boys checked into a room and immediately dumped the loot out on a bed. There wasn't much jewelry, but they counted more cash than they expected, approximately $30,000, mostly in small bills. "Just think," Blackeyes remarked, "I work five years and couldn't even save five hundred dollars. Here only fifteen minutes we make thirty thousand."

The others smiled knowingly.

To Tinh, the robbery seemed so incredibly easy. If he hadn't known better, he might have thought everyone was in on it—the madam, the girls, everyone. It was almost as if it were a preset scheme with rules that had been agreed on beforehand. Later, the others explained it to Tinh. "That's just Chinatown," said Kenny. Robberies happened all the time; store owners and businesspeople knew the routine.

As a newcomer to the underworld, there was a lot Tinh didn't know. He often relied on Kenny, Blackeyes, and the others to fill him in, not just about life as a gangster, but about life in general in New York City.

It was late May 1989, and the others had been committing crimes for months. Most of the time, Blackeyes would choose the target. Sometimes Kenny, Tommy, or a handful of others would venture out on their own, but only after clearing things with their bosses.

Tinh was only vaguely aware of the hierarchy. He knew there was a collection of slightly older gangsters who called the shots for a vast coterie of young Vietnamese males spread throughout much of the city. He was told this gang of criminals called themselves Born to Kill, or BTK for short, and they were fast becoming one of the most feared gangs in the city's Asian community. Some of the gang's members had criminal experience, but many did not. Like Tinh, they were expected to watch and learn as they went along.

In the days following the massage-parlor robbery on Chrystie Street, Tinh's companions often poked fun at him. "Timmy, we thought maybe you piss your pants," joked Blackeyes, referring to the fear in Tinh's eyes when he encountered the Chinese security guy in the basement. Really, though, they were pleased. Tinh had not panicked or done anything stupid, and the robbery had netted a better than average take. As a result, Tinh's stature within the group grew; he could now consider himself one of a legion of young gangsters who committed crimes under the BTK banner. Most likely, he would be invited along on future undertakings.

They would not all be so easy, he was warned. Ripping off massage parlors was one thing, but robbing jewelry stores, restaurants, and people's homes often brought unexpected results. "Sometimes things go bad," said Kenny Vu. "Sometimes, people—they get shot."

The prospect of danger was both frightening and exciting to Tinh. With his small, delicate frame, no one had ever mistaken Tinh for a tough guy. Like most refugees, he had learned to communicate mostly through his eyes, doelike brown orbs that opened wide with fear, wonder, and amazement. Even to the other gang members, most of whom were barely out of adolescence, Tinh seemed innocent and naive. But underneath this facade of unformed virginal acquiescence, Tinh Ngo possessed the soul of a survivor. Already, as a child of war and an exile, he had weathered more than his fill of terror and trauma—an inheritance he shared in common with Blackeyes, Tommy Vu, and all the rest.

In fact, given all that he and his companions had endured, Tinh couldn't help but feel that his arrival as a budding member of the Born to Kill gang was a product of fate. What else could it be but the natural consequence of a grand, cataclysmic journey. A journey that began long ago, before the camps, before the refugee boats, in the bombed-out rice paddies and bamboo groves of his home country of Vietnam.

In 1972, the year Tinh Ngo left his mother's womb, the war in Indochina had reached its most crucial phase. After eight years of unremitting horror, North Vietnamese and U.S. negotiators had finally been forced to the bargaining table. President Richard M. Nixon had reduced the number of soldiers in Vietnam, but he had also increased the frequency of bombing raids, especially in the North. Around Hanoi and Haiphong, napalm rained down from the heavens, tracers lit up the night sky, and the rumble of approaching B-52s was more common than the rooster's call at dawn.

Tinh was born in the South, in the province of Hau Giang, on April 7. The tenth of eleven children, he was fortunate to have been born too late to have any firsthand experience of the war that raged around him. Others in his village were not so lucky. At the time of Tinh's birth, Communist forces from the North had made great inroads into the Mekong Delta, the bountiful agricultural region that encompassed much of Hau Giang. On the outskirts of Can Tho, where Tinh's family lived, soldiers from the North patrolled dusty streets with the arrogance of a conquering army, which they were soon to become.

Tinh's parents were Chinese-born merchants who owned a small pharmacy, which put them in a better financial position than many in Hau Giang. Mostly, the province was inhabited by rural peasants whose dependence on the land for their livelihood meant they would pay the highest price of all. From 1962 to 1970, U.S. forces periodically strafed the delta with Agent Orange, a highly toxic defoliant known to be injurious to humans. By the time of the American evacuation of Saigon and the official end to the war in April 1975, much of the Mekong Delta had been blasted and burned beyond recognition.

As a young boy growing up in South Vietnam in the late 1970s, Tinh was cheerfully oblivious to the war's legacy of violence and devastation. At the time, it seemed perfectly normal to swim in huge bomb craters filled with rainwater. There was nothing odd to Tinh about seeing the carcasses of charred U.S. helicopters and trucks dotting the landscape, or sandbags piled high along the roads. These were the everyday sights of postwar Vietnam, the only world young Tinh knew.

For his parents, however, the turmoil and uncertainty of life under the country's new regime made it seem as if the war had never ended. Drunk with victory, the government had proclaimed Vietnam "the outpost of socialism in Southeast Asia" and rigidly aligned itself with the Soviet Union. American aid, which had artificially bolstered the South Vietnamese economy since the early 1950s, ceased overnight. Inflation skyrocketed, and stores were bereft of basic consumer items. Rice, once the most plentiful commodity in all of Vietnam, was now rationed monthly at state-run rice shops.

Along with the collapse of the country's economy, Vietnam could not escape the continuing ravages of war. In 1978, in reaction to the murderous reign of the Khmer Rouge, Vietnam invaded neighboring Cambodia. In response, China invaded Vietnam from the North. For a time, the country had two wars raging at once, with thousands of young males being conscripted into the military, where they were slaughtered at a terrifying rate.

By 1983, Tinh Ngo's parents surveyed the situation in their homeland and reached an indisputable conclusion: Vietnam was no place to raise a child. They had a family friend who had made his way to California and sent back photographs, glorious full-color snapshots of enormous homes and golden landscapes. If they could get Tinh to a refugee camp in a border country, there was a reasonable chance he would be sponsored by a resettlement agency and sent to the States, where he too might experience the magnificence of American prosperity.

Even with the country's seemingly intractable problems, the decision to cast off their child was a torturous one for Tinh's parents. The Confucian ethic and Vietnamese tradition say that offspring must look after parents when they grow old, and the only real social security that anyone had in Vietnam was the family. But Tinh's parents were both in their sixties. Realistically, they knew there was no future for them in Vietnam—nor would there be for their son if he remained.

On the drive to the refugee boats in Cau Mau, eleven-year-old

19

Tinh cried and cried. As a young schoolboy living through the prime of his childhood, Tinh could not understand the concerns that led his parents to conclude he would be better off someplace else. There had always been rice on the table, a bamboo bed to sleep on, and clothing passed down from one sibling to the next. What could be the problem? he asked. His parent's response that there was no future in Vietnam had not satisfied young Tinh, and he felt cruelly abandoned.

At Cau Mau, on the southern peninsula of the delta, the banks of the Ganh Hao River were packed with refugees. In recent years, Cau Mau had become the favored embarkation point for ethnic Chinese, a minority whom the Vietnamese government had never trusted, fearing they might become a fifth column for Beijing. Many *Viet-Ching* had been expelled in the late 1970s as "boat people" and perished at sea. Now they paid gold to underworld figures to help them flee by arranging illegal shipments of human cargo.

Tinh's parents had made arrangements for him to travel with his oldest sister's husband, whom Tinh knew as Kha Manh. Kha Manh had just spent eight years in a Vietnamese prison camp for the sole offense of having served as an interpreter for the American military during the war. He was thirty-eight years old, spoke good English, and it was believed he would be a wise, able-bodied protector for his young nephew.

As Tinh and Kha Manh prepared to embark, the Ngo family was startled to hear that young Tinh, in fact, would be traveling separately from his brother-in-law. Apparently, the plans had been altered at the last minute. Now, two small vessels, each packed with some thirty people, were to follow a large mother ship through the delta and out to sea. Tinh would be on one vessel, Kha Manh on the other. Both ships were destined for Malaysia, where the castaways planned to throw themselves on the mercy of the refugee camps.

As a surly navigator hollered instructions and rounded up the refugees, Tinh's mother wept and embraced her son. "My child," she explained, "I know you do not understand. But someday you will. And you will realize that what we have done is for the best."

Tinh cried uncontrollably and his nose dripped like a leaky faucet. Standing in the mud on the banks of the river, he waved good-bye to his parents, then disappeared into the crowd of refugees fighting their way onto the boats they hoped would carry them to some faraway world of peace and opportunity.

It didn't take long for Tinh's boat to run into trouble. At the mouth of the Ganh Hao River, after a one-hour voyage through the eerie U Minh forest, both Tinh's and his brother-in-law's boats were stopped by a Vietnamese military patrol vessel. Soldiers stormed onto the boats with guns and began demanding gold and other valuables. When one of the refugees resisted, he was abruptly smacked across the face with the butt of a rifle.

Refugees from both boats were loaded onto the military vessel, stripped naked, and searched. Soldiers turned the contents of the refugee boats upside down looking for precious commodities. By the time the soldiers allowed the refugees to dress and reboard their boats, the mother ship was nowhere in sight.

"You will return to your point of origin," a soldier ordered the navigators of both boats, "or you will perish at sea." The soldiers then drained gasoline from the refugee boats, leaving just enough for the return to Cau Mau.

After the military patrol vessel had safely disappeared, the refugees elected to push on. The two seventy-foot wooden cargo boats powered by truck engines chugged slowly toward the South China Sea, the passengers packed so tightly they were unable to lie down.

Dressed only in shorts, sandals, and a T-shirt, Tinh couldn't help but feel his young life might be nearing a premature end. What few belongings he had were on the other boat with Kha Manh. Feeling destitute and frightened, he cursed his parents once again for throwing him to the sharks.

That night, the sun set on the western horizon and an ominous darkness engulfed both vessels. Navigation had been reduced to a simple maxim: At night, follow the North star; during the day, follow the sun. Unfortunately, this method did not make allowances for the swirling currents at sea, and by dawn the two refugee boats had been separated. Tinh would not see his brother-in-law's face again for many years.

After two days and nights, Tinh's boat was stopped again, this time by a Thai pirate ship. The robbers were dressed like fishermen,

21

and they carried an assortment of weapons, including knives, guns, and a hammer.

"Give us your gold!" shouted one of the pirates in English. A passenger on the boat who spoke English translated to the others what the robbers were demanding. When no one moved, the robbers began angrily ransacking the boat, looking for secret compartments where valuables might be stashed. One of the robbers grabbed a young female passenger and ripped her clothing. She screamed out for help. A Vietnamese male tried to intervene, but he was struck with a hammer and fell to the deck.

Then, in front of everyone, the female passenger was raped. Tinh squeezed his eyes shut, but he could still hear the woman crying, "No, please, I beg you!"

The pirates tied the refugee boat to their own. Another woman was taken at gunpoint onto the pirate boat, where she too was raped and finally released. After two hours, Tinh's boat was cut loose and the pirates sailed away.

The refugees had been told their entire trip to Malaysia was supposed to take three days. They were now in their fifth day at sea, with no land in sight. Without food or water, some passengers became sick and began vomiting blood. Others drank sea water and urine for sustenance.

On the sixth day, the refugees were stopped by another shipload of Thai pirates. More gold was demanded and passengers beaten. Another woman was taken on board and raped.

After that, it was mostly a blur to Tinh. For six more days the boat drifted aimlessly, the fuel tank now bone dry. Many of the older passengers had mercifully passed out. On day twelve, Tinh squinted in the brutal midday sun and watched the buzzards circle overhead. Then, in the distance, he spotted what he first thought must be a mirage: a huge oil tanker with a Panamanian flag on the side. "Look!" young Tinh squealed, pointing toward the tanker.

The other passengers mustered what energy they had left and cried out, "Over here! Help us! Please, help us!"

The Panamanians towed the refugees to a nearby oil derrick, where they were given food and water. For thirty days the oil derrick served as their home, until a boat came and took them to a refugee camp, not in Malaysia, as they had planned, but in southern Thailand.

For the next twenty-two months Tinh lived the life of a camp dweller, first at Songkhla, a camp of mostly Vietnamese, and then at Sikhiu, a larger camp in central Thailand. In the spring of 1985 a U.S. representative interviewed Tinh. He was asked where in the States he would like to be resettled. Tinh knew that his father had an acquaintance in New York, so he suggested the place, knowing almost nothing about it. The only thing Tinh really remembered being told about New York was that the Statue of Liberty was there.

Six months later, Tinh boarded a plane in Bangkok, destined first for a processing center in France, then JFK Airport in New York City. Just thirteen years old, he had survived a perilous, traumatizing voyage out of Vietnam. Now he was heading to the heart of an even larger unknown: life as a *Viet Kieu*, a Vietnamese expatriate in the land of golden landscapes.

On the night of September 30, 1985, a seasonably cool, clear evening, Tinh's plane approached Kennedy Airport. From his seat near the window, Tinh could see the Manhattan skyline, a magnificent display of tall buildings and colored lights that would impress anyone seeing it for the first time, much less someone coming from a flat, squalid refugee camp. Tinh's eyes opened wide and his skin tingled, as if he had passed through some alien force field into a strange, exotic universe.

On the ground, Tinh waded slowly through immigration. In an airport receiving room, he stood anxiously for two hours until a female social worker arrived and asked, "Are you Tinh Ngo?"

Tinh had been taught some English in school and picked up a bit more in the camps, but his command of the language was not great. He was able to discern that the social worker had been sent by the foster agency overseeing his resettlement in the United States.

"Let me introduce you to your new parents," the woman declared. "This is Mr. and Mrs. Simmons."

Tinh was shocked to see an elderly African American couple

standing in front of him. Growing up in Vietnam and living in the camps, he had never seen a black person in his life. On top of that, Mrs. Simmons was blind!

Tinh was overcome by a dizzying mixture of awe, fear, and confusion. *Wow!* he thought to himself. *This is going to be one strange country.*

Tinh moved in with the Simmons family in a compact two-story house in Roosevelt, Long Island, a town of fourteen thousand just a few miles from the New York City line. Mr. and Mrs. Simmons had five foster kids, none of whom were Asian. The first thing Mrs. Simmons told Tinh was to stay away from the other children in the family. "They're bad," she warned. "They sell drugs in the street."

Around the house, Tinh found it difficult to communicate. About the only thing he could enunciate clearly in English were the words "I don't know." Most of his day was spent sitting in his bedroom in the basement staring out the window. Mr. and Mrs. Simmons seemed anxious to help Tinh fit in, but they could never hope to understand his deep feelings of dislocation and abandonment. They fed him heavy American meals, which gave him diarrhea. On Sundays they took him to a Baptist church where parishioners swayed to gospel music and bellowed "Amen!" and "Hallelujah!" in a loud, most un-Vietnamese-like manner.

Simple household appliances were beyond Tinh's comprehension. One day, Mrs. Simmons was excited to put Tinh on the phone to speak with a young Vietnamese boy who had been adopted by a friend of hers. Tinh was relieved to finally be able to speak his native language with someone. The two boys chatted amiably for a while, then the kid asked Tinh for his phone number.

"Phone number?" replied Tinh. "What's that?" The boy explained that there were a series of numbers written somewhere on the phone.

"Oh," answered Tinh. "Okay." He began reciting the numbers on the dial. "One, two, three, four, five . . . ." Even the Vietnamese kid laughed at Tinh's ignorance.

In school, Tinh not only suffered the shame of speaking strange, fractured English, but he had no familiarity with football, baseball, or other American forms of recreation. There were no Vietnamese at Roosevelt Junior High. Mostly, Tinh felt terrorized by African American kids who called him "slant eyes" or "gook" and dumped milk on him in the lunchroom and urinated on him in the rest room.

After six months, Tinh begged his social worker to transfer him somewhere else. He was suffering from bouts of acute depression and loneliness, and his near-sleepless nights were filled with discomforting images from his past.

In April of 1986, Tinh was transferred to a low-income household in Uniondale, another mid-sized Long Island town. His new home was not much of an improvement. His latest mother, a divorced African American woman in her fifties, worked the night shift at a local hospital. While she slept during the day, one of her five foster kids sold crack out of the house. Tinh had never seen crack or powder cocaine before, except on American TV. One day, Tinh watched as his foster brother was beaten to a pulp by a rival drug dealer. Again, Tinh pleaded with his social worker for a transfer.

After eighteen months in Uniondale, Tinh was relocated once again, this time north of New York City to New Rochelle. This situation was a vast improvement. Mr. and Mrs. Rocco were an Italian American couple with two adopted Vietnamese teenagers, one boy and one girl. Tinh could hardly believe that he was now living under the same roof with people his own age born in Vietnam.

Tinh's first agreeable living environment in America didn't last long. Mr. and Mrs. Rocco were an elderly couple approaching retirement. In early 1989 they decided to sell their house and move to Florida. Once again, Tinh would have to find a new place to live. Of all his relocations, this one embittered Tinh the most. He had grown close to the Roccos and made progress in his attempts to assimilate. Now, much like his real parents in Hau Giang, they had abruptly abandoned him.

The social workers informed Tinh that the only family they could currently place him with lived in a poverty-stricken area in Brooklyn. Even *they* were concerned for his welfare in such a difficult environment. But Tinh didn't care. He had lived in so many different houses with so many different parents he figured it didn't really matter where he lived. It was becoming painfully obvious to Tinh that, in the United States, the parents who harbored foster kids did so more for the money they received than out of any true commitment to provide love or support.

In Brooklyn, Tinh wound up in a run-down tenement at 1641 Nostrand Avenue in Flatbush, a tough ghetto neighborhood. His new foster parents were Hawaiian and Filipino; they had adopted three children to go along with the two they already had. Tinh had never seen kids like this. They cursed and threatened the foster parents, smoked crack in the apartment, and came and went as they pleased.

Tinh's new home surpassed even the refugee camps in its level of filthiness. While he lay in bed at night cockroaches and rats crawled brazenly across his body. Outside on Nostrand Avenue, drugs and violence were rampant. And there were no Vietnamese. Mostly, the neighborhood was·a teeming hodgepodge of African Americans and West Indian immigrants from Jamaica, Haiti, and the Dominican Republic.

During the day, Tinh attended Sheepshead Bay High School, where he was enrolled in the eleventh grade. After his classes he headed to Waldbaum's supermarket to work in the produce department. At night, he couldn't wait to get to the local billiard hall, where he was amazed to find dozens of Vietnamese gathered regularly.

It was here that he first met Kenny Vu, Tommy Vu, and others just like himself. They were outcasts, the byproducts of a country traumatized by a war most of them were too young to remember. They had braved refugee boats and survived camps in Thailand, Indonesia, Malaysia, and the Philippines. Many strayed from failed foster homes and some had moved into barren apartments together. As *Viet Kieu*, they shared a common bond: they were *dat khach que nguoi*, lost and lonely in a strange and hostile land.

"Timmy, why you keep this stupid job?" Kenny Vu asked Tinh one night after he arrived at the pool hall still wearing his Waldbaum's work shirt. Tinh said that he needed the money. His foster parents were poor and had little to spare.

Kenny laughed. With hooded eyes, a sinewy physique, and an assortment of outrageous tattoos covering most of his upper body, nineteen-year-old Khang Thanh Vu was the epitome of a young Asian hoodlum. He had been raised in Cam Ranh, a seaside town not far from Vietnam's demilitarized zone. To Tinh, Kenny's cocky and aggressive manner was awe-inspiring. He didn't seem to be afraid of anyone—a rare attribute for a Vietnamese immigrant surrounded by loud, intimidating Americans.

Kenny told Tinh that in New York City there was no reason he had to live the life of the typical subservient refugee, working long hours for low pay, bowing to condescending white people. "You come with us," he told Tinh, "you not worry about money anymore. We take care a you. We get you place to stay."

It didn't take much prodding. Within weeks, Tinh had left his foster home on Nostrand Avenue, dropped out of high school, and moved into an apartment with Kenny, Tommy, and a half dozen other young Vietnamese males.

Tinh knew that the Vu brothers were part of a group that committed crimes. From Kenny, he learned that in New York youth gangs were a way of life. Recently, Koreans and new immigrants from Fukien Province in China had formed upstart gangs to compete with the older, more established Chinese gangs. The Vietnamese, said Kenny, were the newcomers on the block and had only recently begun to organize, to ensure they received their slice of the pie in Chinatown.

At first, Tinh could not have cared less about the money. It was the prospect of brotherhood that appealed to him. In their two-room apartment at 223 Neptune Avenue, in the Coney Island section of Brooklyn, he and the others ate Chinese food and watched videos. At night, they slept three and four to a bed. Among themselves, they spoke mostly Vietnamese. To pass the time they hung out at the pool hall or went to a roller-skating rink in Queens, where they flirted with teenage girls. On trips to Chinatown, Kenny showed Tinh how to mug people in subway stations.

"Give us your money!" they would yell, sounding much like the pirates and rapists they had encountered on the refugee boats. Sometimes Tinh felt guilty stealing tip money from Chinese waiters and garment workers on their way home. He recognized the sadness in their eyes as they relinquished their hard-earned profits, often as little as $20 or $30. But Tinh could not deny the feelings of empowerment he derived from these paltry muggings. And he was easily seduced by the camaraderie they engendered among himself and the others.

In late May 1989, after Tinh had participated in more than a dozen subway muggings, he was introduced for the first time to Tuan Tran, otherwise known as Blackeyes. At a brightly lit billiard hall on Eighth Avenue in Brooklyn, Blackeyes sipped beer and looked sleek in his light cotton suit and black kung-fu slippers with no socks. He had a long, thin "turkey neck," thick black eyebrows, and "Buddhist ears"—pronounced ears with long lobes that indicated a lengthy and fruitful life. Tinh had heard a lot about Blackeyes, an experienced, self-confident criminal whom many considered the *dai low*, or "big brother," of all Vietnamese gangsters in Brooklyn.

"I hearing good things about you," Blackeyes said to Tinh, with Kenny Vu standing at his side. "Maybe you join us on a real robbery, huh? I know a massage place in Chinatown, on Chrystie Street. Very easy. You with us?"

Tinh thought for a moment, then nodded a bit too casually, trying to give the impression he wasn't the least bit scared.

A few weeks after the robbery of the massage parlor on Chrystie Street, Tommy Vu told Tinh, "It's time you officially join gang, Timmy. Come on and get your tattoo. I take you."

Any aspiring young Asian gangster knew the importance of a tattoo. With the Vietnamese, they were like a religion. Since the gang had no initiation rituals, no pricking of blood or burning of incense to symbolize entry into the gang, having a tattoo was the most powerful statement of all. Tinh had been thinking of getting one ever since he moved into the apartment at 223 Neptune Avenue, but he had not wanted to be presumptuous.

Tommy took Tinh to Manhattan's Lower East Side, to a small tattoo shop run by a Puerto Rican ex-con. Most of the gang members had gotten their tattoos there. Tinh scanned the walls of the dingy shop just off Delancey Street, where sailors, bikers, and Asian gangsters had been coming for decades. On the walls were sample designs of dragons, tigers, serpents, naked women, serpents wrapped around naked women, shamrocks, thunderbolts, and flags of every nation. Tinh was overwhelmed; he eventually settled on a huge, menacing eagle with its wings spread wide.

While the tattoo artist ingrained the colorful image onto his left bicep, Tinh sat patiently. After twenty minutes a gauze bandage was taped over the finished tattoo and Tinh was told not to remove it for at least twenty-four hours.

On the subway heading back to Brooklyn, Tinh's curiosity got the better of him. He lifted up a corner of the bandage and peeked at the glistening tattoo, admiring not only the craftsmanship, but all that it represented. The refugee boat, the camps, and the years of humiliation in suburbia were finally behind him. As a member of the expanding brotherhood known as Born to Kill, his life had a sense of purpose.

Maybe now, thought Tinh, he would even get to meet the gang's esteemed leader, a man whose name he usually heard uttered in hushed tones. A man gang members referred to privately as *Anh hai*, a term of endearment and supreme respect. A man known to the people of Chinatown as Tho Hoang "David" Thai.

Chapter 2

In the heart of Chinatown, seated in a small luncheonette in the rear of a hectic shopping arcade, David Thai slurped from a bowl of *pho*, traditional Vietnamese noodle soup. Around him, a handful of young toughs chatted among themselves. A middle-aged Chinese merchant seated across from Thai shifted uncomfortably in his chair. David wiped his chin with a napkin and eyed the merchant with wry skepticism. "Mr. Chang," intoned the thirty-three-year-old gang boss, "you ask me I deliver for you two hundred fifty watches, okay? But last time I deliver, you take maybe half. I forced to unload the rest at basement price. This no good for me, Mr. Chang."

Mr. Chang acknowledged his past transgression with a nervous shrug. "Mr. Thai," he explained, "I sell them all this time, no problem. Rolex sell the best. Best quality."

"Yes, Mr. Chang, best quality. Best quality on all Canal Street."

The Chinese merchant nodded, and David mustered a sly, self-satisfied grin. "Okay," said Thai, "you'll get your two hundred fifty watches. Just fill out the papers. But remember, Mr. Chang. You remember this small favor, yes?" The merchant was handed two forms by a teenager seated nearby. He stood and again nodded humbly, thanking the young gang boss for his indulgence. On his way out the door, the merchant awkwardly bumped into a customer and almost knocked over a stack of boxes. A few of the gang members chuckled; David Thai smiled.

Though Mr. Chang had been a less than sterling customer, Thai could afford to be magnanimous. Over the last two years, while young Tinh Ngo was bouncing from foster family to foster family on Long Island, the Vietnamese gang boss was methodically solidifying his control over the importation and sale of counterfeit watches along Canal Street—the preeminent commercial artery in the largest Chinatown in the Western Hemisphere.

From the hundreds of stalls and shops jammed together over a dense twelve-block stretch, Thai could count on a fantastic monthly volume. Dummy watches, shipped from Hong Kong and stenciled with fake brand names of famous manufacturers like Cartier, Gucci, Omega, and Rolex, sold on Canal Street for $10 to $20. David stood to clear at least $7 per watch. In 1988 alone, he would claim to have sold $13 million worth of merchandise.

It was not all profit, of course. Shipments had to be off-loaded, labeling equipment purchased and maintained, and weekly salaries paid to the young hoodlums whose job it was to protect and maintain a smooth-running operation. Thai often complained of the travails of overseeing an "unregulated" business, but he wouldn't have wanted it any other way. Not only had the counterfeit watch trade made him rich, it had established his reputation as a man to be reckoned with, a key player in Chinatown's venerable and thriving underground economy.

The Asian Shopping Mall at 271 Canal Street certainly did not look like the headquarters of a multimillion-dollar counterfeit watch operation. Under an anonymous green and white awning, elevated slightly above street level, the mini-arcade consisted of a series of small stalls. Individual merchants sold watches from a few of the stalls, sunglasses, wallets, and sweatshirts out of others. Far in the back, partially

31

hidden behind empty boxes and haphazardly scattered merchandise, was the Pho Hanoi restaurant, the tiny luncheonette that often served as David Thai's private office.

On any given day, a dozen or more young Vietnamese could be found eating rice and *pho* at one of Pho Hanoi's six tightly packed tables or hanging out on the sidewalk in front of the shopping arcade. Most were in their late teens or early twenties. Some had already established reputations as gang members and criminals, but the majority were fresh-faced juveniles, newcomers to Chinatown's criminal underworld.

In early June of 1989, after getting his tattoo and officially joining the ranks of the BTK, Tinh Ngo began making regular trips to the Asian Shopping Mall from his apartment on Neptune Avenue in Brooklyn. It was at the Pho Hanoi restaurant that he and David Thai were first introduced, by Tommy Vu.

"This Timmy, *Anh hai*. He with us now," Tommy explained.

David glanced at Tinh, nodded, and asked, *"Con am con chua?* Have you eaten?" It was David's standard question of all new members, a common Vietnamese courtesy that indicated friendship and concern. Tinh bashfully replied, "Yes. We just finish." He was so nervous he could hardly look *Anh hai* in the eye. Thai smiled politely and went on about his business, thinking nothing of this brief, innocuous encounter.

At the time, Mr. Thai was a highly visible presence. When he wasn't conducting business at Pho Hanoi, he could usually be found down the block at 300 Canal, where he maintained another office, this one up a flight of stairs and in the back of a massage parlor. There David presided over yet another lucrative criminal business. It was Thai who imported the young Southeast Asian immigrant women who worked in the parlor, where they sold their bodies for money, of which David Thai retained a sizable percentage.

Usually dressed in the Hong Kong style, with a tailored sport coat, silk shirt, and soft leather loafers, David presented a sleek, intelligent veneer. When he donned his tasteful black-rimmed spectacles, he had the look of a kindly physician. His jet-black hair was neatly groomed, his features smooth and pleasant. When he needed to, David spoke English with confidence. To an outsider, David may have seemed more like a doctor or a businessman than a gangster. Many of Chinatown's residents knew better.

At first, the merchants along Canal Street believed Thai when he told them he could control the unruly Vietnamese youngsters who seemed to appear out of nowhere in the late 1980s, stealing merchandise and extorting weekly protection payments. Over the years, the merchants had grown accustomed to a certain level of harassment from young Chinese gangsters. The fact that much of their trade involved the sale of counterfeit handbags, jewelry, cologne, watches, and other technically illegal items made them susceptible to extortion. Dealing with gangsters and gangster wannabes was an unavoidable part of the business.

Even so, these Vietnamese boys were not like the Chinese. They were disorganized and rude. The merchants were relieved when Thai presented himself as a conciliator, a man who understood these young toughs because he too had once been a lonely refugee lost in the big city.

It was soon clear, however, that David's "concern" for the welfare of Chinatown's merchant class was based more on self-interest than anything else. "If you do not conduct business with me only," Thai warned retailers along Canal Street, "there is no guarantee I can control these boys."

When the New York City Police Department first became aware that Thai was a major supplier of counterfeit watches on Canal Street, officers began making surprise visits to his headquarters. In response, David used his young gang brothers to harass the cops. Once, when a group of uniformed officers gathered on the sidewalk in front of 271 Canal Street, gang members showered them from a building rooftop with "mini-bombs," twenty or thirty firecrackers bound together with string.

Merchants along Canal Street were not amused. Although they harbored no great affinity for the men in blue, it was not in their best interest to encourage their enmity.

David Thai didn't seem to care. A few weeks after the firecracker incident, he stated his case even more boldly. Over the previous week police had been steadily raiding his watch business, confiscating equipment and watches from his Pho Hanoi headquarters. To merchants and his fellow gang brothers, Thai complained they had cost him more than $100,000.

In an attempt to even the score, Thai handed a homemade incendiary device to one of his subordinates, sixteen-year-old Thanh "Eddie"

33

Tran. At five feet four, Tran was small and spindly, with the face of a ferret. Like Tinh Ngo and the other aspiring hoodlums who had begun to gather on Canal Street, Eddie was a wayward foster kid who'd done time in a refugee camp, in his case the notorious Pulau Bidong camp in Malaysia. With the gang as his only family, Eddie Tran was anxious to endear himself to *Anh hai*, no matter how outrageous the request.

It was a pleasant summer evening, just a few weeks after gang members had showered the police with firecrackers. Eddie Tran walked the six blocks from the Asian Shopping Mall to Elizabeth Street, a typically narrow Chinatown lane teeming with pedestrians. He turned right and soon came to the Fifth Precinct, a weathered, white-brick station house in the middle of the block. Eddie lit the fuse on the small bomb David Thai had given him, tossed it in the open window of an unattended police van, and ran.

The explosion sounded with a rousing *ka-booooooooom*, echoing down the street and sending shattered glass flying twenty feet. When the smoke cleared, the van's windows had been blown out, the upholstery shredded, and the dashboard destroyed. Eleven bystanders suffered minor injuries.

The incident was met with alarm by both the NYPD and the people of Chinatown. Gangsters running rampant in the community had been a problem for years, but previous gang leaders had always tried to steer their people away from direct confrontations with the police. To brazenly declare war on the cops by blowing up one of their vehicles was an act no traditional gang leader would have sanctioned. But as the cops and the people of Chinatown were finding out, David Thai was no ordinary gang boss.

Born in Saigon on January 30, 1956, Tho Hoang Thai's experiences as a youth in Vietnam were quite different from those of Tinh Ngo and most of the others who would eventually comprise his gang. Coming of age in the late 1960s, Thai experienced the Vietnam War as it unfolded. He watched his home city transformed from a proud, provincial capital—"the Paris of the Far East"—into a chaotic, slum-ridden warren. Thousands of rural peasants fleeing outlying areas devastated by

U.S. bombing campaigns crowded the city, hoping to find work servicing the military. In downtown Saigon, widows, orphans, and amputees begging for money jammed the sidewalks. Late at night, after curfew, the rats took over, rummaging through huge mounds of garbage left uncollected because municipal workers had deserted to higher salaries at U.S. base sites.

As a youngster on the streets of Saigon, David made the most of the city's wide-open atmosphere. When he wasn't in school, there were GIs to be hustled and money to be made, especially on Truong Minh Gian Street, which lit up at night like a tawdry facsimile of Las Vegas. Prostitutes and their pimps roamed freely; massage parlor "bordellos" and tacky American-style nightclubs abounded. Like many enterprising young Vietnamese, David offered himself as a go-between for the GIs in search of drugs and the *Binh Xuyen*, traditional racketeers who presided over the city's thriving black market.

In Saigon, there was little overt devastation from bombings or the spraying of poisonous defoliants, but David was not immune to the daily terrors. In 1968, on the day after his twelfth birthday, the North Vietnamese launched the Tet Offensive, an audacious attack on major cities in the South. The Thai family cowered in their home on Ton Dan Street as Viet Cong rockets strafed the city and snipers shot their way to the steps of the Presidential Palace.

The following morning, after the seven-hour siege had ended, thousands of civilians lay dead or wounded in the streets. A Viet Cong captive with his hands bound behind him was paraded through Saigon. A South Vietnamese general stepped forward, placed the snout of his revolver against the man's temple, and pulled the trigger. The man grimaced, his legs slowly buckled, and a steady stream of blood spurted from his head. The execution was captured on film and shown over and over for weeks afterward on the government-run television stations. To the citizens of Saigon and people throughout the world, it would become a symbol of the malignant brutality that had engulfed all of Vietnam.

By the early 1970s, it was clear to David Thai's parents that the South Vietnamese government was finished. The American presence in Saigon was diminishing at a rapid rate, and the city's bastardized wartime economy was on the brink of collapse. The war's legacy of inhumanity had turned the people of Saigon inward; corruption and venal self-interest ruled the day. By April 1975, the entire city was caught in a frenzied, desperate rush to evacuate.

As Saigon fell, sixty-one-year-old Dieu Thai was jailed by his Communist enemies. He still had enough pull, though, to secure his son's passage out of Vietnam. In May 1975, David was airlifted by chopper to a U.S. aircraft carrier destined for Hong Kong.

Barely three months passed before David Thai, now nineteen, found himself in the small, alien town of Lafayette, Indiana, living in a home for boys run by a local Lutheran church. Tormented by visions of his father languishing in a reeducation camp, Thai swore not to let his status as a refugee keep him from achieving for himself all the things his father believed possible under the capitalist system. But David had a problem. There was little that was familiar to him in Indiana, a land of big, beefy Caucasians, more than a few of whom held *all* Vietnamese personally responsible for the death of their loved ones during the war. In May of 1976, with $150 in his pocket, Thai ran away from the group home and hopped on a Greyhound bus headed for New York City.

A hardened, headstrong youth, Thai survived in the Big City by bouncing from job to job, working as a waiter and busboy in Manhattan restaurants. For a time, he washed dishes in the kitchen of the Rainbow Room, a plush, upscale eatery on the top floor of the sixty-five-story RCA building in midtown. There, Thai would gaze out the window at the bejeweled expanse of New York City and the surrounding area, an aching reminder of just how far from home and hearth he had been cast.

The pressures of maintaining a steady income were brought to bear in 1978, when Thai met and married Lan Pham, a nineteen-year-old fellow refugee from the city of Danang. They had met when David briefly attended New York University, where Lan Pham was also a student. Within months, Lan became pregnant with their first child. They both dropped out of school and moved into a cramped studio apartment in Hell's Kitchen, a notoriously rough Manhattan neighborhood.

Being a busboy or waiter was okay if you had only yourself to support. But to be an adequate provider, a young man with a family needed something more.

Since arriving in New York, David had spent a considerable amount of time in Chinatown. At first, it had been merely to soak in the familiar sights, smells, and cuisine of a thriving Asian community. Before long, David was making daily trips to Canal Street to explore the economic possibilities.

In New York's Chinatown, there was no such thing as an independent operator. For a young person hoping to get started in a business that could be deemed illegal or even criminal, there was an elaborate protocol that had to be followed, one that often began with membership in a youth gang.

Sometime in 1983, David Thai became a member of the Flying Dragons, one of Chinatown's largest gangs. The Dragons controlled an area of the city near Pell Street, in central Chinatown. Dozens of restaurants, grocery stores, and other commercial ventures were located in the district. Since the early 1970s, the Flying Dragons had served as both plunderer and defender of the region and had engaged in frequent turf wars with their primary rivals, the Ghost Shadows, another strong Chinatown gang.

Because he was Vietnamese, David Thai knew he would never amount to much as a Dragon. There were few Vietnamese in Chinatown in the early 1980s. David and a handful of others were allowed to form a smaller unit known as the Vietnamese Flying Dragons, but they were cut off from the gang's more lucrative rackets. Established Chinese gangsters tended to view the Vietnamese as "coffee boys," using them to run errands or, in some cases, commit the more dangerous and violent crimes that might result in jail time or death.

David wasn't a very active member of the Dragons. Although he took part in a few robberies, he was never arrested and never did time in prison. He didn't seem to have much interest in the dirty hands-on work of being a gangster. Although few people knew it at the time, his criminal affiliations were a purely practical consideration; mostly, he was creating a base for his future ambitions.

In late 1987, Thai began positioning himself to branch off on his own. The time was right. After years of allowing the gangs to rage virtually uncontested, law enforcement had cracked down. The previous year, the rival Ghost Shadows had been hit with a massive racketeering indictment that sent twenty-one of its members off to prison. A few months later eight members of the United Bamboo, a Chinatown gang with strong ties to the Taiwanese government, were convicted on similar charges. Chinatown's traditional gang structure had never been weaker.

Weaned on Saigon's thriving black-market economy, Thai knew an opportunity when he saw one. Already, he had established an impressive economic foundation with his budding counterfeit watch business on Canal Street. All he lacked was manpower.

As Thai's watch business grew, word spread throughout the pool halls, coffee diners, and skating rinks where young Vietnamese gathered that there was a businessman on Canal Street who took care of his own. Vietnamese kids who were new to New York, or who had recently deserted their foster homes or just gotten out of prison, came to Thai for assistance. "Mr. Thai, I have nowhere to live," they would say. "Mr. Thai, I need money for food." Usually, David freely offered money and advice, seemingly with no strings attached.

In some cases, Thai's benevolence may well have been genuine. David had been around Chinatown long enough to know that the Vietnamese were not always welcomed with open arms. These sentiments were based, in part, on deep-rooted animosities between the Chinese and Vietnamese that went back centuries. Some of it also had to do with fear: The Vietnamese were the product of a violent, war-torn country, and some Chinese believed them to be similarly violent, unstable people. Mostly, though, prejudice against the Vietnamese was class-based. They were simply the most recent Asian immigrant group to arrive in Chinatown, and were therefore on the low end of the pecking order.

Whatever the reasons for their ostracism, Thai knew that his fellow Vietnamese could not rely on Chinatown's traditional support structure. At the time, there were no Vietnamese business associations or Vietnamese banks. Most social-service agencies catered to the Chinese, where only traditional Mandarin or Cantonese dialects were spoken. Since there were no residential areas where Vietnamese passed along apartments from one generation to the next, finding, much less being able to afford, a place to live seemed insurmountable.

David Thai was hardly a blithe village benefactor, however, doling out favors solely to promote the edification and advancement of his people. First and foremost, he was a gangster on the rise. As such, his compassion carried a price tag. To most young men who received an indulgence from Thai, it was simply understood that they owed him one. If David needed someone to frighten a merchant on Canal Street into purchasing only his product, his brothers were there. If Vietnamese gangsters beholden to Thai ventured out on their own, robbing a restaurant, massage parlor, or jewelry store, they kicked a percentage of their take up the chain of command, either to their local *dai low* or directly to David.

Thai's reputation was so great that even youngsters who were not criminally inclined were intrigued by the prestige and power the gang offered. David's expanding fraternity promised something no young Vietnamese male was going to find anywhere else in American society—a feeling of belonging. For those like Tinh Ngo who had suffered through the worst of the refugee experience, this was no small matter.

Sometime in late 1988, Thai called his first sit-down, a gathering of people considered to be high-ranking members of a gang then known mostly as the Canal Boys. At a modest dim sum restaurant on Broadway just off Canal Street, approximately twenty young Vietnamese feasted on soy-stewed pork buns, moo-shu pancakes, lotus pastries, and other delicacies. Blackeyes was there, as was Eddie Tran, the young gang member who'd thrown a bomb into the police van on Elizabeth Street. Also in attendance was twenty-year-old Vinh Vu, known to all as Amigo, the gang's popular Canal Street underboss.

"Think of what we have here as a business, not a gang," Thai urged, standing before his ragged, upstart crew.

Little of importance was discussed at this small gathering, but for those in attendance it was a point of considerable pride. Relationships were solidified and egos stroked.

Within months, however, whatever prestige gang members acquired from that meeting was quickly surpassed by word of an upcoming one that promised to be even more important. This gathering would involve not only high-ranking gang members in and around Chinatown, but virtually every aspiring Vietnamese gangster throughout New York City and the entire surrounding region.

It would be the first official gathering of the gang known as Born to Kill.

Young Tinh Ngo arrived at the plush, upscale Japanese restaurant in midtown Manhattan feeling as if a butterfly were loose in his stomach. It was a balmy evening late in June 1989, just three weeks after Tinh met David Thai for the first time, and he was nervous. With Tinh were members of his Brooklyn crew—Tommy Vu, Kenny Vu, and Vinnie, a gang member who had just recently moved into their Coney Island apartment.

For such a momentous occasion, the boys had donned their most fashionable clothing. They wore loose-fitting linen sports coats with matching black pants, fashionable collarless shirts buttoned to the neck, black leather loafers without socks, and of course, black sunglasses that usually remained on even indoors.

Located on West Thirty-sixth Street, far from Chinatown, the restaurant had been chosen for its anonymity. Since it wasn't Vietnamese or Chinese, presumably the meeting could be held in secret. Still, it had to be Oriental, a place that served food familiar and agreeable to the gang members' palates.

When Tinh entered the restaurant, he was amazed by what he saw. Inside a spacious front room, a dozen tables were filled with gang members seated five or six to a table. Apparently, the entire place had been reserved for tonight's event. The food was spread out smorgasbord style, with gang members helping themselves to sushi, tempura, and heaps of Japanese noodles—all at David Thai's expense.

Nearly every Vietnamese person Tinh had ever met on Canal Street was in attendance. Along with rank-and-file gang members, there were *dai lows* from all over the area. Dung Steven, the *dai low* from across the river in Jersey City, was there, as was Jimmy Wong, the new *dai low* in Brooklyn. Michael Lam, the *dai low* in Queens, was there with a person Tinh knew only as Sonny, a *dai low* from the Bronx. The *dai low* in Connecticut, Phat Lam, was also in attendance. The various underbosses were accompanied by members of their crews, some of whom Tinh knew, some of whom he'd never even seen before.

In the back of the restaurant, near the head table, a large banner had been tacked high on the wall. On the banner was stenciled a coffin with three candles on top and the letters BTK engraved on the side. The purpose of the banner was clear. From here on out, the name Born to Kill, or BTK, would override Canal Boys or any other designation different gang units might have chosen for themselves. The coffin with three candles, which signified no fear of death, would be the gang's logo.

Many gang members would later claim credit for having come up with the gang's name. Everyone knew it originated from a slogan American GIs used to write on their helmets and helicopters during the Vietnam War. Even to a group of youths with little education or appreciation of irony, the name seemed deliciously appropriate. The phrase Born to Kill evoked the appropriate measures of fear and nihilism these young gangsters were trying to project.

Tinh and his crew grabbed one of the last remaining tables, located not far from the entrance. As they served themselves food and ate their meal along with everyone else, an air of excitement filled the room. Just months earlier, many of these same people had been scrounging along Canal Street asking for handouts. For some, the ink on their tattoos had barely dried. Now, here they were, feasting like Mafia chieftains, like important criminals who had arrived at a position of significance and respect.

"I must thank you all for coming," David Thai noted humbly, standing to speak midway through the meal. For the next ten minutes or so, Thai sounded his usual themes. As Vietnamese, they were embarking on what David liked to call a "journey," one that would hopefully bring them respect and make them rich. As relative newcomers to the New York area, they would need to band together if they hoped to overcome the powerful forces aligned against them.

With his gang brothers listening in rapt attention, David advised, "*Con kien cong con vua*"—a Vietnamese saying that meant, "By sticking together, the tiny ants can carry the elephant."

After the meal, David circulated among the gang members, who sipped cognac and smoked expensive French cigarettes. Although few were older than their late teens or early twenties, they behaved as they thought seasoned ganglords should. To those with a sense of history, the evening's gathering may have even had a noble purpose. After all,

41

centuries ago similar assemblies had been held by Vietnamese man-
darins, the natural leaders of a people whom foreigners had repeatedly
sought and failed to pacify. David Thai, so poised and seemingly generous, was their new mandarin leader, a man of "higher destiny," chosen
to lead his minions through the travails of life.

Of course, the image of David Thai as a prince presiding over his
chosen people had been carefully crafted by Thai himself. It was he
who had arranged the meeting and commissioned the banner that hung
from the wall. As Thai moved from table to table, working the room like
an old-time Chicago ward heeler, he was not only affirming his position
as *Anh hai*, the oldest and wisest brother, but as the most powerful
business, community, and spiritual leader these young men would ever
know.

With Amigo by his side, David chatted amiably with the gang
members at Tinh Ngo's table. There were no conditions for joining the
gang, said Thai, except for one. "You must sign this agreement," he
explained, pointing to a piece of paper Amigo held in his hand.

The paper outlined the rules of the Born to Kill gang. First and
foremost, it stated, gang members would not betray their gang brothers
in any way. Second, they would not cooperate with the police. Third, if
a member left the gang, he was required to have his tattoo scraped from
his skin. New York members who deserted the gang would also have to
leave the New York City area. The fourth and final condition, emphasized David, was especially important. Before any criminal act was undertaken by a BTK gang member, it had to be cleared with the local
dai low.

The paper had already been signed by most of the people in the
room. It went around Tinh's table with almost everyone, including Tinh,
signing his name after giving the rules a cursory glance. Andy, one of
the gang members who had accompanied Tinh on his first armed robbery
of the massage parlor on Chrystie Street, demurred. "I just don't see
why we have to sign this paper," said Andy.

There was a hushed silence at the table. Andy's response could
have been taken as a test of David Thai's authority, if David wanted to
take it that way. Instead, with his usual smooth persuasiveness, Thai
seized on the occasion to present a favored image of himself, that of the
velvet glove pulled smooth and tight over an iron fist.

"Little brother," he responded calmly, "go home and think about it. No one should have to make such an important decision right away. The door is always open. But remember: You must sign this paper if you call yourself a member of our organization."

Tinh and the others at the table were impressed. Thai handled Andy's challenge with such a cool head, standing up for his own position without needlessly embarrassing his challenger. In fact, as Tinh watched David move so confidently from table to table, dazzling his guests with charming small talk and easy laughter, he wondered how Thai had developed such a fearsome reputation.

Tinh may have been young, but he had experienced enough in life to know that leadership was based on power, and power, especially in the underworld, was based largely on fear. How could anyone be afraid of David Thai, thought Tinh, when he appeared to be so benevolent, so understanding?

Three weeks later, after the cognac had been downed and the words of solidarity had receded into the atmosphere like so much cigarette smoke, Tinh would have his answer.

Stretched out on a bed in a small hotel room, Tinh was awakened from his nap by a knock at the door. Clad only in his underwear, he got up, went to the door, and inched it open. Through the crack, he could see Phu, a short *Viet-Ching*.

"*Anh hai* want to see you," Phu told Tinh.

"*Anh hai?* He here? At this hotel?"

"Yes," nodded Phu. "He want to talk to you. Room 308."

"Okay. Give me one minute, I get my clothes on." Tinh closed the door and pulled on his pants, wondering what on earth David Thai was doing at the Carter Hotel.

Located directly across from the offices of *The New York Times* on West Forty-third Street in midtown Manhattan, the Carter was a cheap hotel trying to look expensive. The lobby was spacious, with lots of mirrors and gold lamé, but the rooms were small and spare.

Lately, the hotel had become a favored hideout for BTK gang members who needed to lie low after assorted criminal activities. Surrounded by the continuous tumult of Times Square, the gangsters figured a few tough-looking Asian kids would hardly be noticed at the Carter. It was not the kind of place a smooth operator like David Thai would usually be found, unless he had a reason. Tinh knew of one possibility, and it made his stomach muscles tighten with fear.

Just two days earlier, Tinh, the Vu brothers, and Phu had raided another Chinatown massage parlor, this one at 54 Sixth Avenue. It had been a daring 4:00 A.M. heist in the middle of Ghost Shadows territory, and the net had been an impressive $15,000.

After the robbery, as they hightailed it to the Carter Hotel, Tinh had secretly taken $1,000 from the bag of stolen money and stuffed it in his underwear.

Tinh knew it was a dangerous thing to do, but he didn't care. Months earlier, after his first massage-parlor robbery, the Brooklyn *dai low*, Jimmy Wong, had taken nearly all of Tinh's cut, claiming he needed it to buy food and pay rent.

Tinh knew gang protocol specified that the *dai low* was authorized to control the distribution of proceeds from all robberies. And he knew that a percentage of the proceeds from all robberies was used to cover living expenses in the various "safe houses," or apartments, that the gang members used. But Tinh had come away from the Chrystie Street robbery with a measly $100, and he was determined to make sure that this time he received his fair share.

Tinh took the elevator down to the third floor and knocked on the door of room 308. Phu opened the door and motioned Tinh inside.

"Hello, *Anh hai*," Tinh said, as he entered. Looking around the room, Tinh saw worried looks on the faces of Tommy Vu, Jimmy Wong, Sonny, and others who were there.

David Thai stood up, walked over to Tinh, and brusquely slapped him across the face. Then he kneed him in the groin. When Tinh fell to the ground in pain, David began kicking him.

"Motherfucker!" screamed Thai, kicking and kicking. "You motherfucking motherfucker! How dare you steal from me! How dare you steal from BTK!"

"Sorry, *Anh hai*," cried Tinh, between blows. "I know I make mistake. Please. Sorry."

When Thai finally stopped kicking, Tinh pulled a wad of cash from his pocket and thrust it toward David. "Here, *Anh hai*, this all the money I have. I know the mistake, *Anh hai,* so I won't make mistake again."

David was breathing heavily from the exertion. He took the money from Tinh and turned to the others. "Who take care a this guy?" he asked. "Who does he follow?"

"Uh, I take care a him," answered Jimmy Wong, Tinh's official *dai low.*

"Jimmy, take this guy home. Take this motherfucker outta my sight."

Jimmy Wong walked over and helped Tinh to his feet.

Wincing in pain, Tinh glanced around the room at the others, who looked chastened. For good reason. Whether David Thai knew it or not, it was a common practice for gang members to skim money from robbery proceeds if they thought they could get away with it. Tinh had seen others do it, including many of those standing by as he took his beating.

"Sorry, *Anh hai,*" mumbled Tinh one last time as he was led to the door.

In the days that followed, Tinh nursed his cuts and bruises. He figured it was Phu who had squealed on him. He knew he should be mad about it, but he wasn't going to worry for now. After all, the incident had taught him an important lesson. He had seen the iron fist in the velvet glove. To Tinh, the moral was as plain as the hair on Ho Chi Minh's chin.

Unless you had a taste for punishment, you didn't fuck around with David Thai.

Chapter 3

It was just after five o'clock on the afternoon of August 5, 1989, and traffic on Canal Street was backed up as far as the eye could see. Huge trucks and commuter vehicles idled their engines, some waiting to head west toward the Holland Tunnel, others due east toward the Manhattan Bridge. Many motorists, their vehicles belching noxious fumes, angrily honked their horns and screamed obscenities. Others sat comatose, resigned to their fate as victims of a predictable New York City horror: rush hour congestion in Chinatown.

At 271 Canal Street, in front of the Asian Shopping Mall, two teenage males approached David Thai, who was chatting idly with a few associates. The two boys were both members of the Flying Dragons. It had finally become clear to the larger, more established gang that the BTK was a force to be reckoned with, especially here on Canal Street. Accordingly, the Dragons had been harassing Born to Kill gang members throughout the city.

"You think you big man," said one of the boys,

46

fifteen-year-old Duc Ly. "You think you important guy. But nobody respect you, David Thai. Nobody respect BTK." With Duc Ly was an equally young companion named Thanh Lai. Together, they stood on the sidewalk taunting David in broken English, as throngs of rush-hour shoppers obliviously passed by.

The BTK leader was clearly annoyed. "Hey, little boys," he replied, "go home. Your mothers call for you."

Then Duc Ly did something everyone knew spelled trouble. He spit on the sidewalk, a gesture of disregard for BTK territory, the BTK, and David Thai himself.

For a moment, Thai froze, so startled he was unable to think of an appropriate response. Then he turned and abruptly stormed toward the rear of the shopping mall. Duc Ly and Thanh Lai continued laughing and making comments about Thai and the BTK. Although the passersby may have been oblivious, the Chinese and Vietnamese merchants and street peddlers were not. They looked down and avoided eye contact with the young troublemakers, hoping the tenseness of the moment would pass.

In the rear of the mall, Thai brushed past a handful of BTK gang members and disappeared through a door that led to a small cellar below the Pho Hanoi luncheonette. When he reappeared seconds later, he was holding two handguns. "Here," he said, handing one gun to gang member Eddie Tran and the other to nineteen-year-old Lam Trang, another BTK *sai low*. "Go shoot those motherfuckers."

Ferret-faced Eddie Tran had not hesitated when David asked him to blow up the police van in front of the Fifth Precinct, but murder in broad daylight was another matter. He stammered and tried to disappear into the crowd. Lam Trang, on the other hand, seemed enthusiastic. With his unruly mop of black hair greased into a bad version of a 1950s ducktail, he was anxious to distinguish himself from all the others making daily pilgrimages to Canal Street.

Lam Trang ran to the front of the mall. As dozens of onlookers watched in horror, he raised a .38-caliber revolver and fired two shots. One bullet struck Duc Ly squarely in the face, another in the side of the head, sending him crashing to the pavement.

Thanh Lai tried to flee but didn't get far. Lam knelt on the sidewalk to steady his aim and fired two more shots. Ten feet away, Thanh

47

Lai was struck twice in the back, with one bullet piercing his left lung and another his aorta.

The BTK gang members scattered; David Thai went one way, Lam Trang another. By the time police arrived, both victims were lying in glistening pools of blood. They were also both dead.

Along Canal Street, most shop owners quickly pulled their gates down and closed for the day. Despite the many merchants and shoppers on the street at the time of the shooting, no local residents would admit having witnessed this outrageous double homicide on one of the city's most crowded streets in broad daylight.

Stark terror had a lot to do with their reluctance. For some time, tensions had been building along Canal Street and throughout Chinatown. The manner in which Born to Kill had taken over such a lucrative commercial strip called for some sort of response from the powers-that-be. In the past, disputes of this nature were sometimes settled through gang warfare. Turf-related shootings were not uncommon.

Even so, this was something new. Gang shootings in Chinatown were usually carefully orchestrated affairs. A group of hitmen would go into a rival disco, video arcade, or restaurant and open fire on a specific target. It may have been brutal, and sometimes innocent bystanders did get killed. But at least it was planned.

Rarely were gangland shootings as wild and spontaneous as this stupefying double murder on Canal Street. To old-timers—even those merchants and residents who had lived through previous periods of gang violence—this shooting represented something altogether different, a tear in the fabric of the community that suggested Chinatown, as they knew it, was beginning to come apart at the seams.

To an outsider, Chinatown in the late 1980s probably looked much the same as it always had. Business was booming as usual. The neighborhood's narrow, craggy streets were alive with the customary swarm of Asian immigrants. Dining in one of the area's many dozens of restaurants was still the pleasant, affordable experience it had always been for tourists and Wall Street types, people who enjoyed the more obvious aspects of Chinatown's commercial prosperity without ever looking beyond the garish signs, the quaint shops, the cheap prices.

Maybe the rest of the city didn't see it, but the locals were abundantly aware that Chinatown was in the midst of a startling transformation. Among other things, in the last decade the city's Asian population had nearly doubled, further crowding an already tight-knit, densely populated stretch of real estate covering just forty square blocks on Manhattan's Lower East Side. To accommodate the influx, the community's traditional boundaries had expanded north, well past Canal Street into Little Italy. Newer Asian communities in Brooklyn and Queens were also growing at an astonishing rate.

The geographic changes were only the most conspicuous aspect of the community's metamorphosis. Even the average Caucasian could see that Chinatown was growing and reinventing itself, in slightly smaller versions, throughout the five boroughs of New York. What most New Yorkers did not know was that, as a result of the diverse nature of recent immigration, the community was being transformed at its core.

In the past, Chinatown had been comprised overwhelmingly of immigrants from Mandarin-speaking regions of China. The 1965 Immigration Act had opened the door to a new generation of immigrants, and they had gone about the business of establishing a vibrant, largely self-sustaining society. In America, they spoke mostly Cantonese and saw themselves as Chinese subjects living in a country that held little interest beyond the clearly defined boundaries of their own community.

Now, the community moved to the rhythms of an array of nationalities from all over Southeast Asia. Not only were the Vietnamese arriving in sizable numbers, but immigrants had also been flooding in from Cambodia, Laos, Malaysia, and Fukien, a rural province in southeast China with its own unique dialect. Like the Vietnamese, these newer immigrants were mostly from Third World countries in the throes of political turmoil. They spoke their own language. They came to Chinatown with little education or material wealth, straining the community's already overburdened social-service organizations.

From the beginning, Chinatown had always preferred to take care of its own problems, free of meddling by *low faan*, which is short for *guey low faan*, or "barbarian"—a term used to describe know-nothing outsiders. For decades the community's unique isolation from mainstream American society was both its great strength and its most crippling weakness. The image of Chinatown presented to the general public by its inhabitants was of a "Gilded Ghetto," a thriving business community where any impoverished immigrant could make a living. In truth, Chinatown's housing, health, and labor conditions were among the worst in the city, and they were getting worse.

The community's insular structure may have been counterproductive, but the reasons for its existence were not hard to fathom. Few ethnic groups in the history of the United States had been as systematically discriminated against as the early Chinese settlers who came to California during the years of the Gold Rush. The Chinese Exclusion Act of 1882 barred further Chinese laborers and their wives from legally entering the country. It excluded Chinese from most occupations, including manufacturing and mining. It also forbade them to become citizens. Many states even denied Chinese the right to testify against Caucasians in court.

Unlike American immigrants of Irish, Jewish, and African descent who fought against the pernicious stain of racism, the Chinese tried to make the best of a bad situation by drawing inward. Rather than face the risk of death at the hands of government-financed mobs, they formed their own internally governed societies, first in major metropolitan areas on the West Coast, then later in New York, Philadelphia, Boston, Chicago, Washington, D.C., and other cities.

The youth gangs that would eventually become a major problem in nearly every Chinatown throughout the United States were a product of this process. Before the gangs, there were the tongs. Initially, the tongs had been established as self-help organizations designed to assist new immigrants in adjusting to life in *Kam San*, or Gold Mountain, as the United States became known. Since there were few women in Chinatown as a result of the Exclusion Act, tongs were exclusively fraternal organizations. For a small fee, any adult male could join. Regular meetings were held at the tong headquarters, which was housed in a building owned by the tong and presided over by a duly elected leader.

Eventually, the tongs became the primary overseers of Chinatown's various criminal rackets, which included gambling, prostitution, and the sale of opium. Since local police either stayed out of Chinatown or were bought off, there was plenty of room for territorial disputes and other violent altercations. From 1910 to the early 1930s, bloody tong wars were a rite of passage for many young Chinese males.

50

The tongs were themselves patterned after ancient secret societies known as triads, revered organizations once lionized in epic poetry and song. First formed in China in the seventeenth century, triads began as part of an underground political movement that sought to overthrow the corrupt Ming dynasty. Later, triads evolved into a sprawling criminal fraternity with membership in virtually every Chinese community throughout the world.

The triads were less an organization than a loose brotherhood, similar to the Freemasons or the Knights of Columbus. The fact that they were secret only enhanced their mystique. If the Asian underworld was a rich, bubbling kettle of hot and sour soup, then the triads were the secret ingredient that gave it its unique tang.

Most tongs maintained elaborate initiation rituals based on triad legend. In a secret ceremony, an aspiring tong member would have his finger pricked with a needle, then mix a drop of his blood with water and drink it down. With the leader of the tong presiding, the inductee then knelt before a Buddhist shrine and recited the Thirty-six Oaths, pledging loyalty and fidelity to the tong. The triad mystique made being a member of the Asian underworld seem like a noble, even sacred endeavor, and it has continued to serve as a persuasive means of recruitment for tong and gang leaders to this day.

Beginning in the mid-1970s, the tongs—once composed of assorted hooligans and "hatchet men"—sought to change their image. The tongs had never been *legally* defined as criminal organizations, but their primary function within the community was well known. Now, however, they tried to pass themselves off as fully legitimate business associations. From here on out, the daily details of overseeing the community's still burgeoning criminal rackets would be handled by youth gangs, who were just beginning to emerge as a persistent force.

Over the decades that followed, reporters, some cops, and even representatives of the U.S. government would often try to define the relationship between the tongs and the gangs. Even though gang members worked as guards in gambling dens located in the basements of buildings owned by the tongs, even though gang members were sometimes known to *live* inside the tong headquarters, the leaders of these business associations denied there was a relationship. Most tong members had themselves never been implicated in any crime and steadfastly refused to accept characterizations of their organization as a criminal enterprise.

Nonetheless, throughout most of Chinatown, the relationship was understood. The On Leong and Hip Sing tongs, the community's two most powerful business associations, had been around since the dawn of Chinatown. Beginning in the mid-1970s, periodic gang wars raged, establishing certain alliances. The Ghost Shadows became closely identified with the On Leong tong, the Flying Dragons with Hip Sing. The police referred to the gangs as the tongs' "youth wing" or "standing army."

Through it all, gambling and prostitution remained two of Chinatown's healthiest rackets, though the early twentieth-century brothels had long since been replaced by slightly more respectable massage parlors. Extortion of local merchants by gangsters became such a common practice that most merchants didn't even think of it as such; they willingly paid a weekly fee for the promise of protection. This caldron of illicit activity sustained Chinatown's underground economy well into the 1980s, until heroin entered the picture.

While U.S. law enforcement focused virtually all of its energies on the worldwide cocaine scourge that reached its zenith during the years of the Reagan/Bush presidency, Chinese criminals had been systematically consolidating the production and wholesale distribution of heroin. Contrary to popular opinion, heroin use in the United States remained steady throughout the 1980s. Through a loose international network based in Hong Kong, Chinese gangsters met this demand by offering a product that was cheaper and more potent than anything that had ever been seen before. Southeast Asian heroin, known as China White, flooded the market. Chinatown became the place where massive heroin deals were initiated and where the criminal proceeds—unprecedented amounts of dirty money—were laundered through local banks and used to open businesses and finance major real-estate purchases.

Ironically, at the same time tumultuous social changes in Chinatown were making it possible for newer gangs like the BTK to gain a toehold, Chinese crime lords were consolidating their control of the heroin trade, the largest cash business in the world. Attitudes about crime in Chinatown were being redefined; no longer was it the quaint, localized undertaking portrayed in the mainstream media. Now when cops and federal agents talked about triads, tongs, and gangs, they usually used the term "Asian organized crime." In early 1989, congressional hearings were held to discuss a troubling new problem—the Chinese Mafia—believed to be centered in New York City's Chinatown.

With stakes so high, renegade factions like the BTK, though they may have been relatively low in the pecking order, were a potentially serious problem. For the Asian underworld to operate properly, certain rules had to be adhered to. Hong Kong drug lords funneled money into Chinatown banks and real estate, which enhanced local business interests represented by the tongs. Youth gangs, at the behest of the tongs, protected everyone's interests at the street level. Supposedly, the triad mystique made everybody feel like they were in it together. If the various criminal divisions fulfilled their duties as they were supposed to, it was a thing of beauty. The Asian underworld prospered and Caucasian law enforcement stayed away.

The more the BTK challenged the status quo by brazenly carving out turf for itself, pissing off the police, and engaging other gangs in violent conflict for the flimsiest of reasons, the more it disrupted the flow of commerce. The gang's intemperate murder of two Flying Dragons on Canal Street was a prime example. The BTK's antics were attracting unwanted attention. The gang did whatever it wanted, with little or no regard for Chinatown's larger criminal framework. Given the number of factions who were affected, from rival gang members to tong leaders to international brokers of China White, it created a situation that was simply intolerable and would have to be dealt with soon, lest the activities of a lumpen street gang began to do irreparable damage to a vast, hugely profitable underworld conglomerate.

53

As a veteran member of Chinatown's criminal establishment, David Thai knew full well the threat his budding gang posed to the powers-that-be. Thai's minions, on the other hand, were mostly oblivious. The ranks of the BTK were satisfied with the eminence the gang gave them within the community, and they felt honored by the sense of brotherhood they were able to derive from it. As for the larger galaxy of tong bosses and heroin traffickers who presided over the underworld, they were as far removed from the daily lives of Tinh Ngo and the others as the moon, the stars, and other far-off constellations.

If the Chinese gangsters who now controlled the upper echelons of Asian organized crime were indeed comparable to modern-day *capo regimes*, their young BTK counterparts resembled some earlier incarnation of *Cosa Nostra*. Tough and unvarnished, they were the contemporary Asian equivalent of the Sicilian Black Hand, *Cosa Nostra* in its incubation stage, when *padrinos* and their henchmen were content to prey exclusively on recent immigrants within their own community.

Like the Black Hand, the BTK understood that most immigrants were cut off from the protections of mainstream American society. It was Jimmy Wong, the gang's Brooklyn *dai low*, who told young Tinh Ngo when he first joined the BTK, "We rob and steal only from other Asians. They don't know anything about U.S. law and don't go to police. They afraid. They afraid to even report the crime."

The BTK's practice of preying entirely on Asians only reinforced the gang's inherent isolation. The Vietnamese, in general, had not been warmly embraced in Chinatown to begin with. Now that the BTK was muscling its way onto the local scene in such a seemingly disrespectful fashion, Chinese stereotypes about the Vietnamese were conveniently substantiated.

It wasn't fair, of course. Most Vietnamese in Chinatown were hardworking and law-abiding, as were most Chinese. But the antics of the BTK reinforced negative perceptions, pushing the gangs' members further and further from any hope of ever integrating into Chinatown's legitimate social framework. They became outsiders in a community already far outside the mainstream.

In the larger arena of American life, these young Vietnamese hoodlums didn't even exist. At Brooklyn's Coney Island, where Tinh Ngo, Tommy Vu, Kenny Vu, and others from their crew maintained a safe-house apartment, they walked around largely unnoticed by the local citizenry. Coney Island was the last stop on the subway, as far out as you could get without sinking into the Atlantic Ocean. Once home to earlier generations of Russian Jews and other Eastern Europeans, the neighborhood, like most of Brooklyn, had been through a cultural wringer. On Neptune Avenue, near where the BTK brothers rented their apartment, the restaurants and shops were now mostly Indian and Pakistani. The rest of the neighborhood was a mishmash of white ethnics, African Americans, and a smattering of Chinese who lived over the storefronts along Coney Island Avenue.

Hanging out in the weathered video arcades near the once-proud Brighton Beach boardwalk, Tinh and the others sought to approximate the mores and mannerisms of the American kids around them. Like most urban youth, they patterned their behavior after young African Americans, who seemed to rule the streets. Their conversations, whether in English or in Vietnamese, were peppered with exclamations like "yo" and "man," and they frequently called each other "homeboy," as in, "Yo, man, this is Quang. He my homeboy."

It was here in Brooklyn that Tinh Ngo first partook of another custom common to American youth—the purchase and consumption of illegal narcotics.

As a relative newcomer to the gang, Tinh was the one who often had to buy the drugs. Usually, Kenny Vu would send Tinh out to Coney Island Avenue to purchase dime bags of marijuana and crack cocaine. The first few times, Tinh was terrified. But he knew it was a rite of passage he had to go through.

On the Avenue, black males lingered in shadowy doorways while white cops cruised by in squad cars. Using the lingo he'd been taught by Kenny, Tinh would ask a street peddler, "You got the good stuff?"

"Yeah, my man," he would answer. "How much you need?"

After buying a couple of dime bags of crack and two or three bags of smoke, Tinh would head back to the Neptune Avenue safe house, located in a three-story, red-brick building. Tinh and the others lived on the first floor, next door to a Spanish bodega and directly above a street-level exterminator-supply shop.

At first, Tinh stayed away from crack. He had seen how wild it made his assorted foster siblings. But almost everyone else in the apartment got high, especially Kenny Vu. Soon, Tinh also was taking hits of the powerful cocaine derivative, usually by inhaling from a compressed beer can, which, when properly dented and perforated, served nicely as a crude pipe.

Early one morning in August 1989, Tinh, Kenny, and a few other gang members had been up all night drinking and smoking crack. Dawn had begun to lighten the sky outside, and the salty ocean air provided a respite from the inevitable mugginess just hours away. The small apartment, practically devoid of furniture, was a mess. Empty beer cans and cartons of Chinese take-out were strewn about the floor, and dirty dishes were piled high in the kitchen.

In the front room Kenny Vu was standing in his underwear, whacked out of his mind and holding a gun. The others were greatly amused. It was not uncommon for Kenny to parade around with at least his shirt off, to better display his impressive array of tattoos. On his right arm, from his shoulder to his elbow, was a naked woman with wings. Below the elbow on his forearm was an elaborate, multicolored dragon. On the other arm was a large black panther; below that, a menacing cobra coiled and ready to strike. On his chest was a jagged red and blue rendering that looked more like a gaping wound than a lightning bolt, which was what it was supposed to be.

Kenny staggered to an open window at the front of the apartment, aimed his gun, and fired. He liked to pop off rounds in the apartment, which sometimes annoyed the neighbors. Sure enough, within seconds there was a banging from the apartment above.

Once before, the two elderly Russian ladies who lived above had complained when Kenny fired shots in the apartment. Kenny didn't seem to care. He would aim and fire at kitchen appliances, mirrors on the wall, or out the window at the moon, the clouds, and the sky.

Kenny fired another shot out the window. The banging persisted until, suddenly, there was a loud *thump!* as if someone had fallen to the ground.

The boys didn't think anything of it. Within ten minutes, however, they heard the sound of an approaching siren, which got louder and louder. Eventually, an Emergency Medical Service vehicle pulled up in front of their building.

It was now around 7:00 A.M. Out of curiosity, a smattering of neighborhood onlookers gathered on the street. Tinh, Kenny, and a few others also went outside to see what was going on. When they did, they saw one of the old ladies from the second floor being carried outside on a stretcher.

"What happen?" Tinh asked a bystander.

"I guess she had a heart attack and died," the guy answered.

Tinh went upstairs and told Kenny, "Hey, you better get outta here. You fire the gun and one a those ladies fall down dead from a heart attack. Any minute cops come looking for you."

The gang members quickly rounded up what was left of their drugs and flushed them all down the toilet. Kenny gathered the half dozen or so guns around the apartment into a gym bag, climbed out a back window onto a fire escape and disappeared. When the cops finally knocked on the door, the boys played dumb, using the standard ruse of pretending they couldn't speak English.

The next day, Kenny called Tinh from the Chinatown safe house where he was hiding out. "Those cops still around?"

"No," answered Tinh, "but you better stay away. Maybe neighborhood people point the finger at you."

"Nah, Timmy. There's no problem. We invisible to those people. They don't even know we alive."

The following day Kenny returned to the apartment on Neptune Avenue. As he had predicted, nobody in the neighborhood seemed to notice.

That night, after the sun disappeared over the horizon, Kenny sat by the front window of the safe-house apartment and resumed firing. Below him, a sign on the building's facade read, simply and eloquently, EXTERMINATOR. RETAIL/WHOLESALE.

"Everybody on the floor!" shouted Kenny Vu, standing inside the door of the Sinta Lounge, a Chinatown bar. For emphasis, he pulled the plug from a nearby juke box and fired a gunshot into the ceiling. The bar's thirty or so patrons immediately hit the deck.

Tinh Ngo and two other BTK gang members went to work. Tinh hopped over the bar counter and began loading money from the register into a plastic bag while Bao Hung Tran, a gang member known as Nicky, fleeced the patrons for cash, jewelry, and other valuables. Within minutes, they were out the door, where a getaway driver awaited. They raced to the home of Amigo, the Chinatown *dai low,* and counted the proceeds—$15,000 in cash, plus assorted watches, rings, and credit cards.

Ever since the brazen double homicide of two young Flying Dragons on Canal Street six weeks earlier, the BTK had been committing crimes that seemed designed to provoke a reaction from Chinatown's more established`gangs. The robbery of the Sinta Lounge was a good example. Located on Reade Street just a few blocks from City Hall, the bar was a well-known hangout for members of the Ghost Shadows. Tinh and the others were familiar with the bar because Kenny Vu had a friend who was a member of the Ghost Shadows. Kenny and Tinh had been allowed to drink there before, and they used the opportunity to familiarize themselves with the bar's layout and lax security.

During the robbery, the BTK gangsters hadn't bothered to wear masks or hide their identities in any way. The message they sought to deliver was blunt: Here's my face. Take a good look. I dare you to do something about it.

In numerous meetings with his *dai lows*, David Thai had made it clear that because Chinatown's traditional power structure did not include the Vietnamese, the Vietnamese were therefore not bound by the rules and laws of the community. BTK members would play, rob, and even kill wherever they wanted.

Their audacity was alarming. Around the same time as the Sinta Lounge heist, a BTK crew robbed a gambling den at 1 Catherine Street, the largest of Chinatown's dozen or so illegal casinos. Charging into the basement of a building that housed two up-and-coming tongs—the Tung On and Tsung Tsin—a crew of six gang members not only stole the casino's proceeds, but lined up the customers, who included some of Chinatown's most reputable businessmen and tong leaders, and stripped them of cash, jewelry, and credit cards.

Robbing a well-populated gambling den was serious business. It signified the BTK was intensifying its campaign, committing crimes that more directly affected the tongs, raising the level of its criminal activity higher and higher up the community power structure.

In a little over a year, from the time David Thai first established the Pho Hanoi luncheonette as an informal headquarters, the BTK had mushroomed to nearly one hundred members in the New York area alone, a rapid expansion that may well have given the gang delusions of grandeur. Chinatown's other criminal groups were taken aback. The Flying Dragons, after all, had insulted David Thai's BTK and received a rude awakening, i.e., two dead Dragons sprawled on Canal Street at rush hour. Now, many in Chinatown figured the Ghost Shadows would have to step up and meet the BTK's challenge or risk losing stature within the community.

By late 1989, the level of gang activity in Chinatown had gotten so outrageous that even the cops were finding it hard to ignore. The fact that the BTK was willing to blow up a police van in front of the precinct house should have tipped the NYPD off that they weren't dealing with the usual Chinatown crowd. In the past, when gang activity got out of hand, the police would usually go directly to the tong leaders, who were expected to control the gangs and keep the situation from spinning out of control. But since the BTK had no tong affiliation, the police had so far been unable—or unwilling—to take any other meaningful action.

Like everything else in Chinatown, the relationship between the cops and the community's organized criminal element was complex. Since the earliest days of Chinatown, police had developed a habit of staying out of the way when it came to underworld crime—especially if it involved crimes committed by one gang against another. Partly, this stemmed from certain cultural realities. To initiate a criminal investigation, you needed an official complaint from the victim. Since people in Chinatown were discouraged from taking their problems outside the community, crimes very often went unreported.

An even greater problem was that, in the past, cops had been encouraged—sometimes even paid—by tong officials to look the other way. Ignoring crime in Chinatown was not hard, since the community traditionally was one of New York City's safest, with little of the random street violence that bedeviled much of Manhattan and the other boroughs.

To rationalize taking payoffs and disregarding gang activity, an attitude developed among the ranks of the NYPD that Chinatown was a hopelessly enigmatic netherworld that could never be understood by anyone who wasn't Chinese. This "truism," adhered to by non-Asians throughout New York, became a convenient excuse for a tradition of apathy and outright negligence toward Chinatown that never would have been tolerated in most other ethnic communities.

One NYPD officer with more knowledge than most of the unusual dynamic that existed among the cops, the criminals, and the people of Chinatown was Detective Douglas Lee. Born in Hong Kong and raised in New York City, Lee was a rare item on the force—a Chinese-American cop who spoke Cantonese, Mandarin, and also Toishanes, a village-style Chinese spoken by many neighborhood elders.

In 1987, Lee became a member of the Jade Squad, a unit of five detectives assigned to the Manhattan District Attorney's Office whose sole bailiwick was Asian crime gangs. The Jade Squad had been started specifically as a way to circumvent the neglect that existed in other areas of law enforcement when it came to gang crimes in Chinatown. The unit was given a citywide mandate to gather intelligence that might help the police spot developments in Chinatown's vast underworld before they exploded into embarrassing newspaper headlines.

In numerous trips around Chinatown, Lee had been getting an earful from local merchants about the BTK. "These Vietnamese boys crazy," the people told him. "They have no control. We give them money they ask for, they still push us around, throw chairs, break things up."

Many Chinese merchants were willing to talk with Lee, not only because he spoke their native tongue but because his manner was exceedingly respectful. At an even six feet, Lee was tall for a Chinese male, but he spoke in a soft, deferential tone that matched his gentle smile and kindly features.

As a child of Chinatown, Lee understood the importance of "face," the universal Asian term for acknowledging an individual's dignity and prestige. He knew that if you showed another Chinese person face, they would feel compelled to return the courtesy. Face was like respect, only more subtle and multifaceted. Face could be expressed in a gesture, a manner of speech, or through a person's general attitude. You could achieve face through proper behavior and high social standing. If you bestowed the proper degree of face on others, you were blessed. If you caused someone to lose face, you stood to suffer the consequences.

Since arriving in Chinatown with his family at the age of thirteen, Lee had become well acquainted with the corrupting influence of the gangs. In the days of his youth in the late 1960s it had been the Black Eagles and the White Eagles who recruited fresh blood by hanging around local high school playgrounds. Sometimes kids were physically intimidated into joining the gang; other times they were lured through the promise of girls, money, and excitement.

Lee himself had friends and knew of fellow students from Chinatown's Seward Park High School who had forsaken their education to become gangsters. Some were from respectable middle-class families. Unlike their immigrant parents, they had been raised in an aggressive, consumer-oriented society and had no intention of working long hours at a dry cleaner's or a fish and produce market. Being a gang member meant fast cash and, in some quarters, "big face."

Of course, most of what Lee knew about the gangs, both as a former resident of Chinatown and as a member of the police department's preeminent Asian gang unit, did not apply to the Vietnamese. They had not grown up in Chinatown, and few of the gang members lived there. They had no family or community restraints that might cause them to feel shame or embarrassment at provoking so much trouble in the community.

In early February 1990, in response to complaints about the BTK throughout the city, Lee and his Jade Squad partners increased their surveillance in and around Chinatown. They checked in often with restaurant owners and merchants in the area, and sometimes spoke with the gangsters themselves, who usually snickered disdainfully at the police and went on their merry way.

Lee even approached David Thai, whom the Jade Squad had long since identified as the leader of the BTK. Thai often double-parked in front of the Asian Shopping Mall in a sleek 1985 Jaguar he had recently leased. "David, how are you?" Lee would ask, approaching Thai either on the sidewalk or inside the mall. "Where are your boys today? Out causing trouble?"

David usually frowned. "Detective Lee, I tell you so many times. I don't control those boys. I only a businessman."

In recent weeks, the incident that Lee and his fellow officers had become most concerned about was yet another shocking double homicide. During the early morning hours of February 8, four young BTK members had strolled into Winnie's Bar on Bayard Street, a revered Ghost Shadows "tea room," as Chinatown saloons were still sometimes known. A few Ghost Shadows gang members approached the BTK gangsters and told them they were not welcome in Winnie's Bar and would have to leave.

The BTK members went outside and huddled across the street in Columbus Park, where they smoked cigarettes and cursed the Ghost

Shadows for the insult they had been forced to endure. The oldest of the group handed a 9mm semi-automatic pistol to fifteen-year-old Qui Tran, a relative newcomer to the gang. "You call yourself BTK, you must prove you belong," he said. "Go in there. Wave the gun around. Scare them."

Qui Tran went into Winnie's Bar and pulled out the handgun. Almost immediately, the Ghost Shadows pulled out theirs. A wild shootout ensued, with automatic gunfire shattering glass and ricocheting off the ceiling and walls. Within seconds, two Ghost Shadows lay dead and two more were seriously injured, including a girlfriend of one of the gang members.

Qui Tran fled the bar onto Bayard Street. His companions were nowhere in sight. Before he had time to react, Tran spotted an NYPD paddy wagon barreling down the street in his direction. Without hesitation, he ran.

The paddy wagon, with two cops inside, pursued Tran through the deserted streets of Chinatown. Near Canal Street, Tran ducked behind a parked car and aimed his 9mm at the cops. Officer James Meyers hit the brakes, drew his weapon, and fired off three rounds at Tran, one of which nailed him in the shoulder. The young gangster fell to the pavement. Meyers and his partner jumped from the wagon, handcuffed the assailant, and immediately took him into custody.

Within days, news of the shootout at Winnie's Bar wafted through Chinatown like the smell of rancid fish, malodorous but not altogether unfamiliar. Lee knew it spelled trouble. First, the BTK had murdered two Flying Dragons in broad daylight on Canal Street. Now they had perpetrated an incredible double killing in one of the Ghost Shadows' favored tea rooms.

A few weeks after the shootout at Winnie's Bar, Lee and his partner, Detective James Donovan, spotted David Thai as he pulled up in his Jaguar in front of the Asian Shopping Mall. They watched as he parked, entered the mini-mall, and soon reemerged with two other BTK members, including his right-hand man, Amigo.

Lately, Thai was rarely seen without Amigo, an increasingly popular figure on Canal Street. Despite the tensions between gangs, Amigo was known to have acquaintances that crossed gang boundaries. He was particularly cozy with the Fuk Ching, an up-and-coming gang that controlled one of Chinatown's most lucrative new rackets: the smuggling of illegal Chinese aliens into the United States.

The cops watched as Thai, Amigo, and their companion climbed into David's Jaguar, pulled away from the curb, circled the block, and headed east on Canal Street.

"Let's follow these guys and see what they're up to," suggested Lee. He knew it was unlikely they would catch someone like Thai in the act of committing a crime, but it was useful to know his daily routine.

The cops pulled out into traffic on Canal Street. It wasn't hard to follow David's Jaguar, with its distinctive grayish tint that seemed to change color slightly depending on the light of day. They followed the car to the Manhattan Bridge, across the East River and into Brooklyn. From there, David drove onto the Brooklyn-Queens Expressway and headed north into Queens.

The Jaguar left the expressway, with the cops trailing at a safe distance. They watched as the car stopped in front of a combination gun shop and military supply store. David waited in the car while his two henchmen went into the store.

Lee and Donovan parked their car and idled the engine. Soon, Amigo and his companion came out of the store with two large boxes. David got out of the car, opened the trunk, and helped load the boxes into the back. Then they all got into the car and drove off.

"What was that all about?" Donovan asked the store's clerk a few minutes later, his detective's shield dangling prominently from his breast pocket.

"You mean those Chinese guys?" the female clerk asked.

"Vietnamese," replied the detective.

"They were here to pick up an order. Twenty-seven bulletproof vests."

Donovan had to hear that again. "Bulletproof vests?" he asked.

"That's right," answered the clerk, "bulletproof vests, police issue. Just like you guys wear."

On the drive back into Manhattan, the detectives shook their heads in dismay. They knew the BTK had stirred up tremendous bad blood between themselves and Chinatown's traditional criminal factions. They could smell it in the air. But twenty-seven bulletproof vests!?

63

It was impossible to know exactly what the gang up was to. But Lee was certain of one thing: David Thai loading up on bulletproof vests gave the distinct impression that the local underworld was about to erupt, perhaps raising the standard for gang violence to new heights. Which did not bode well for the Gilded Ghetto.

Chapter 4

In October 1989, a few months before detective Doug Lee spotted David Thai buying bulletproof vests in Queens, Tinh Ngo got himself arrested. Given the level of serious criminal activity under way in the Asian community at the time, Tinh's incarceration was petty. He, Kenny Vu, and three other gang members had been caught driving around Brooklyn with four unregistered handguns in the car. Tinh was ready to plead guilty as charged, but a court-appointed attorney told him to wait. Two of the guns weren't even in working order—lowering the infraction from a felony to a misdemeanor—and two other gang members had already pleaded guilty to possession of one gun each. Eventually, Tinh's case was dismissed, but not before he'd spent six long months in the notorious Rikers Island Correctional Facility, New York City's preeminent penal institution.

At Rikers, Tinh had occasional flashbacks to the refugee camps, where a similar institutional drudgery prevailed. Given the twenty-two months he spent within the confines of a fenced-in compound in Thailand, Tinh seemed prepared for his time behind bars. But at least in the camps he had been surrounded by fellow countrymen, some even from Hau Giang, his home province. Rikers Island was an ethnic polyglot, with a seething criminal population fiercely divided along lines of race, color, and sexual predilection.

In his first week at Rikers, Tinh was taken under the wing of a renowned Vietnamese inmate known as LT, the unofficial *dai low* of the prison's Asian population. "In here," LT told Tinh, "we speak only to other Asians. If Chinese or Vietnamese get in a fight with some people, we must back them up. Don't be afraid of black people, white people, Puerto Ricans. We defend you."

LT explained that the other prisoners rarely messed with Asians, thanks to an incident that had occurred one year earlier. According to LT, some black inmates had been harassing him. So one night around Christmastime, LT and another Vietnamese inmate known as Shadow Boy went on a rampage, slicing the faces of black inmates with a straight razor. Said LT to Tinh, "We told them, 'We have no gifts to open for Christmas, so we must open faces.' "

Despite LT's paternalism and expressions of solidarity, Tinh found Rikers terrifying. Physically, few inmates were as diminutive as the Vietnamese. At five feet five and 125 pounds, Tinh was the norm for his group. He was afraid to go anywhere without at least three or four other Asian inmates.

66

On C Wing, where Tinh was housed, there were Vietnamese and Chinese representatives from all the Chinatown gangs. On the street, many of these people would have been rivals. Within the prison walls, they banded together as protection against a hostile, mostly non-Asian population.

Though small in stature, the Vietnamese inmates Tinh met at Rikers were among the toughest gangsters he had yet come into contact with. Many, like LT, were in for murder and assorted other harsh crimes. On those rare occasions when Tinh witnessed altercations between Asian and non-Asian inmates, the Vietnamese were always the first line of defense, their BTK tattoos serving as proud, garish badges of distinction. Tinh left Rikers Island with his convictions deeply reconfirmed that the only people he could count on in this mean, menacing world were his fellow gang brothers.

Upon his release in March 1990, Tinh used the BTK pipeline to facilitate his resettlement in the outside world. At Rikers, a gang member had given him Amigo's pager number and told him to contact the Chinatown *dai low* as soon as he got out. Sure enough, Tinh beeped Amigo and was called back right away.

"Timmy," said Amigo, "you out now? Good. Yes, we have a place for you."

Since Tinh was identified with the Brooklyn faction of the BTK, Amigo set him up in a safe house in Bay Ridge, an old Italian and Irish working-class neighborhood in the shadow of the Verrazano Bridge. There were five or six other gang members already living in the two-room apartment at the time. The day after moving in, Tinh took the subway to lower Manhattan, where he met Amigo at 267 Canal Street, a shopping arcade just a few buildings east of David Thai's Pho Hanoi headquarters.

Tinh's time in prison had altered his physical appearance in subtle but significant ways. No longer the wide-eyed innocent, he was leaner and harder, with the gaunt, feral look common to many Vietnamese gangsters.

"Timmy, you look like you get skinny in that place," joked Amigo. "I better get you something to eat." After stuffing himself with a huge bowl of *pho*, Tinh was told by Amigo, "Come on, I take you to see *Anh hai*."

Tinh hadn't had direct contact with David Thai in many months, not since the afternoon at the Carter Hotel when *Anh hai* smacked him around for stealing robbery proceeds. He was worried David might still be angry, but he needn't have been. Thai knew how to play his role as both gang boss and benefactor. He knew that, unlike Chinese gang members, few Vietnamese coming out of prison had any family connections to depend on. David's willingness to take care of his brothers, to provide food, rent, and companionship at such a vulnerable point in their lives, was one way of ensuring that the gang remained the center of all that was reliable and important to the boys of the BTK.

"Timmy," offered David, "here's two hundred dollars. Come by tomorrow, we have more for you."

Anh hai also hooked Tinh up with a new beeper, second only to a tattoo as an important status symbol for Asian gangsters. Tinh simply walked over to E-5 Communications, an electronics store on Centre Street, one block north of Canal. In the past, the BTK had extorted money from and then robbed E-5 Communications until a special arrangement was worked out. Now, all a gang member had to do was show up with Amigo and say, "My name's so-and-so. Born to Kill." A special BTK notation was made by the customer's name, and he was given unlimited free service on the finest beeper in the shop.

Armed with a new beeper and a fresh sense of freedom, Tinh was soon back into his usual routine, hanging out on Canal Street, at Chinatown amusement arcades, and at Maria's Bakery, a large coffee and Chinese pastry shop where young gang members often gathered to plan crimes and engage in small talk.

While in prison, Tinh had heard about the shooting at Winnie's Bar and other outrageous acts perpetrated by the BTK against the Ghost Shadows. The fact that bad feelings between the two gangs had escalated to the point where everyone seemed to think a war was imminent concerned him greatly. After all, Tinh had taken part in the robbery of two Ghost Shadows establishments—the massage parlor on Sixth Avenue and the Sinta Lounge. Neither time had he or his fellow bandits bothered to wear a mask or disguise. Before, their brashness had kept victims and rivals off-balance. But with a full-fledged gang war under way, there was no telling who might come looking for revenge.

Along with the obvious tension between gangs, Tinh was equally concerned about a story making the rounds in Chinatown that, if true, suggested the BTK was headed toward a day of reckoning that would make its current problems pale in comparison.

Apparently, the so-called Godfather of Chinatown, Kai Sui "Benny" Ong, had called for a meeting with David Thai. The eighty-one-year-old Ong, known in the community as *Chut Suk*, or Uncle Seven, was an "adviser-for-life" of the powerful Hip Sing tong. There was no figure more legendary and no leader more revered than Uncle Seven, an owlish, iron-willed octogenarian whose personal history seemed to encompass the entire dramatic chronicle of twentieth-century Chinatown.

Born the seventh of nine sons to a poor bricklayer in the Toishan village of Harbin, Benny Ong had emigrated to the United States in

1921, at the age of twelve. Soon after his arrival in New York City, he took a two-dollar-a-week job in a laundry, developed a taste for gambling, and, on his eighteenth birthday, followed his older brother Sam into the Hip Sing. Like many young men of his generation, Benny Ong had played a role in the great tong wars of the 1920s and '30s, during which territories and criminal rackets were established by the Hip Sing and On Leong tongs that remain deeply imbedded in the structure of modern-day Chinatown.

In 1935, Ong was arrested in connection with the death of a man during the robbery of a gambling game run by a rival tong. Legend has it that Ong was innocent and went to jail rather than implicate another Hip Sing member. Later newspaper reports revealed, however, that he admitted his guilt and provided the identities and whereabouts of three alleged accomplices. Either way, Ong was found guilty of murder and served the next seventeen years in an upstate New York prison. When he was paroled in 1952, he returned to Chinatown and picked up where he'd left off, eventually assuming leadership of the Hip Sing tong from his brother, who died of cancer in 1974.

Uncle Benny may have had a checkered past, but he was still a tong leader, which afforded him a position of considerable power. And his stature increased even more when, in the mid-1970s, he became a ranking member of the Chinese Consolidated Benevolent Association (CCBA), Chinatown's official governing body, comprised of leaders from the abundant family associations, district associations, and tongs.

As leader of the Hip Sing, Uncle Benny was believed to have been the first to establish strong ties between the tongs and the gangs. At the time Uncle Benny took over, the gangs were getting uppity, shaking down merchants, robbing tong-sponsored gambling parlors, and showing a general lack of respect toward community elders. Ong saw the value in incorporating gang members into the tong structure, where their activities would become more organized and perhaps less wantonly destructive to the community at large.

Of course, paying gang members to protect Hip Sing gambling halls and to apply pressure during territorial disputes was also a great personal benefit to Benny Ong. Benny's power in Chinatown continued to grow, even though he was jailed again briefly in 1977 on charges of having bribed an immigration official.

The lengths that Uncle Seven was willing to go in utilizing the leverage of the gangs became a matter of great controversy in December 1982, following one of Chinatown's most well-known gangland slaughters. Two days before Christmas, four gunmen from the Flying Dragons walked into the Golden Star tea room, a Chinatown saloon on East Broadway. Using an assortment of automatic weapons, they let loose a barrage of gunfire. Patrons dove for cover behind tables and booths. Shattered glass littered the room like confetti. By the time the gunmen fled, three people lay dead and eight more had been seriously injured.

The Golden Star was a popular gathering place for members of the Kam Lum, an upstart tong recently begun by a disaffected Hip Sing member. In Chinatown, trying to start a new tong in another tong's territory was like trying to eat a bowl of chicken broth with chopsticks—it simply wasn't going to work. Benny Ong viewed the very existence of the Kam Lum as a challenge to his authority. In a rare instance of public frankness, he was quoted in *New York* magazine as saying of the Kam Lum leader, "Sixty year I build up respect and he think he knock me down in one day?"

After the shooting, the angry Kam Lum leader first accused Ong of having masterminded the bloodbath, then had grave second thoughts. Eventually, he apologized to Uncle Seven and his tong all but disappeared from the scene.

Now, eight years after the Golden Star massacre, Benny Ong was faced with a new challenge in Chinatown—the sprawling aggregation of Vietnamese gangsters who had, among other things, disrupted the flow of commerce in Chinatown's underground economy. From his familiar perch at the Hong Shoon restaurant on Pell Street, where he appeared daily wearing a short-brimmed gray fedora, Uncle Benny heard stories of these young Vietnamese hooligans who were challenging the community's traditional power structure. Ong was not about to let a group of boys who had only recently arrived in Chinatown create such chaos, so he demanded a *kong su*, underworld slang for "negotiation."

There were many in the community who felt that David Thai should have been flattered to share a plate of rice with Benny Ong. The very fact that Thai would be sitting at a table with the venerable Godfather of Chinatown was, in a way, a significant acknowledgment of the niche David had carved for himself. Presumably, in exchange for David's reining in his gang brothers, the elderly tong leader would suggest some sort of power-sharing arrangement by which Thai could hold on to his lucrative Canal Street rackets.

Given the honor-bound nature of Chinatown's underworld, the worst thing David could have done was ignore Benny Ong's request for a meeting. Which is exactly what he did.

Of course, Thai knew that to ignore Benny Ong would be viewed as an unforgivable slight. The BTK had already offended everyone else in Chinatown by publicly trading gunfire with rival gangs. Although no blood had been shed, this was the worst insult of all. By not even responding, David was openly disparaging Uncle Seven, causing him to lose face. Uncle Benny would have to answer the insult.

Throughout history, Chinatown had experienced tong wars, gang wars, and retribution hits of every variety. In the lexicon of the triads, revenge was a god that required human sacrifice. Ominous forces had been put into play, and it would not take long for destiny to reveal itself to the members of the BTK, the people of Chinatown, and beyond.

On the morning of July 26, 1990, Tinh was asleep on a single mattress on the floor of his bedroom in the Bay Ridge safe-house apartment when one of his roommates shook him awake. "Timmy, Timmy, wake up," urged Richie Huynh.

"What?" responded Tinh, still half asleep. "What is it?"

"You hear the news?" asked Richie.

"What news?"

"It's Amigo," said Richie. "He got killed last night." Richie explained how Amigo had been gunned down on Canal Street while waiting for a taxi outside David Thai's massage parlor.

Like everyone else, Tinh was deeply saddened by news of Amigo's death. He could imagine no greater outrage than rival gangsters brazenly murdering one of the BTK's most revered members in the middle of their home turf on Canal Street.

Two days later, Tinh would be forced to amend that evaluation when three Chinese hitmen sprayed the crowd at Amigo's burial with gunfire, sending hundreds of mourners fleeing in a mad rush to avoid a sudden, unspeakable demise. From that point on, the BTK and their "journey" would never be the same.

BLOODY BURIAL, screamed the front page of the New York *Daily News* on Sunday, July 29, 1990. GANG WARFARE ERUPTS AT CEMETERY, trumpeted *Newsday*. Television and radio accounts added their own loud voices to the commotion. One national news program dusted off an old report suggesting that Vietnamese gangs like the BTK must be financed by powerful anti-Communist groups such as the National United Front for the Liberation of Vietnam, or the Frogmen, a California-based gang comprised of former South Vietnamese soldiers trained in assassination and the sophisticated use of explosives.

It was hardly surprising that these reports lacked any direct evidence of a link between the organizations mentioned and the shooting at the cemetery. The mainstream media were like the cops, handicapped by a long tradition of neglect in regard to Asian issues. Now, a seething Chinatown gang war had burst into the open, and in the frenzy that followed, a bewildered media was flailing in search of an explanation.

Staged like a scene from a movie, with hitmen dressed in long black coats bearing flowers, the shooting was certainly dramatic. In fact, the hit may well have been styled after the Hong Kong gangster flicks that gang members—both Chinese and Vietnamese—viewed so assiduously at the Rosemary, the Sun Sing, and other Chinatown movie theaters.

Since the mid-1980s, the Hong Kong film industry had been producing a seemingly endless stream of highly distinctive, hugely popular movies set in the Asian underworld. In *Bullet in the Head, A Better Tomorrow,* and *Love and Death in Saigon*—to name a few—moments of romanticized male bonding were interspersed with images of balletic, slow-motion violence. Some gang members viewed these movies as idealized versions of their own lives, and they reveled in the heavily stylized carnage and deliriously high body counts.

Most popular of all were the films of director John Woo, the Sam Peckinpah of the Hong Kong cinema. Woo's movies always contained at least one epic shootout in a dramatic setting. In *The Killer,* a few dozen gangsters wage war in a Gothic cathedral backlit with thousands

72

of candles. In *Hardboiled*, gangsters open fire on the movie's hero in a large, hectic urban hospital.

The gangsters who sprayed the BTK with gunfire at the cemetery in New Jersey had outdone even John Woo. The setting was not only picturesque, it also contained a cultural subtext that most Asians would immediately recognize.

While virtually all societies treat the burial of a loved one as a sacred ritual to be conducted with reverence and respect, Eastern religions have a uniquely holistic view of the afterlife. The overwhelming majority of Chinese and Vietnamese, steeped in the traditions of Buddhism, are raised to believe that after death comes rebirth and then life again, on and on in a cycle. Death is viewed not as a conclusion, but as a reunification of the deceased with his or her ancestors. The burial process is especially important, because it determines the degree of tranquillity a being will have as he or she passes from life on earth into the afterlife.

Apparently, Amigo's passage was going to be a bumpy one. The gods had every reason to be offended by what took place at Rosedale Memorial Park Cemetery. More than just an attempted gangland hit, it was a desecration, one that had been carefully orchestrated to exhibit the same level of disrespect toward the BTK that the BTK had shown toward Chinatown's underworld traditions.

After the shooting, the myriad forces that had brought about the murder of Amigo and the bloody aftermath remained murky. For such an important sequence of events to have taken place, however, knowledgeable observers both in Chinatown and in law enforcement felt certain that Uncle Seven must have played a role. They also knew it was unlikely that anyone would ever prove that in court. For his part, David Thai was convinced that whoever gave the actual go-ahead, the muscle was provided by the Ghost Shadows.

73

Even before Amigo's funeral, Thai had sworn vengeance. "We going to kidnap Ghost Shadows leader, chop his head off and throw it in the street," he told Tinh Ngo and a handful of other BTK members at the Pho Hanoi luncheonette. Later, he claimed he was going to detonate a homemade bomb on Bayard Street, in the middle of Ghost Shadows territory, at the exact moment Amigo's body was being lowered into the ground out in Jersey.

The Great Cemetery Shootout quieted David down. He had been chastened, perhaps, by the magnitude of the event. Besides, all this media attention was not good for business. For the time being, the best course of action was to take no action at all.

An eerie calm descended on the streets of Chinatown. For the first time in a while, merchants on Canal Street opened their shops early and closed late. Tourists bought counterfeit merchandise at outrageously low prices and went home happy. Local restaurants were packed with smiling American customers.

It was inevitable, however, that the ranks of the BTK would be forced to reassert themselves. Not all of the gang's members were as free of financial concerns as David Thai. More than most of the many mobsters, punks, and white-collar charlatans operating within America's huge criminal underground, BTK gang members were motivated by a simple, irrefutable instinct for survival. They may have worshiped *Anh hai* and tried to endear themselves to him by following his every command. But they still had to eat.

By the end of the summer, after a few weeks of lying low, their collective stomach had definitely begun to growl.

Tinh Ngo stood at the front counter inside Maria's Bakery, a bustling cafeteria and catering shop located on Lafayette Street, one block north of Canal. He ordered a soda and a Chinese pastry. Behind him, the room was filled with afternoon idlers and high school kids just out of classes for the day. American pop music and the din of assorted Chinese dialects filled the air. On a plastic tray, Tinh carried his food and beverage to a Formica booth in a far corner, where four BTK brothers were sitting.

"Timmy," said one of the gang members. "You hear what happen?"

"Oh, no," moaned Tinh, taking a seat. "What now?"

The gang member filled Tinh in on the latest BTK escapade.

The previous day—around 10:00 A.M. on the morning of August 27, 1990—a group of five gang members stormed a wholesale produce warehouse at 380 Broome Street, just a few blocks from where Tinh and the others were now sitting. During the robbery, the gang members shot thirty-eight-year-old Sammy Eng, son of Kan Wah Eng, the owner of W. C. Produce. After ransacking the market's small front office, they began tying up Kan Wah Eng and the three or four store employees who were unlucky enough to be on the premises at the time.

While sixty-year-old Kan Wah Eng was on the floor, he made the mistake of looking up briefly.

"I told you not to look at me!" admonished Jimmy Nguyen, the lead robber. "Why you look at me?"

Another gang member, a slight *Viet-Ching* named Cuong Pham, was in the process of tying up Kan Wah Eng with a telephone cord. Just as he bent down to wrap the cord around Kan Wah Eng's ankles, an enraged Jimmy Nguyen fired a shot at the elderly store owner. He missed, hitting Cuong Pham instead in the back of the head, blowing his brains all over Kan Wah Eng, the floor, and a nearby wall. Frantically, the robbers fled W. C. Produce before the cops arrived.

"Oh, man," said Tinh, when he heard the story. "What did David Thai say?"

"He mad," replied the gang member. "He real mad."

Among other things, the robbery attempt at W. C. Produce revealed a gap in leadership within the BTK. The produce market was in the middle of Amigo territory. With Amigo gone and nobody yet chosen to take his place, the BTK gangsters had embarked on the robbery without the knowledge or approval of any *dai low*. Coming just four weeks after the Great Cemetery Shootout, this wildly inept, accidental killing of one BTK gang member at the hands of another received significant local coverage in that morning's *Newsday*—an occurrence that did not sit well with David Thai.

Tinh Ngo sipped his soda and shook his head in astonishment. As the gang members gave him more details on the shocking death of Cuong Pham—a gang member Tinh knew well—he couldn't help but think: That could easily have been me.

Nearly all robberies were conducted amid a high level of chaos. The idea was for the robbers not only to get the goods, but to generate terror. This way, the victims wouldn't dare think of reporting the crime to the police. Furniture and other items were usually thrown around; victims were sometimes beaten and yelled at in an assortment of languages. Occasionally, shots were fired into the ceiling to scare people.

Tinh felt lucky. Of the half dozen or so robberies he had taken part in, none had yet erupted into serious violence. There was a time when he was turned on by the prospect of danger and the adrenaline rush that came from robbing people at gunpoint. But not anymore. After the cemetery shootout, where he hid behind a tombstone and watched as some of his fellow gang members were felled by gunfire or fled in horror, the harsh realities of violence suddenly became much more acute.

Now this—the stupid, careless death of a gang member during a sloppy attempted robbery that never should have taken place to begin with.

For the first time since he joined the gang, Tinh began to ponder what life might be like were he not a member of the BTK. The subject, quite frankly, made him feel bleak and depressed.

For Tinh and other BTK members, being a gangster was not the same as being a member of *Cosa Nostra*, or being a Colombian drug dealer, or even an African American gangbanger. A Mafia *soldato* lived a life separate from his criminal deeds. He had a wife and children at home and traveled in quasi-legitimate circles. A Colombian cocaine dealer reaped huge profits and presented himself to his community as a legitimate businessman. Members of the Crips and Bloods led halfway normal lives; many went to school and held jobs while fulfilling adolescent fantasies by being part-time gangsters.

But there was nothing part-time about being a member of the Vietnamese underworld. For Tinh and many of the others, the BTK was their entire life. They lived with gang members, ate with gang members, and socialized only with other gang members. In recent months Tinh had even cut off all communication with his family back in Vietnam. As far as he was concerned, he had no past. And like many teenagers his age, he never thought much about the future. His daily existence was entirely dependent on the various robberies and extortions he committed with other gang members.

About the only non–gang-related outlet Tinh had was a relationship he had struck up with a seventeen-year-old Chinese-American girl named Sandy. He first met Sandy earlier that summer, through Kenny Vu. She was slim and delicate, with porcelain features and beautiful, translucent skin. Her parents were immigrants, but Sandy was New

York-born, or ABC, as American-born Chinese were commonly known in Chinatown.

Tinh liked Sandy, but he couldn't really say he was crazy about her. In fact, he had never officially asked Sandy out on a date at all. They were simply paired up one day by a group of mutual friends while on their way to a party in Queens. Afterward, they took occasional trips together to the Coney Island amusement park. There they passed the hours in the penny arcades along the boardwalk and drove the bumper cars. Their favorite ride was the Wonder Wheel, Coney Island's age-old Ferris wheel, which took them high in the sky, overlooking the ocean, the beach, and the elevated subway trains that brought thousands of people to the far-flung reaches of Brooklyn.

Tinh had always been timid and awkward around girls. Many gang members had taken advantage of David Thai's stable of young prostitutes, the immigrant women who worked at his Chinatown massage parlor. Kenny and Tommy Vu were at the massage parlor all the time. A gang member named Hai had fallen madly in love with one of David's girls and even followed her back to Malaysia. But Tinh had never gone to the massage parlor as a customer. And he'd never really had a serious girlfriend before.

In the beginning, what Tinh liked most about hanging out with Sandy was the stature it brought him among his friends. Although women were never allowed to take part in the gang's activities in any substantial way, a gang member's standing seemed to increase if he had young girls trailing after him. Sandy also seemed to gain respect and even awe from friends of hers who were impressed that she went to parties and occasionally danced at nightclubs with notorious members of the underworld.

"What's it like?" Sandy once asked Tinh about his life as a gangster.

"It's really nothing special," Tinh answered modestly.

Eventually, Sandy took matters into her own hands and introduced Tinh into the world of the flesh. One afternoon while no one was at home at the safe-house apartment, Sandy offered, "Here, Timmy, this is how it's done."

On a mattress on the floor, with horns honking and sound of children playing outside, Sandy guided Tinh through his first sexual en-

77

counter. Tinh was relieved, since many of the other gang members had been making fun of him for being so inexperienced. He also felt it was appropriate that he should lose his virginity in a BTK safe house.

As he got to know Sandy better, Tinh tried to express his budding feelings of disenchantment about his underworld life. Tinh had never experienced this level of physical intimacy with anyone before. Moreover, as an outsider, Sandy seemed like the only person who might understand why Tinh would feel trapped by a life-style that pushed him further and further from any prospect of a normal, well-adjusted existence. But Sandy wasn't interested. All she wanted to know was whether Tinh had ever killed anyone.

"I have no desire to kill any person," Tinh told Sandy.

Later, Tinh asked Sandy why she had never taken him to meet her parents.

"Oh," she answered, "I couldn't do that. My parents tell me to stay away from Vietnamese people. They would never approve of me having a boyfriend who was Vietnamese."

Tinh had heard these sentiments expressed before, especially by other ABCs, who regarded the Vietnamese as crude and untrustworthy. Few self-respecting Chinese parents would hire a Vietnamese kid to work in their restaurant or market, much less allow one to go out with their American-born daughter.

After that, Tinh saw less and less of Sandy. In a way, the relationship succeeded only in driving him further back into the arms of the gang, convincing him that there was no life outside the closed criminal brotherhood that had become his family, his lifeline, his entire existence.

More than ever, Tinh became convinced that his lot had been decided long ago, when he first entered the world as a vulnerable, terrified newborn in his home country of Vietnam, the Land of the Ascending Dragon. Everything after that was *dao lam nguoi*—natural law, universal law, the law of karma.

Chapter 5

At the same time Tinh Ngo was having his emotional ties to the BTK reaffirmed, the relationship between Chinatown's various criminal factions was turning ugly once again.

On the morning of October 15, 1990, a parking-lot attendant arrived for work in lower Manhattan and made a grisly discovery. In the rear of the lot, amid debris and behind billowing plastic bags of garbage, the bodies of three young Asian males were found piled one on top of another. Each had been shot through the head at close range.

It didn't take the police long to piece together a thumbnail sketch of what had happened. The parking lot was on Reade Street, across from the Sinta Lounge in Ghost Shadows territory. Through various witnesses, the police established that the three murder victims had definitely been in the bar earlier that morning. A neighborhood resident reported hearing shots fired around 3:15 A.M., just after the boys had been marched outside at gunpoint. Apparently, they had been made to put their jackets on backward, making it virtually impossible for them to defend themselves. Then they were executed; two youths were shot twice in the back of the head, a third once.

All three of the victims were Vietnamese, with an assortment of tattoos identifying them as members of Born to Kill.

To the people of Chinatown and the city at large, the killings struck an unusually grim note. Chinatown had seen gang wars before. In 1976, a series of tit-for-tat gang hits resulted in more than a dozen deaths over a twelve-month period. In the mid-1980s, when Chinatown's ethnic makeup first began to diversify and there was a frantic scrambling for turf, gang members were gunned down in gambling dens, barber shops, and neighborhood video arcades. The shooting at the cemetery effectively established that the rules had changed—for the worse. Now it was as if Chinatown's gang wars had descended to the level of barbarism.

One member of the community who felt that the time had come for drastic action was Virgo Lee, the city's director of Asian affairs. Lee heard about the triple homicide on Reade Street on his car radio while driving home. Like most everyone else, he was sickened, especially when he heard the victims had been shot and left to die in a parking lot less than two blocks from his City Hall office.

The next morning, Lee picked up the phone.

"Let me ask you something," he said to an acquaintance, a well-known restaurateur and member of the all-powerful Chinese Consolidated Benevolent Association. "If I were to call for a meeting between myself, business leaders, community leaders, and the police department to discuss what we can do about the gang problem in Chinatown, would you show up?"

"Well, yes," the restaurateur answered. "If you asked me, I would."

Lee hung up the phone, called another businessman he knew and asked the same question. "I suppose so," the businessman answered.

Lee hung up, made a few more calls, and got generally the same answer. He was greatly encouraged.

In most communities, what Lee was proposing was hardly revolutionary. An exchange among representatives of city government, local police, and community leaders might seem like a logical first step toward overcoming a crisis like the one currently bedeviling Chinatown. Few people knew better than Lee, however, just how different Chinatown was from most communities.

Though he had only recently been appointed to the job of Asian affairs director by the newly elected mayor, David Dinkins, Lee was, at the age of thirty-nine, a product of the community. Since arriving from his native Boston as a teenager, he'd spent much of his adult life butting heads with the community's traditional powers. As an activist and union advocate in the 1970s trying to organize working-class and poor immigrants, Lee had learned that social activism was rarely appreciated in Chinatown. Even his parents, rural peasants originally from Toishan province, thought he was "insane," a rabble-rouser who had come under the sway of bad influences in America.

It was through his experiences as an activist that Lee first began to fully understand the ubiquitous power of the CCBA, the traditional nemesis of younger, more progressive Chinese-Americans.

Made up of representatives from most of the community's family, district, and business associations, the CCBA was Chinatown's official governing body. The association's president was sometimes referred to as "the Mayor of Chinatown." CCBA members saw themselves as arbiters of Chinese tradition and culture. Mostly, they comprised a powerful business lobby that refused to deal with any Asian-American group or social-welfare organization not sanctioned by the CCBA.

Headquartered in several buildings on Mott Street, in the heart of old Chinatown, the association was fully legitimate, but it conducted business amid great secrecy, behind closed doors and only in Chinese. The ways in which the CCBA arrived at decisions that affected the lives of nearly all Asians living in the city had contributed greatly to Chinatown's reputation as a mysterious, closed society.

As a representative of city government, Virgo Lee had to deal with the CCBA, whether he liked it or not. Its members' power as decision-makers reached far beyond the organization itself to encompass a stratum of Chinatown society known simply as "the elders." Mostly conservative Cantonese-speaking residents who had fled China in the thirties and forties, the elders were the official voice of Chinatown. No

81

meeting that Lee might hold would have any credibility unless they were included.

Getting their cooperation was problematic, to say the least. Although most elders had never been directly linked to the criminal rackets or the gangs, they supported a system of commerce in which the tongs and the gangs played an important role. If a well-known restaurateur and CCBA member was having a labor problem, gang members might be used to harass picketing employees. In fact, nobody liked to talk about it much, but it was common knowledge that a sizable portion of Chinatown's labor pool was composed of illegal immigrants smuggled into the United States by gangsters. A number of prominent tong bosses who were also CCBA members were believed to be key players in the smuggling process.

Given the symbiotic relationship between Chinatown's business community and the criminal element, the elders had never been out front on the issue of gang violence. For years, most elders refused to admit publicly that gangs existed at all, much less that they were a problem. This attitude had prevailed for so long that even most of Chinatown's social activists had come to believe the gang situation could never be seriously addressed.

As a community veteran, Virgo Lee knew what he was up against. Which made him doubly surprised as he continued flipping through his Rolodex, calling virtually every community and business leader he was on speaking terms with. His idea for a joint community/city government/law enforcement meeting was being met not with terseness, as he expected, but with general acceptance. Even when Lee emphasized that this would be a public gathering attended by members of the Chinese-language press, and not a secret closed-door meeting, no one hung up on him.

By late afternoon nearly two dozen community leaders, including some of the most powerful businessmen in Chinatown, had pledged their willingness to take part in the meeting.

The director of Asian affairs was astounded. The prospect of the community's most powerful forces coming together to officially acknowledge the gang situation was unprecedented. To Lee, it was as startling an indication as any underworld shootout could have been that the current wave of gang activity represented something new, something even the most revered and powerful leaders in Chinatown felt had moved beyond their control.

The most reluctant participant in Virgo Lee's plan for a high-powered summit meeting on gang violence was none other than the New York City Police Department.

"Why should we be negotiating with gangsters?" one high-ranking lieutenant bluntly asked Lee when the subject of the meeting was broached.

"Hey," answered Lee. "If you have evidence any of these people are engaged in criminal activity, then arrest them. Otherwise, you're going to have to deal with these people because of who they are and who they represent."

One reason for police reticence when dealing with community elders was the still-smoldering memory of Chan Tse-Chiu, a legendary tong leader better known as Eddie Chan. In the late 1970s, after an especially violent period of gang warfare, Chan emerged as a key force in the Asian community. With impressive financial power and friends in high places, Chan was a classic example of the type of Chinatown power broker who frustrated lawmen most—outwardly respectable, close to powerful politicians, and thoroughly corrupt.

Theoretically, the cops should have liked Eddie Chan. He was, after all, one of them. Chan first come to New York from Hong Kong, where he had served for many years as a detective sergeant with the Royal Hong Kong Police. In the early 1970s, a corruption scandal forced five notorious police sergeants to flee the colony, though not before they amassed a small fortune from gambling, extortion, prostitution, loansharking, and other criminal rackets. As rich exiles in Taiwan and later Canada, the former police officers became known as the Five Dragons. Though his name had not yet surfaced in the ongoing corruption probe, Eddie Chan also fled Hong Kong at the time of the scandal. In New York's Chinatown, he became known as the Sixth Dragon.

A stout, balding, moon-faced man with a Fu Manchu mustache, Eddie started slowly in New York, first by opening a small jewelry and antiques store. Then he bought a funeral parlor, two or three restaurants, a vegetable market, and several buildings in Chinatown and Little Italy.

When young gangsters from the Ghost Shadows inevitably tried to shake Eddie down, he invited them to lunch. Seated around a restaurant table, the lead gangster asked Chan, "You used to be a police officer in Hong Kong, right?"

"That's right," answered Eddie.

"Well, you arrest a friend of ours one time. He was tortured and crippled, so now you owe us money."

As the gang leader spoke, Eddie calmly arranged his chopsticks, salt shaker, teacup and other table implements to indicate that he was a high-ranking member of a well-known Hong Kong triad. Although the gang youths were impressed enough to suggest Eddie forgo payment, the next day Chan gave them $2,000 anyway. Clearly, Eddie Chan knew the game and was willing to play by the rules.

In 1978, Chan's wealth and triad connections got him elected president of both the local On Leong tong and its national chapter—the largest Chinese fraternal organization in the United States. In just three years, Chan had achieved a stature equal to that of Benny Ong, the Godfather, who was then serving time for his bribery conviction.

Unlike Uncle Benny, who tried to keep a low profile, Chan assumed his role as community leader with a flair for the limelight. He wore suits hand-tailored to fit his sumo-wrestler physique, rode around in a chauffeured Rolls-Royce owned by the On Leong, and was a featured attraction at Chinese civic and political functions. He also became vice president of the United Orient Bank, located on the ground floor of the four-story, pagoda-style On Leong headquarters at Canal and Mott streets.

Along with his flashy personal style and lucrative business ventures, Chan was known as a man who had mastered the art of *guon xi*, the cultivation of influential connections. He became friendly with and contributed to the campaigns of a number of local politicians, among them Mayor Edward I. Koch and Congresswoman Geraldine Ferraro. In 1984, he contributed generously to the reelection campaign of President Ronald Reagan.

Chan's facade of respectability began to crumble in 1983, when a triad leader in Hong Kong first identified him as a major organized-crime figure in the States. Other revelations followed. An indicted Chinese criminal in the United States told federal investigators that Chan "controls the activities of New York criminal gangs through his influence as leader of the On Leong tong." Canadian authorities reported that the head of a prominent triad in Toronto had made a secret trip to New York to slip Chan $130,000 in cash.

Late in 1984, amid rumors that Chan's United Orient Bank was in trouble because of these and other criminal allegations, Chinatown depositors withdrew $6 million in the space of a few days. In a stunning turn of events, Chan was forced to resign as vice president and director. Federal investigators suspected Chan had been using the bank to launder money for triad gangsters and heroin dealers. Before he could be questioned, Chan did what he had done earlier when he got into trouble in Hong Kong—he disappeared. Some say Eddie currently lives in Singapore or Taiwan. Other sightings have been reported in Manila, Paris, and the Dominican Republic.

The NYPD and the Jade Squad had been onto Eddie Chan from the start. But attempts at an investigation were always stymied by Chan's veneer of political respectability and civic high-mindedness. When everyone's worst suspicions about Chan were finally confirmed, an attitude took hold in law enforcement circles that all rich business leaders in Chinatown were triad gangsters in disguise.

The fallout from Eddie Chan's short but heady reign also deeply embittered the CCBA, for entirely different reasons. Business and community leaders in Chinatown felt the case of Eddie Chan—a prominent CCBA member—was being used by the cops and city government to indulge in age-old racist stereotypes. Not all CCBA members were gangsters, they argued—though few non-Asians listened.

For Chinatown's elders to now be willing to sit down with representatives of city government and the NYPD, Virgo Lee knew, had to be because they saw it in their own self-interest to do so. Since the meeting he proposed would be focusing not on traditional tong-associated gangs but rather on the BTK, the elders were being given a rare opportunity to take the high ground. Since they weren't being directly implicated, they could condemn gang violence and conveniently blame the entire problem on the Vietnamese.

There was another, even more obvious consideration, one that Lee stressed often when making his initial pleas to community elders. "You know and I know," he told them, "that all this gang activity has to stop;

it only brings unwanted attention to Chinatown, which is not good for business."

This was an argument the business leaders could get behind. Nothing meant more to the *kiu lings*—the "big shots" who comprised the bulk of the CCBA—than the opportunity to exercise their rights as capitalists, free of unwanted attention from meddlesome outsiders.

It was early in the afternoon of October 17, 1990, when the group of thirty people began to gather at One Police Plaza, the NYPD's drab, twelve-story headquarters just a few blocks from Virgo Lee's City Hall office in lower Manhattan. It was a brisk fall day, with billowing cumulus clouds hovering in the sky amid various shades of gray—a somber tableau that seemed to fit most everyone's mood.

That morning, the police commissioner's office had issued a press release containing additional information about the Reade Street homicides. The three victims were identified as Yu Kim Ly and Phong Thien Nguyen, both seventeen, and Bang Nhu Nguyen, age sixteen. Characterized by the police as low-ranking BTK members, they had been drinking at the Sinta Lounge. Witnesses claimed that one of the BTK members may have used a rival gangster's cellular phone without permission, while another made the fatal mistake of asking his wife to dance. As far as the cops could tell, these were the only reasons the three youths had been marched outside and brutally executed.

The senselessness of the killings gave an added impetus to the meeting, as the business leaders and law enforcement personnel took their seats in a medium-sized conference room on the eleventh floor at police headquarters.

"I think we all know why we're here," began Virgo Lee, standing before the group. "Given all that has happened in recent months, clearly something has to be done. The mayor has voiced his concerns to me. But we need the cooperation of community leaders if we hope to get control of this gang activity."

Lee introduced Chief of Detectives Joseph Borrelli, who was there representing the police commissioner's office. Borrelli had been one of the high-ranking officers who initially balked at participating in the

86

meeting. Now that he was here, he made his remarks in a perfunctory manner, imploring the community leaders to encourage victims of crime in Chinatown to come forward, particularly those whose businesses were located in BTK territory on Canal Street.

Because of his long criminal history and alleged underworld affiliations, Benny Ong had not been invited to the meeting. Even Virgo Lee had to admit Uncle Benny's presence would have been a bit much. Nonetheless, there were others present with similarly controversial reputations. Manson Lau, president of the Fukienese American Association, presided over a tong that police believed had become a haven for members of the Fuk Ching gang. Also present was Paul Lai, adviser-for-life to the Tsung Tsin Association. Headquartered in a building at 1 Catherine Street, it was the Tsung Tsin Association whose illegal gambling casino had only recently been rousted and robbed by the BTK.

Paul Lai was the first community representative to speak. Standing before the group, the elegant, fifty-eight-year-old tong leader expressed his concerns for the community's "image," which was dependent on the appearance of a safe, crime-free environment where New Yorkers and tourists alike could shop and dine comfortably.

"This trouble with the gangs is not good for the livelihood of our citizens," said Lai.

Other community members rose to put prepared statements on the record. Even those whose reputations remained unfettered by alleged links to Chinatown's criminal underworld voiced concerns similar to Lai's. The current situation was bad for their image, they reiterated, and therefore bad for business.

Near the end of the meeting, a slight, soft-spoken businessman with a wispy mustache addressed the group. Cambao de Duong, leader of the Greater New York Vietnamese-American Community Association, was a relative newcomer to Chinatown. The people de Duong represented—respectable Vietnamese citizens attempting to establish themselves within New York's entrenched Asian community—were among those most directly affected by the gang problem.

Struggling to articulate his concerns in halting, heavily accented English, de Duong spoke of the unique difficulties faced by young Vietnamese refugees. Most came from families that had been shattered by traumatic circumstances, he reminded the gathering. In America, these boys were thrown into schools at a level commensurate with their age, not their educational abilities. Many were humiliated by the experience, and sought refuge and a sense of self-worth through the gang, where their desire to be accepted made them vulnerable to manipulation by the older, more hardened criminals among them.

"Where are the social programs and community centers that might help these youths feel they have a place in the community?" asked de Duong. "We are quick to condemn the youths for choosing crime. What do we offer as an alternative?"

The assemblage sat in silence as he made his plea. De Duong, of course, was attempting to address large social issues, perhaps even broaden the discussion to get at the root causes of Chinatown's long tradition of gang activity. Most of the others at the meeting were concerned simply with protecting their own interests. The Chinese business leaders nodded and listened attentively, but given the tangled relationships that sometimes made strange bedfellows of Chinatown's criminal element and its business leaders, nobody seemed anxious to talk about root causes.

After an hour or so, the meeting broke up. There had been no acrimony. Virgo Lee went home happy, believing there was reason to hope that the gathering—the first of its type among these people on this particular subject in the long history of Chinatown—was a significant first step toward making the community more open, more democratic.

For the business leaders and tong bosses who attended the meeting, the possible benefits were less grandiose. The fact that the elders had been willing to sit down with the Caucasian power structure was an unprecedented acknowledgment on their part that the problem did exist. They had been willing to make that concession for a larger gain, although that larger gain, like many things in Chinatown, was not exactly what it seemed to be.

To the tong bosses and some business leaders who participated in the meeting, the motive was simple. A pesky gang of unschooled newcomers was turning Chinatown on its head, and the elders had been unable to alleviate the problem, no matter how violent things got. For those with "alleged" connections to the community's traditional underworld structure, the meeting would be deemed *successful* only if it fulfilled its ultimate purpose as a further marshaling of forces against the ranks of the BTK.

"Three of our boys get murdered and they have a meeting to discuss violence committed by *us*!?" David Thai exclaimed to Tinh Ngo and others during an afternoon visit to the Brooklyn safe house. The *World Journal* and *Sing Tao Jih Pao,* Chinatown's two largest newspapers, both reported that the high-powered summit meeting at One Police Plaza had been held primarily to discuss "the growing problem of BTK violence." Without even finishing the articles, Thai threw the newspapers across the room.

As far as he was concerned, the press coverage of the meeting continued a trend that had begun around the time of the cemetery shooting. Even though the ceremony had been held to mourn the murder of a cherished BTK member, and even though it was BTK members who were the *victims* of the graveside fusillade, these events were presented as further examples of Vietnamese gang violence in Chinatown.

Now this. In a way, it reconfirmed a self-image that Thai and his BTK minions had always cultivated—that of eternal outsiders in a strange, hostile land. The cops hated them. The Chinese resented them. Now the city of New York wanted them to serve as scapegoats for all the violence that occurred in the Asian community.

Even though David seethed with a sense of injustice, he knew there was little he could do. Thai had been around Chinatown long enough to know how unusual it was for such a meeting to have taken place. He suspected that some sort of strange, nefarious power play was under way, with the BTK being used as a pawn.

Already, *Anh hai* had begun to distance himself from his Canal Street operations. In the months leading up to the meeting at NYPD headquarters, Thai was rarely seen at Pho Hanoi, or the massage parlor at 300 Canal Street, or most of the other Chinatown locations he previously frequented.

In fact, much had changed in David Thai's personal life since the BTK emerged as Chinatown's most notorious new criminal scourge. Among other things, he had suffered a fate not unfamiliar to other obsessive, super-ambitious men on the make: His wife left him.

Thai had been spending so much time hatching schemes with his gang brothers, either on the phone or during visits to the numerous BTK safe houses around New York, New Jersey, and Long Island, that his wife had begun to doubt his commitment to her and their two children.

"You have two families," she admonished David. "One on the street and one at home."

Whatever disappointment Thai may have felt at his wife's departure was tempered by the fact that he quickly acquired a new, far more understanding female companion. Among the seven or eight immigrant women imported to work as prostitutes in Thai's massage parlor on Canal Street was an alluring Malaysian named Kim Yee Ngoh. Born in Kuala Lampur, Malaysia's capital city, she went by the name Sophia in the States. Just twenty-two years old, she was five feet one and barely one hundred pounds. She had lovely almond-shaped eyes, silky black hair, and a head-turning smile that could be both innocent and seductive.

Along with her exotic appearance, Sophia had an eye for business. Almost immediately after her arrival in Chinatown in late 1989, Thai moved her from the back rooms at the parlor—where young women administered hand jobs, fellatio, and whatever else was required to satisfy a customer in need—to the front, where she served as bookkeeper and madam.

For a while, David and Sophia lived together in a modest split-level house on Round Swamp Road in Old Bethpage, Long Island, a middle-class suburb not far from the city limits. For security reasons, David tried to keep the whereabouts of his house a secret as long as he could. But there were always gang members coming and going. Once the location became common knowledge to a dozen or so BTK members, David moved, this time to another split-level home in Hicksville, another anonymous Long Island suburb.

For some time now, Thai had been thinking about taking advantage of the BTK's criminal connections beyond New York state. It was at Amigo's funeral, when nearly two hundred Vietnamese mourners showed up from locations throughout the eastern United States, that Thai first began to think seriously about the gang's potential for expansion. Mobility had always been one of the BTK's more distinguishing features. With none of the family and community ties that kept Chinese gangsters local, Vietnamese gang members were free to roam, their common language providing immediate entrée to Vietnamese underworld circles throughout the country.

It had become clear to David Thai that in Chinatown, the BTK could extort, rob, and kill, but they would never be Top Dog. They were Vietnamese, doomed to be outcasts forever.

The realization had been painful, but illuminating. The time had arrived for the BTK to leave the confines of Chinatown, to take their act on the road.

Already, *Anh hai* had been laying the groundwork. In Bridgeport, Connecticut, a mid-sized industrial city ninety miles north of Manhattan, a BTK emissary named Phat Lam had established roots. Earlier that summer, Thai had begun visiting Phat Lam on a semi-regular basis, and together they opened a massage parlor. Thai had even sent Sophia to Bridgeport to oversee the business.

Phat Lam made a list of Asian restaurants, gambling joints, and massage parlors in the Bridgeport area, many of which seemed like easy prey. A handful of BTK gangsters with faces unfamiliar to local police could hit these establishments and be out of town in a few days.

The prospects looked good to David Thai. Only this time he would not entrust the planning and execution of the robberies to his more amateurish gang brothers. Lately, they seemed to be chalking up a high casualty rate with diminishing returns.

The time had come for David to fully utilize the skills of Lan Ngoc Tran, a mysterious, slightly older gang member. Born and raised in the coastal town of Hue, Vietnam's ancient imperial capital, Lan Tran had lived through the heaviest years of the war. It was an experience he and David Thai shared in common, one that made their relationship stronger and more intimate than the sometimes remote affiliations Thai had established with his younger, rank-and-file gang brothers.

Most gang members knew little about Lan Tran's past, though they referred to him respectfully as *Bac Lan,* or "Uncle Lan." The story most of them had heard was that after the fall of Saigon in 1975, young Lan Tran had stayed in South Vietnam to become a freedom fighter. Supposedly, he followed Communist leaders to their homes, where he robbed and killed them. Once, he took part in the bombing of a Communist office building in downtown Ho Chi Minh City, as Saigon was rechristened after the war. After serving a few months in jail, where he was hung by his feet and whipped, Lan escaped South Vietnam and made his way to the United States.

In America, Lan Tran was a transient, living briefly in Texas, California, Toronto, and Georgia before finally settling in New York in the mid-1980s. Even then, Lan Tran came and went so often that, initially, some BTK members didn't know he was in the gang.

Others who had known Lan for a long time gave him credit for coining the gang's moniker. Supposedly, while riding the subway one day with three young gang brothers, Lan had nodded toward a huge subway station poster for a Hollywood movie. The advertisement depicted an American soldier in Vietnam with the words "Born to Kill" scrawled on his helmet.

"What, *Bac Lan*?" asked one of the gang members. "What is it?"

"Here," Lan supposedly remarked, pointing to the slogan. "From now on, this is what we call the gang."

Whatever its origin, the name stuck.

Lan was just five feet four, with a slight, almost emaciated frame, and clothing that hung from his body as if from a wire hanger. He sometimes changed his appearance. One month his hair was wild and spiky, with a yellow streak, the next short and neatly combed. His eyes were always the same: sad and squinty. His perennially jaundiced pallor made him look frail and harmless. But David Thai knew better.

Lan was a true killer, Thai told his gang brothers. A real professional. He was the ideal person to spearhead the BTK's first foray beyond the familiar confines of New York City into the dark American night.

"You watch Uncle Lan," David advised Tinh Ngo and others. "You listen to what he have to say. Lan don't fuck around. When he got a problem during a robbery, he take care of it right away."

At the time, *Anh hai*'s gang brothers didn't really know what he was talking about.

Within a few short weeks, his words would seem like prophecy.

Chapter 6

"**D**o as I say, or else you die!" warned Lan Ngoc Tran.

He was standing inside the Bang Kok Health Spa, a small, neatly organized massage parlor in downtown Bridgeport. Lan's English was heavily accented, but the message was loud and clear. Two young women in the reception area of the parlor cowered in a far corner. Near the door, Chin Suk Ruth, the proprietor, gasped with fear.

"Open the door! Let my guys in! *Now!*" ordered Lan, his 9mm pressed to the back of Chin Suk Ruth's skull. Because he had been alone, Ruth had allowed Lan entry, no questions asked. Now she walked to the front desk and carefully pressed a buzzer, allowing Kenny Vu and a gang member named Tung Lai to enter.

"You got any customer in back!?" Lan Tran asked, barking at the proprietor as if it were an interrogation.

Although Chin Suk Ruth had come to the United States from her native Korea more than twelve years ago, she found it hard to speak clear, concise English with a gun pointed squarely at her head. "Yes, yes," she stammered. "American customer somewhere back there."

Lan nodded to Kenny Vu and Tung Lai to check the back. Tung Lai soon reemerged with a large, slovenly American with unruly black hair and a droopy mustache.

"Sit down," said Lan to the American, gesturing toward a sofa against the wall.

"Can't I just go?" the American asked, his eyes wide with fear.

"No. Nobody hurt you," answered Lan. "We not here for you. Just sit." The fat American plopped down on the couch.

The two girls were told to sit next to the American and keep their heads lowered. Lan Tran began rifling through the drawers of the reception desk until he found a pair of pliers, which he used to snip the extension cord on the telephone. Then he ripped the cord out of the wall.

"Where you keep safety box!? Where you keep money!?" Lan barked at Chin Suk Ruth.

She was nearly overcome with fear. "We n-n-not have m-m-money," Ruth stuttered.

Tung Lai, the youngest of the robbers, stepped forward and slapped the thirty-eight-year-old woman across the face with an open hand, screaming, "You lie, motherfuck!"

Dazed from the blow, Chin Suk Ruth staggered to the desk and took out a metal box, which she opened with a small key. Inside was $1,800 in cash. Lan Tran quickly stuffed the money in a canvas bag he was holding.

One at a time, Tung Lai led the girls to the back rooms. "You give us money, jewelry, everything!" he commanded. When one of the girls protested, Chin Suk Ruth could hear her being smacked around, her cries echoing down the long hallway.

Meanwhile, in the reception area, Lan Tran grabbed everything of value he could find—a VCR, two expensive leather jackets, credit cards, and other personal belongings. When he spotted a twenty-dollar bill that had been shellacked onto the wall for good luck, he carefully sliced it off with a pocket knife.

After ransacking the entire establishment for seven or eight minutes, the three robbers gathered everyone in the front room again. "You call police, you make big mistake," warned Lan Tran, a rictus grin on his face. "We come back here and fuck you up, every one a you!"

Then they were gone.

It took Lan and his crew barely ten minutes to drive through the streets of Bridgeport back to the house at 223 Wayne Street. It was just after 9:30 P.M. David Thai and his girlfriend, Sophia, were there waiting when they arrived.

"Good," said David. "That was fast. How much you get?" He gathered the bags of loot and handed them to Phat Lam, who disappeared into a bedroom to count the proceeds.

It was November 3, 1990, and most of Thai's BTK road crew had arrived at the house in Bridgeport the day before. A few, including Kenny Vu, Tung Lai, and Phat Lam, had been living there off and on for months. As the designated *dai low* in Connecticut, Phat Lam was responsible for paying rent, stocking the house with food, and making sure everyone was accounted for.

Despite its seemingly innocent, suburban appearance, the split-level, wood-shingled abode on the outskirts of town was, in fact, a thriving bordello. For the last few months, Sophia had been serving as the house madam. David made sure there were always plenty of working girls on the premises by shuffling women back and forth between Bridgeport and his massage parlor in New York City. The bordello was closed while the BTK was using the place as a safe house.

That night, everyone in the house was given $200 from the robbery proceeds, whether they had been in on the heist or not. "Next time," said Thai, "we get maybe twice this much."

Over the next few days, Thai's BTK crew ventured out on more robbery attempts. The most ambitious, a planned shakedown of a large Laotian wedding reception, fell through when the gang members realized the reception hall was across the street from the Bridgeport police department. But it would take more than one little derailed robbery to slow them down. They had a long list of Asian establishments waiting to be hit. Some would work out, some wouldn't. The important thing was to keep moving.

For young Vietnamese gangsters looking to ply their trade, Bridge-

95

port was a hospitable place, nestled on the northern banks of Long Island Sound. The city's modest skyline was dominated by cranes and silos. Once a proud factory town, until all the factories closed down and sent their workers packing, Bridgeport was suffering a fate familiar to many mid-sized American cities. Unemployment rose every year and municipal funds slowed to a trickle. About the only thing that remained healthy in Bridgeport was the crime rate, which meant the city's over-burdened police force wasn't likely to pay too much attention to a group of Vietnamese criminals who preyed only on other Asians, many of whom never reported the crimes anyway.

One week after the Bang Kok Health Spa robbery, Lan Tran walked into a small Laotian restaurant and take-out joint on Main Street, near downtown Bridgeport.

"Don't move! Get down!" Lan shouted at the owner of the Vientiane Restaurant after pulling his 9mm from inside a zippered bag. At first, the restaurant owner was confused. How could she not move and get down at the same time?

Uncle Lan was dressed in a slick, disco-style gray suit, his spiked black hair sculpted with heavy mousse. Tattoo-laden Kenny Vu stood behind Lan, wearing dark sunglasses and holding a .38. Outside, in front of the restaurant, Little Cobra stood guard with a .357 tucked inside his black leather jacket.

The owner, her husband, and her niece were all forced to lie down on the floor. In the kitchen the owner's cousin, who was the head cook at Vientiane, was chatting on the phone. Lan Tran grabbed the receiver from his hand and ripped the cord from the wall. The cook got down on the floor without even being asked.

Lan cleaned out the cash register while Kenny Vu snatched an expensive-looking bracelet, earrings, and a necklace from the women on the floor. When they headed for the door, Lan pulled back the slide on his gun, chambering the round in the breech, which made a loud metallic noise. "Stay down," cautioned Lan, "and maybe you live." Then he and Kenny scuffled out the door.

Back at the house on Wayne Street, Tinh Ngo had just arrived from New York City, and David Thai was angry. "Timmy, what happen to you?" Thai demanded to know. "Why you get here so late? The robbery almost done now." Tinh had been given instructions to pick up

Nicky in Chinatown and drive to Bridgeport in time to help with the
Vientiane Restaurant robbery.

"I was speeding and the police stop me, *Anh hai,*" explained Tinh.

As Tinh spoke, Lan Tran and the others walked in the door.

"How did it go?" David Thai asked Lan.

Lan Tran shrugged, as if to say, "No problem."

Thai beamed with admiration at the cool and efficient way Uncle
Lan conducted his duties, terrifying shopkeepers and restaurant owners
without even breaking a sweat.

"Okay, everybody. Listen up," instructed *Anh hai.*

While Sophia toiled in the kitchen preparing dinner, the gangsters
gathered in the living room. Kenny Vu and Little Cobra, still pumped
up from the robbery they had just pulled off with Uncle Lan, set their
guns aside.

"Tomorrow," said David, "we go back to New York. I want everybody get plenty of rest in next few days. Then we take long trip. Drive
maybe twenty hours. We do couple a robberies somewhere else."

"But we here only one week," interjected Tung Lai.

"I know," replied *Anh hai.* "This how we gonna do it now. This
new BTK. We keep moving. This way, they never catch us doing any
crimes."

Later that night, Sophia finished cooking a large pot of *pho* and
the gang members sat around watching a Hong Kong gangster video
on TV.

David pulled Tinh aside. Whatever ire he might have been feeling
toward Tinh earlier had passed. "Here, Timmy," he said, handing Tinh
$300. "This for you. For gas." David rested his hand on Tinh's shoulder
and spoke in a grave, conspiratorial tone. "Remember. Not tomorrow
but next day, meet on Canal Street and I have somebody out there to
give you directions and everything, to go. This job a big one, Timmy.
Big fucking job. Understand?"

Tinh nodded and stuffed the cash in his pocket. He was flattered
that David was speaking to him directly, as if he were on a par with
Uncle Lan. "Yes, *Anh hai,*" Tinh reassured his boss. "I be there for
you."

Three days later Tinh and the others were on the road once again, heading south along Interstate 85, which cut through the flat, industrial expanse of the eastern United States. Tinh piloted a Monte Carlo Supersport registered to David Thai's brother, with Nicky riding shotgun. Tinh's eyes were fixed on the taillights of a 1990 Oldsmobile driven by Tung Lai. In the car with Tung Lai were Kenny Vu and a gang member known as Black Phu. The two-car caravan proceeded at a brisk pace, stopping only for gas and food, as they hurried to their rendezvous with David Thai, Lan Tran, Little Cobra, and others who had already arrived in the small Southern town of Gainesville, Georgia.

By embarking so quickly on another out-of-state sojourn, the BTK had adopted a ritual familiar to young Vietnamese gangsters throughout the United States. Even before David Thai's New York gang had begun to establish itself on Canal Street, Vietnamese criminals were making their presence felt in a surprising variety of geographic locales. Unlike the BTK, most of these gangs were not operating out of a huge, thriving community like New York City's Chinatown. Most had no set base of operation. Secure in their knowledge that, as Vietnamese, they would hardly be noticed by most Americans, they roamed from state to state, city to city, preying on hardworking immigrants who were themselves existing on the fringe of American society.

On the loose in the country's vast, rambling terrain, the BTK and other Vietnamese criminals were, in a way, mimicking the kind of gangsterism first pioneered during the years of the Dust Bowl and the Great Depression. Legendary bandits like Pretty Boy Floyd and John Dillinger had also been intoxicated by the seemingly limitless possibilities afforded by a huge landscape divided into differing states, with separate criminal justice systems and law enforcement departments that were, if not downright hostile toward one another, sometimes less than cooperative.

Rootlessness has obvious advantages for all sorts of criminals operating in the United States, from bank robbers to serial killers. But for Vietnamese gangsters, the motivating factors were more than just practical. For most, their lot in life had been predetermined. As the residue of an unpopular war and the byproduct of refugee camps half a world away, they had no real roots to begin with. Like Tinh Ngo, most had lived unsettled lives, bouncing from foster family to foster family. Even other Vietnamese, those who were able to live quiet, law-abiding lives, saw these troubled, transient youths as lost and lonely souls. *Bui doi*— "the dust of life"—they were called by the older, more established Vietnamese, who both sympathized with and feared the young gangsters in their midst.

By 1990, more than half a million Vietnamese refugees had arrived on United States soil since the fall of Saigon fifteen years earlier. The first to arrive were those lucky enough to get out before or soon after Communist troops rolled into central Saigon. By airlift and by sea, more than one hundred thousand Vietnamese had been transferred to safe havens in Hong Kong, the Philippines, and other locations throughout Southeast Asia where there was an American military presence. By the late 1970s, the Americans were long gone and the method of emigration became more horrific. In a three-year period, from 1977 to 1979, nearly three hundred thousand refugees fled as "boat people," a path later followed by Tinh and many of his BTK brothers.

Of course, the majority of Vietnamese immigrants who made it into the United States did not become criminals. In fact, the relative ease with which the earliest generation of refugees adapted to American society may have lulled some U.S. citizens into thinking the Vietnamese possessed an innate ability for adjusting to alien environments. Having escaped the clutches of a victorious Communist regime bent on exacting revenge and imposing its will, most postwar refugees accepted their reincarnation as Americans with diligence. Many achieved financial success as small-business owners, and their children often excelled in U.S. schools.

But these initial refugees had come overwhelmingly from Vietnam's educated class, those with ties to the military power structure in Saigon. The boat people in the late 1970s and those who followed throughout the eighties were not so well scrubbed. They were poor and mostly from the countryside. Predominantly young males, they were set adrift by their families, a tradition known as "throwing out the anchor." It was hoped that, as males, they would be better equipped to survive the refugee experience and find work in Australia, Canada, or the United States, then bring family members to live with them.

Arriving as "unaccompanied minors," many young, shellshocked refugees simply cracked under the enormous pressures. Like Tinh Ngo, they bounced from foster family to foster family. From Florida to Washington State, they dropped out of school and hung out in pool halls with other young Southeast Asian refugees. Some banded together and committed crimes, establishing links with other Vietnamese criminals in far-flung towns and cities.

By the late 1980s, wayward Vietnamese hoodlums had become associated with a particularly brutal type of crime known as "home invasions." Home invasions were like robberies, only the perpetrators planned the crime so as to deliberately find the home's occupants within. During a home invasion a family might be tied up with electrical cord, rope, or duct tape while gang members ransacked the house looking for cash, jewelry, and electronics. Terror tactics and sometimes torture were used to coerce the victims into producing valuables like gold or expensive family heirlooms locked away in a safe.

The victims of these home invasions were always Asian—Cambodians, Koreans, Laotians, Malaysians, Chinese. Communities with large segments of Vietnamese were especially susceptible. In Southern California, where more Vietnamese immigrants reside than anywhere else in the United States, over two hundred home invasions were *reported* in 1989 and 1990, meaning maybe twice that many actually occurred. To the north in San Jose during that same period, home invasions were taking place at a reported rate of four a month.

By 1990, home invasions and other violent crimes committed against Asians by Vietnamese gangs were on the rise in a staggering variety of cities, including Houston, suburban Washington, D.C., Boston, Minneapolis, and Toronto.

Because of the nomadic nature of this unusual new breed of gangster, local lawmen around the country weren't having much luck prosecuting cases. In New York and other major cities where Chinese gangs had been around for a while, at least local cops had a frame of reference. But Vietnamese gangsters often hit in communities off the beaten track. Even on those occasions when witnesses and victims did come forward, there weren't many cops or agents with an understanding of the culture.

Like the Chinese, Vietnamese names were written with the family name first, though this was usually changed once a person settled in the United States. There were only around two hundred family names

100

in the entire Vietnamese language, leading U.S. lawmen to think that because there were so many criminals named Nguyen or Tran, the two most common Vietnamese surnames, the criminals were either using an alias or were all related. To add to the confusion, Vietnamese gangsters had adopted a certain patented appearance carried over from city to city that made them look strikingly similar.

In 1987, a systematic attempt to deal with the problem was undertaken by two enterprising cops outside Washington. James Badey, a Vietnam War vet and detective from Arlington, Virginia, and Detective Phil Hannum from neighboring Falls Church, were both battling an increase in crimes committed against Asians in their respective communities. In response, they started the International Association of Asian Crime Investigators, an information network they hoped would become a nexus for investigators working on all types of Asian crimes. Much to their surprise, the IAACI's quarterly newsletter soon became almost exclusively devoted to the exploits of the Vietnamese underworld, which they described as "the most rapidly expanding criminal phenomenon in the United States."

Unlike the ranks of the BTK, who were operating mostly within New York City's highly structured criminal underworld in Chinatown, most Vietnamese brotherhoods were made up of "parasitic groups," a term used by Badey and Hannum to describe small, roving bands of gangsters who struck wherever and whenever they wanted. As yet, there didn't seem to be any clearly defined structure that linked these groups in any hierarchical way. There was no *capo di tutti capi,* or boss of bosses. But the possibilities were disquieting. With such a vast reservoir of criminal talent, how long would it be before some strong-willed, charismatic leader had the vision to seize the reins?

Despite the efforts of the IAACI, few lawmen were paying attention to the country's growing Vietnamese underworld, especially at the federal level. At the time, the FBI and DEA were busy chasing *mafiosi* and megabuck dope dealers; they weren't likely to focus on a group of "fringe" criminals who targeted only East Asians, seemingly one of the country's quietest minorities. Even in New York's Chinatown, where David Thai was well known to cops with Asian crime expertise, there was little knowledge of the gang's out-of-state connections—which was hardly surprising. In New York, a police officer's performance is judged on his or her local arrest rate. There was simply no impetus for NYPD detectives to concern themselves with what might be happening beyond the boundaries of the city or the state.

If they had, they might have foreseen that David Thai had big plans when it came to the Vietnamese underworld. Up to now, those plans involved occasional BTK crime sprees in disparate locales like Connecticut and Georgia, the gang's current destination. Beyond that, the stakes only got bigger. Although *Anh hai* didn't talk about it much, Tinh Ngo and the other BTK *sai lows* began to see that their leader was driven by a deep, powerful ambition. Thai knew that, even if the BTK were never to be Top Dog in Chinatown, Chinatown would serve nicely as a stepping-stone, a foundation from which he could tap into a larger criminal network of Vietnamese gangsters and racketeers scattered throughout the United States.

As far as Tinh Ngo and the others was concerned, it was a given: If anyone was going to emerge as supreme commander of America's sprawling, expanding Vietnamese underworld, it was very likely going to be their esteemed boss, Mr. Tho Hoang "David" Thai.

When Tinh and the other BTK gangsters arrived in two carloads at a Dunkin' Donuts just off Highway 129 near Gainesville, it was well past midnight. There was a whiff of juniper in the air and a stillness unlike anything the boys had ever experienced back in Chinatown. From a pay phone, Kenny Vu dialed the number they had been given by *Anh hai*. An American woman answered with a lyrical Southern accent that sounded funny to Kenny.

"David Thai there?" he asked.

"You better call back tomorrow," answered the lady. "Everybody here's had so much to drink they fell right asleep."

Kenny told the lady to let David Thai know they would be staying at Days Inn, located across the street from Dunkin' Donuts.

At nine o'clock the following morning, *Anh hai* knocked on the door of the motel room, fresh and wide awake. He greeted his young brothers like an eager conventioneer, instructing them to follow him to Cafe Huong, a Vietnamese coffee shop on the outskirts of Gainesville, where he bought everyone breakfast. After they'd eaten, David handed each gang member $100. "Put this in your pocket in case you need it," he said, playing his usual role as big brother and benefactor.

The gang members were still exhausted from the twenty-hour drive from New York City. But David already had business on the brain. "Today, we gonna check out a couple jewelry stores near Atlanta," he told the gang.

In Georgia, the BTK contact was a lanky, rugged auto mechanic named Quang Van Nguyen. Quang served the same function as Phat Lam in Bridgeport, making up a list of local Asian establishments that looked like good robbery targets.

That afternoon, David Thai and his BTK brothers met Quang Nguyen and drove to Doraville, a placid Atlanta suburb fifty miles south of Gainesville. Doraville was small, with barely eight thousand residents, but the town had a sizable outdoor shopping center located alongside Buford Highway, a broad six-lane thoroughfare that connects Doraville with other Atlanta suburbs. Known as Northwoods Plaza, the shopping center was an ethnic mix of *taquerías* and Chinese groceries, with a few Vietnamese establishments thrown in.

David Thai himself went into the Sun Wa Jewelry Store, a compact retail outlet sandwiched between a Spanish-language video shop and a Dollar-Mart. Ostensibly, Thai had a ring that needed fixing. Really, he was casing the place to see whether it was worth robbing.

"This one easy to take," said *Anh hai* to the others after coming out of the store. "They got big inventory, no security."

After checking out a few more Asian stores, the boys drove back to Gainesville.

The house where Thai and the others were staying was a squat, ranch-style dwelling at 2904 Maverick Trail Road, a rural, wooded cul-de-sac. The house was surrounded by leafy oak and sycamore trees; there were no streetlights, shops, or other urban amenities in the area. During his years in Georgia, Lan Tran had lived in another part of Gainesville with the couple now residing at the house, Lan's former roommate and his American girlfriend, Kathy Ivester—the woman with the Southern accent Kenny Vu had spoken with on the phone.

With nearly a dozen gang members now staying at the modest two-bedroom home, the place was a swirl of activity. The boys had barely settled in when, the next night, they were off to Atlanta again, this time

103

for a little entertainment. A nightclub in Atlanta was having a party, and the featured attraction was Diem "Linda" Trang, a sexy Vietnamese pop singer from California.

What the Vietnamese referred to as a "party," most Americans would probably call a concert. For weeks leading up to the event, flyers are posted in Asian restaurants and pool halls throughout the area. Young men and women come from miles away, paying anywhere between $25 and $100 to see a familiar, top-name entertainer. The parties, held in big cities across the United States, are a rare opportunity for Vietnamese youths to get dressed up and meet other Vietnamese from outside their community.

On occasion, these parties also served as convenient meeting places for members of the underworld. It was not unusual for elaborate crimes to be hatched at tables and booths where young males sipped on expensive cognac while their girlfriends swirled around them on the dance floor.

At approximately 10:00 P.M. that night, David Thai and his BTK brothers arrived at the Atlanta party in two carloads. Right away, *Anh hai* got angry. The doorman at the club had the audacity to actually make Thai and his BTK crew pay to get in. As leader of the largest and most infamous Vietnamese gang in the United States, Thai was accustomed to dropping his name and getting in free most places.

Inside, while nearly five hundred men and women danced underneath a disco ball and strobe light, *Anh hai* glowered. He declared to his gang brothers, "I tell you what we gonna do . . ."

Around one o'clock, when the club approached closing time, Kenny Vu, Black Phu, and a few others were to start a fight inside the club. That would draw the two security officers outside the club inside. Then Tinh Ngo and Nicky were to jump the doorman, who was standing just outside the front door. "He got big pockets on that jacket," said David. "I bet he got something like a thousand dollars on him."

By the time the club was starting to close, everyone had a few beers under his belt. Tinh and Nicky went outside. As planned, a commotion started inside the club, and the security guards were called in. At that moment, Nicky asked the doorman, "Hey, you know how we get to North Carolina?"

"Yeah," answered the doorman. "Where your car?"

Like most gang members, Nicky was small, with a look of permanent bemusement on his face. He, the doorman, and Tinh ambled out into the parking lot.

Without warning, Nicky swiftly pulled out a gun and put it to the doorman's head. "Don't make me have to shoot, motherfuck," he advised, using the BTK's favorite curse word—a word used variously as a noun, an adjective, and an exclamation point.

Tinh began rifling the doorman's pockets. Except for a few pieces of paper, they turned out to be completely empty.

Nicky had his arm around the guy's neck, trying to hold him still. But the doorman broke free and began to run through the parking lot. "Ping! Pang! Pong!" sounded the shots from Nicky's gun as he fired at the doorman, who danced through the parking lot like a monkey high on crack cocaine.

Meanwhile, inside the club, Black Phu had taken his role in the charade far too seriously. A dark-skinned Amerasian—the child of an African American soldier stationed in Vietnam during the war—Phu was notoriously high-strung. On top of that, he'd had too much to drink, turning what was supposed to be a fake altercation into a real one by pulling out *his* gun and firing a few shots into the ceiling of the nightclub.

The BTK members inside fled at the same time the doorman outside was scampering through the parking lot. Police sirens could be heard getting closer. Nicky stopped shooting and ditched his gun underneath the fender of a huge truck. The gang members piled into their two cars, then raced through the streets of Atlanta until they found the expressway.

As they drove through the pitch darkness on I-85 back toward Gainesville, Tinh told David Thai what had happened with the doorman. He was certain *Anh hai* would be mad. Instead, David laughed, his usually reserved chuckle building into a full-blown guffaw. This pleased Tinh, who rarely saw Thai express pleasure of any kind. Tinh also laughed, and so did the other gang members, until the entire car was filled with the sound of howling, knee-slapping BTK gangsters.

Over the next forty-eight hours, everyone in the crowded house on

105

Maverick Trail Road began to get antsy. On Thanksgiving, a holiday that meant little to the boys of the BTK, a handful of gang members headed north across the state line into Chattanooga, Tennessee. Led by Jimmy Nguyen—the gang member who had accidentally shot and killed a fellow BTK gangster during the robbery of the produce warehouse in Chinatown three months earlier—the crew robbed a small jewelry outlet just as the store's owner was closing for the day. They blindfolded and tied up the middle-aged Vietnamese woman with duct tape and set her on a large bag of rice in the back of the store. Little Cobra stabbed the bag threateningly, then Jimmy Nguyen pistol-whipped the woman until she mercifully passed out. The boys arrived back at the house in Gainesville with a bag of jewelry.

The next morning, David Thai, Lan Tran, Tinh, and a few others walked across Maverick Trail Road to a wooded area not far from the house. Another local gang member, Hoang Ngo—better known as Jungle Man—had just dropped off a small cache of handguns purchased at a pawnshop in nearby Braselton. Located sixty miles from Atlanta, Braselton was a sleepy Georgia town that became famous when it was purchased a year earlier by its most renowned native daughter, the sultry actress Kim Basinger. Like most Georgia towns, Braselton was a convenient place to purchase guns. The only requirement was a Georgia state driver's license and one other piece of ID.

Near a pond in the woods, the gang members took target practice, firing at empty beer bottles and the trunk of a large sycamore tree. The report from the weapons echoed across the pond and through the trees, and soon Kathy Ivester, the gang's hostess, came out to complain.

"Are you trying to get us evicted?" she yelled at David Thai.

For days, Ivester had been aiming caustic barbs at *Anh hai*, mostly because he tied up her telephone for hours at a time, making long-distance calls to New York, California, and God knows where else. "You think you can just come out here and fire your guns and nobody's gonna notice? Well, you better think again, mister. We got neighbors here. They might just call the police."

Then she stormed back into the house.

David winced, as if maybe he was developing an ulcer. "Man, this lady getting on my nerves," he said to no one in particular. "I think maybe we go do this robbery and get the fuck outta here."

Late on the morning of November 26, 1990, forty-six-year-old Odum Lim was seated in the back of the Sun Wa Jewelry Store, fixing the clasp on a diamond necklace. Lim's work space was cramped, which was just the way he liked it. Tools hung from nails on the wall around him, his bench was messy, and a glaring fluorescent desk light was pulled in tight on the job before him.

A buzzer on the store's front door sounded. Lim looked out from behind his workbench to see four well-dressed Vietnamese males enter the store. To Lim, they seemed a little *too* well dressed for an uneventful Monday afternoon in Doraville. He got up from his bench and came out to the front of the shop, where his wife and two young daughters were standing behind a glass showcase.

The interior of the Sun Wa Jewelry Store was not spacious, but Lim and his wife had a sizable inventory displayed in a series of eight glass cases arranged in a U-shape. Customers could peruse the expensive gold and diamond jewelry arranged on velvet trays inside each four-foot-high case, but could not get behind the counter without being buzzed in through a security door—or jumping over the top of the counter.

Lan Tran, Nicky, Little Cobra, and Kenny Vu pretended they were looking at the merchandise. Nicky eventually approached Lim's wife, Kim Lee, with a broken neck chain that needed fixing. At that moment, Tinh Ngo and Tung Lai entered the store.

From the door, Tinh watched as Nicky leaned over the counter to speak with Mrs. Lim. On the other side of the store, Lan Tran was pointing out a ring inside one of the glass cases that he wanted Mr. Lim to show him. Otherwise, the store was quiet, and Tinh wondered what the hell was going on. The plan had been for him and Tung Lai to enter after the others, when the robbery would already be under way. For a second, he thought maybe the job had been called off.

Just then, Tung Lai, standing on the right side of the store next to Nicky, called out, "Mr. Owner, will you please help me with this one, this ring right here?" He pointed to a piece of jewelry in the case.

Odum Lim looked suspicious, but he came over anyway.

"This one," insisted Lai, "this one right here."

As Lim bent over to see which ring Lai was pointing at, Lai abruptly reached across the counter and grabbed him by the tie. It was a bold maneuver to start the robbery, except for one thing: The tie was a clip-on, and it immediately came off in his hand.

Before the store owner had a chance to react, Little Cobra, standing next to Tung Lai, pulled out a .38 special and stuck it in his face. "This a robbery! Everybody down on the floor! Now!" he barked.

Tung Lai, Little Cobra, and Nicky all vaulted over the glass counter in unison. Nicky grabbed Mrs. Lim by the throat and began pushing her toward the rear of the store. "Follow me or I hurt your mother!" he commanded the two young girls, ages nine and six.

"Please don't hurt mommy! Please!" begged the younger of the two daughters while following Nicky and Mrs. Lim toward a room in the back of the store.

The robbery had been carefully planned, with specific duties assigned to each of the robbers. Lan Tran hopped over the counter on the far side of the store and began trying to break the lock on a safe-deposit box. Kenny Vu whipped out his gun and stood guard at the door. Little Cobra, Tung Lai, and Tinh were supposed to clean out the glass showcases, dumping the contents into pillow cases they had brought with them.

Tinh hopped over the counter in the far right corner, directly across the store from Lan Tran. The glass jewelry cases were locked, and Tinh began frantically searching for a key. There was none that he could see. He spotted a plastic Nintendo play gun on the counter, picked it up, and banged it against the case, trying to break the glass. Instead, the flimsy plastic gun cracked and shattered in his hands. Tinh looked around for something harder, spotted a large stapler, and again began *thump, thump, thumping* on the glass.

To his left, Tinh could see that Tung Lai and Little Cobra were having problems with Mr. Lim. A Cambodian refugee who had spent years in a work camp at a time when the murderous Khmer Rouge ruled his country, Odum Lim might have been twenty-five years older than most of the robbers, but he was tough. Lim was not about to let these young Vietnamese punks endanger his livelihood and threaten his family without a fight.

"*Motherfuck!*" exclaimed one of the gangsters.

"I get you!" grunted Odum Lim. He reached out, attempting to grab Little Cobra's gun, then smashed Tung Lai in the face with a forearm.

Lim, Lai, and Little Cobra began wrestling. They banged against the glass case in front of them, toppling it over with an ear-splitting *crash*! That's when Tung Lai pulled out a six-inch bowie knife and began sticking and stabbing Odum Lim, the knife piercing Lim over and over in the arm and neck.

Meanwhile, Tinh had shattered his glass case and was hurriedly dumping trays of jewelry into the pillowcase. He could see Tung Lai stabbing and wrestling with Mr. Lim, but continued to do what he had been told. "No matter what happens, Timmy," David Thai had said, "you just keep taking jewelry. You got most important job of all."

BAM! A piercing gunshot rang out, the bullet ricocheting off a far wall and into the ceiling. A startled Tinh Ngo looked over to see that despite multiple stab wounds and being covered with blood, Odum Lim had gotten his hands on Little Cobra's gun, which had discharged. Tung Lai cried out, "Look out! The owner have the gun, the owner have the gun!"

On the other side of the store, Lan Tran looked up from trying to open a bulky, gray safe-deposit box, saw his fellow gang members wrestling with the store owner, and got up with an expression more of annoyance than concern.

Tinh was still shoving jewelry into the pillowcase when he saw Lan come from the far side of the store, moving so quickly that Tinh could have sworn he saw a blaze of color trailing behind him. Gracefully, in one quick, fluid motion, Lan whipped out a gun from inside his waistband, placed it an inch away from Odum Lim's left temple, and fired.

To Tinh, the sequence seemed like a dream. He saw smoke and a burst of fire emanate from Lan's gun. Then he saw blood spurt from the store owner's temple and heard his muffled cry. Tung Lai and Little Cobra recoiled in shock. The store owner slumped to the floor.

Slowly, Lan Tran turned toward Tinh. His eyes were cold. Empty. Looking at Uncle Lan, Tinh felt as if all his senses had been heightened. He could hear a clock ticking across the room; the wind blowing through the trees outside; a baby crying half a world away in a small bamboo hut somewhere in Hua Giang province.

Then came an explosion of noise and confusion as they all ran. Tung Lai and Little Cobra practically tripped over one other trying to get to the door. Kenny Vu had already split. Lan Tran disappeared in a cloud of smoke. Tinh, jewelry dribbling from his pillowcase, stumbled for the door as quickly as he could.

In the small storage room in back, Nicky had been attempting to handcuff Mrs. Lim to a metal bar on the wall. He heard a loud commotion and then silence.

Looking more bemused than ever, Nicky peeked out from the back room, then gingerly crept to the front. His eyes opened wide. The gang members were gone, and the store was a shambles. There was blood on the carpet, starting where Odum Lim had been shot, then trailing across the floor and out the front door. Lim himself was nowhere in sight.

Mrs. Lim and her two children also ventured to the front of the store. They stood in shock and surveyed the damage, their eyes slowly following the ominous blood smears.

Outside, the gang members darted into two getaway cars. They drove two blocks east to a gas station parking lot, where David Thai and the local contact, Quang Nguyen, had been waiting patiently in a Jeep Cherokee.

"*Anh hai,*" Lan Tran said to David, "the whole thing get fucked up. The owner—he get shot."

"You get the gold?" asked David.

Tung Lai, his shirtfront covered with the store owner's blood, proudly held up the bag of jewelry.

"We better get out a here," advised David. "Meet back at the house."

All three getaways cars sped down Buford Highway onto I-85, heading north to Gainesville.

It was a good forty-five minutes before anyone realized that Nicky had been left behind in the store.

Chapter 7

"You motherfucking stupid motherfuck," *Anh hai* yelled at Tung Lai. "Nobody say nothing about you fuck around with the owner. You supposed to get the jewelry, like Timmy."

The gangsters were standing in the front room of the house on Maverick Trail Road. Tung Lai had removed his bloody shirt and was trying to explain how he got involved in the tussle with the store owner. "I just try to make sure the owner don't have some weapon."

"No," snapped David Thai. "No, no, no. Your job was to break the glass and steal jewelry. That what you supposed to do."

"Hey," interjected one of the gang members. "Where's Nicky?"

Everybody looked at one another in stunned silence, realizing that a colossal fuck-up had just gotten worse.

"He's not with you?" somebody asked.

"No, I thought he with you," someone else replied.

"He not with us. Didn't he come with you?"

"Awww shit," said David Thai, rolling his eyes.

Anh hai and Quang Nguyen jumped back into the Jeep Cherokee and headed toward Doraville. They were only gone about thirty minutes when a Doraville taxi pulled up in front of the house and Nicky got out.

"How you motherfuck leave me like that?" he screamed, storming in the front door. "You set me up."

"No, no," replied Uncle Lan, trying to calm Nicky down. "It just a big mistake. We think you with them, they think you with us. David Thai just go to pick you up."

An hour later David Thai and Quang Nguyen came back to the house. Thai looked shaken. "We better get outta Georgia. Fast. I think that store owner dead. I see police everywhere."

Thai had seen Odum Lim on a stretcher in front of the Sun Wa Jewelry Store. Lim's face was a bloody mess, and his left arm was perforated with a dozen stab wounds. After the robbers fled, Lim had managed to drag himself to the front of the store, pull open the door, and crawl out onto the pavement. When the police and medical personnel arrived, he was lying in a pool of blood with his distraught wife and two children sitting on the sidewalk next to him, sobbing quietly.

"Gather your things," Thai told the others. "We get outta here soon as we can."

"*Anh hai*," said Kenny Vu firmly. "We don't want Tung Lai in our car. Let him go somewhere else. This guy fuck up so bad, he bad luck for us."

"Hey," interjected Nicky. "You think we want this motherfuck with us?"

Tung Lai hung his head sheepishly.

David Thai was exasperated. "Well, somebody gotta take him back to New York."

"We take him, *Anh hai*," offered young Tinh Ngo. "We take him back with us."

Within a few hours, the BTK gang members were back on the road, driving through the dead of night along the interstate. Seated behind the wheel of the Monte Carlo, Tinh passed a blur of exit signs: Kannopolis, North Carolina; Savage, Maryland; Swarthmore, Pennsylvania. The names seemed otherworldly to Tinh and his Vietnamese brothers.

With the car radio droning in the background, Tinh tried to make sense of all he had seen that day. The sound of Lan Tran's gun was still ringing in his ears; the sight of blood spurting from the store owner's head was still vivid.

It was an event Tinh had been dreading for some time. Violence had been exploding all around him for months. Now, he was himself an accomplice in a stark, cold-blooded killing.

One thing seemed clear to Tinh: This shooting was not right. To kill a man with his family nearby—a man who had done nothing but try to defend himself and his livelihood—was wrong, wrong, wrong. Tinh scoured his conscience, trying to find some excuse, any excuse, that might justify what had taken place.

There was no excuse.

Visions of the shooting at the Sun Wa Jewelry Store swirled inside Tinh's head throughout the twenty-hour drive to New York City. They would continue to do so, taunting and tormenting him in the days and weeks that followed.

Back in Chinatown, merchants and residents alike had enjoyed a brief respite from the persistent violence that had become synonymous with the BTK. Altogether, David Thai and the handful of key gang members who accompanied him on his out-of-state crime spree had been gone for the better part of a month. During that period, the tit-for-tat gang warfare of the last year and a half, which resulted in a string of dead gang members from most of Chinatown's major gangs, had subsided. The city's newspapers turned their attentions elsewhere. In December 1990, John Gotti, the Mafia's *capo di tutti capi*, was arrested on federal racketeering charges, an event that would keep many of the city's best crime reporters occupied over the weeks and months that followed.

In part, the relative peacefulness that had now descended on Chinatown's underworld could be attributed to the meeting held two months earlier by Virgo Lee, the mayor's Asian affairs director. Typically, no official decrees had been announced or official truce declared. The CCBA had resumed its closed-door meetings; no one outside a handful of Chinatown's most powerful tong and business leaders would know what sort of an arrangement was reached. Nonetheless, the Flying Dragons and the Ghost Shadows had backed off, and the shootings all but ceased.

Not only that, but a fundamental change in the attitude of many in the community toward the BTK had taken place. As long as the gang stopped overstepping its boundaries by hitting commercial establishments in other gangs' territories, it was as if Chinatown's power structure had all but ceded Canal Street to David Thai's Vietnamese gang.

Of course, the BTK themselves had played a role. Even while *Anh hai* and his road crew were off haphazardly expanding the gang's profile in Connecticut, Tennessee, and Georgia, the gang's other members had not been idle. Although the exact number of gang members tended to ebb and flow depending on who was in prison or who had been killed lately, there were still believed to be somewhere around seventy-five BTK members in the New York vicinity alone. Thai had left strict instructions with numerous *dai lows* to maintain a strong presence on Canal Street.

Every Saturday a handful of gang members made extortion rounds, demanding anywhere from $20 to $200 from the approximately seventy shops packed tightly along a four-block stretch of Canal Street, between the streets of Centre and Lafayette. Up to now, some merchants had resented making extortion payments to the BTK, not so much because they didn't want to pay but because the Vietnamese gangsters had lacked the proper authority. In the wake of the big meeting between the NYPD and the CCBA, most merchants were glad to cough up the money, believing—perhaps wishfully—that it was a small price to pay for order and tranquillity on Canal Street.

Now that Chinatown's criminal element had, for the time being, ceased shooting at each other, the citizens of the community could turn their attention to more worthy matters. As the chill of December gave way to the deep freeze of January, all of Chinatown rallied to celebrate the New Year's season, an annual, ongoing festival that ran from late January until February 15. Neighborhood restaurants and markets bustled with shoppers, and the sound of firecrackers and the smell of brimstone filled the air day and night. Drifts of debris from shredded firecrackers littered the streets like new-fallen snow.

The celebration culminated with the Dance of the Dragons, a grand Chinatown tradition. In different parts of the community, five different dragons operated by a dozen young males gyrated back and forth through the streets. Trailing behind the dragons was a parade of Chinatown's citizens, who clanged cymbals and banged on drums. Revelers lined the streets and watched from windows and fire escapes, clamorously ushering in the Lunar New Year, in this case the Year of the Ram.

To the Vietnamese, the New Year's season is known as Tet, the Festival of the First Morning of the Year. Their celebration is designed to unite all Vietnamese—Buddhist and Catholic, Marxist and capitalist. Firecrackers are exploded to ward off evil demons and spirits. The first distinct sound heard in the new year is most important. Traditionally, a cock's crow signals hard work and a bad harvest. The lowing of a buffalo heralds a year of sweat and toil. A dog barking signifies confidence and trust.

In 1991, one of the first sounds heard by a Chinatown store owner named Sen Van Ta was the *thwaaack* from the butt of a gun being smashed against his skull. This is not a sound explained in Vietnamese mythology, but its implications were clear enough.

It was early in the evening of January 21, 1991, the beginning of Tet. Sen Van Ta was shutting his clothing outlet at 302 Canal Street after a busy day. Ta was the landlord of a sizable commercial space that included his store and a subtenant, the Golden Star jewelry store. Ta stood outside the store on the sidewalk, pulling down a metal security gate. Inside, three employees were putting jewelry and cash into a large safe.

Out of nowhere, three BTK gangsters appeared on the sidewalk. "Open this gate and let us in," demanded one of them, pressing the barrel of his gun against Sen Van Ta's ribs. They forced the landlord back inside his store, where the startled employees looked up just as one of the gangsters smacked Sen Van Ta in the head with a handgun.

After that, the robbers followed the usual routine. They made all the employees lie facedown on the floor. Then they ransacked the store and robbed each employee, kicking one of them in the ribs when he removed a ring from his finger too slowly. They fled the store with an impressive $350,000 worth of jewelry and close to $1,000 in cash.

Outside on Canal Street, two getaway cars awaited. Three of the gangsters piled into a powder-blue Cadillac with New Jersey plates. Behind the wheel was Jungle Man, the Georgia-based BTK member who'd served as a getaway driver during the bloody Doraville heist and was now living in New York. Little Cobra, another of the Doraville robbers, jumped into the backseat of the Caddie along with Nguieu Tun, a sixteen-year-old gang member known as Teardrop because of a small, teardrop-shaped tattoo under his left eye. (During the robbery, Teardrop covered the easily identifiable tattoo with a flesh-colored Band-Aid.)

Darkness had descended on the streets of Chinatown. The Cadillac, its headlights not yet turned on, zoomed west on Canal Street. Three cops in an unmarked police vehicle saw it go speeding by. They turned on their siren, put a flashing red light on top of the car, and took off after it.

When Jungle Man saw the cops in pursuit, he stomped on the accelerator and led them on a wild chase through the streets of Chinatown and Little Italy. The Cadillac raced through a number of red lights, sideswiped a car, and narrowly missed plowing head-on into an NYPD squad car. An all-points-bulletin went out, and approaching sirens resounded throughout Chinatown.

After a fifteen-minute chase through heavy traffic, the Cadillac was finally cut off at the intersection of Chrystie and Broome by police cars converging from all sides. The BTK gangsters were dragged from the car by nearly a dozen cops, all of whom had their guns drawn.

"Down on the pavement! All of you!" commanded one of the cops, his gun aimed at their heads.

The gang members dropped to the ground.

The police searched the Caddie and found some jewelry. When they retraced the route of the chase, they found a .380 handgun and an Uzi submachine gun used in the robbery that had been tossed from the speeding getaway car. Jungle Man, Little Cobra, Teardrop, and one other gang member were taken into custody.

The next day, Sen Van Ta and two employees from the Golden Star jewelry store were brought to the First Precinct to view a lineup. From behind a two-way mirror, Sen Van Ta identified both Little Cobra and Jungle Man. Later, Teardrop and the fourth participant were also identified. They were booked on charges of robbery in the first degree, with Sen Van Ta listed as the main complainant.

Because of the high-speed car chase through Chinatown, the jewelry store robbery had quickly become the talk of the community. The heist was of particular interest to David Thai, who had selected the target for the robbery—a jewelry store located right next door to his Canal Street massage parlor. It was *Anh hai* who decided which gang members would commit the crime, and it was *Anh hai* who received the stolen jewelry after the robbery, delivered to him at a safe house in Long Island by the robbers in the second getaway car.

The arrest of four gang members had not been anticipated, though occasionally these things did happen. Usually, gang members in Chinatown—Vietnamese, Chinese, or whatever—could rest assured that witnesses would not come forward and their victims would not file charges. That was the way Chinatown operated, through a code of silence that had made it possible for generations of gangsters to continue plying their trade.

This time, the complainant had not only come forward—he seemed determined to see the case brought to justice.

Sen Van Ta, age twenty-nine, was not naive in the ways of Chinatown. Born in rural South Vietnam, he had come to New York as a penniless refugee after a two-year stint at a camp in Galang, Indonesia. In 1983, he began his business career as a street vendor. Along with hundreds of other Chinese and Vietnamese immigrants hoping to make their way in Chinatown's highly competitive marketplace, Ta sold batteries, headphones, cassette tapes, and other inexpensive merchandise from a small, folding card table on Canal Street.

Driven by a desire to make something of his life, Sen Van Ta was proof that Chinatown, however crowded and perilous, still functioned as a vehicle of hope and opportunity for even the most destitute Asian immigrants. For two years, from 9:00 A.M. to 7:30 P.M. seven days a week, Ta stood behind his table on Canal Street selling trinkets. He saved nearly everything he earned. In late 1985, he and a friend—a fellow refugee he first met at the camp in Indonesia—pooled $15,000 each and opened a small store that sold jeans and T-shirts. At the time, commercial rents were still reasonable in Chinatown, and within the first twelve months of business Sen Van Ta and his partner were already turning a small profit.

By the late 1980s, Sen Van Ta had become well aware of the BTK. Most merchants he knew were inclined to pay the young gangsters who came into their stores demanding "protection money." At the time, brazen thefts—mostly by African American teenagers—were common on Canal Street. If these Vietnamese toughs were able to prevent shop-lifting and harassment by menacing outsiders, many store owners felt they had no choice but to pay.

In the beginning, Sen Van Ta also paid. But he had stopped. For one thing, at five feet nine and 175 pounds, Ta was reasonably sturdy for a Vietnamese male; he didn't need to pay young hoodlums to look out for his physical welfare. Furthermore, Ta was infuriated by the ra-tionale these gangsters used when they made their extortion demands. They would say, "We are Vietnamese, just like you. We are hungry and we need money to eat."

Sen Van Ta felt he was just as much a humanitarian as the next person, but he too knew a few things about what it meant to be destitute. Just like these gangsters, he had been displaced by the Vietnam War at a young age. He too had been sent out to sea by his parents, spent years in a refugee camp, and arrived in America as a lonely, unwanted outsider. But Sen Van Ta had not chosen a life of crime. He worked for a living, sinking every penny he made back into his business ven-tures until he could stand proudly on his own two feet as a reputable, taxpaying citizen. As such, Ta could not see why he had to pay money to hoodlums who were unwilling to make the same sacrifices he had made.

Sen Van Ta knew his unwillingness to continue making extortion payments was probably one of the reasons his commercial space had been targeted for robbery. The blow to the head—a nasty gash that required ten stitches—was an added indignity that only strengthened his determination to stand up to the dreaded BTK.

As a seasoned Chinatown merchant, Ta knew there would be re-percussions. The first was a piece of mail delivered to the shop on February 7, two weeks after the robbery. Inside a plain white envelope Ta found an article on the robbery and subsequent arrests clipped from the *Downtown Express*, a free weekly newspaper distributed in Chinatown restaurants. Accompanying the article were a few shards of broken glass.

"What does this mean?" an employee asked him.

"This mean maybe they blow up the store," answered Ta.

A few days later, Sen Van Ta was enjoying the early morning sunshine on Canal Street, standing on the sidewalk in front of his store. He had just unlocked the security gate to open for the day when he was approached by a well-dressed Asian male he immediately recognized as David Thai.

"Don't open this store," David Thai told Sen Van Ta. "Instead, go to court and say those four boys did not rob you. Then maybe you get your jewelry back and we can forget this unfortunate incident."

In the past, Thai might have made this threat by proxy. After all, it was unseemly for a boss to directly involve himself in the gang's street-level intimidations. But now that the BTK had confined its New York operations almost exclusively to Canal Street, it needed to enforce its territorial imperative more emphatically than ever before. By visiting Sen Van Ta in person, David Thai was drawing the line. He was making it clear to *all* merchants on Canal Street that defiance of the gang was an offense that would simply not be tolerated.

Sen Van Ta was not intimidated. He ignored the BTK leader and opened his store. With ten fresh stitches in his head, he couldn't have forgotten the incident even if he wanted to. And he wasn't about to let David Thai or anyone else scare him into dropping the charges.

119

Around the same time that Sen Van Ta was entering into a war of wills with the BTK, Tinh Ngo was slipping deeper and deeper into an emotional morass. Ever since the robbery and brutal assault in Georgia, he had been walking around in a daze.

The Doraville jeweler, in fact, had not died. Despite a gunshot wound to the head and multiple stab wounds, he recovered. But Tinh didn't know that. He saw the guy take a bullet in the cranium and assumed he had been abruptly reunited with his ancestors. Guilt-ridden by his own complicity in what he believed was a cold-blooded murder, he had started smoking crack again, something he hadn't done with any regularity in many months. Living with four or five other gang members in yet another BTK safe house in the Sunset Park section of Brooklyn, he was sleeping no more than three or four hours a night. His dreams were haunted by images of Lan Tran pressing his gun to the store owner's head, the trigger being pulled, blood spurting upward.

The lack of sleep and occasional use of crack heightened Tinh's sense of paranoia, which brought about an altercation with the law that, under the circumstances, seemed inevitable.

A few weeks before the robbery at Sen Van Ta's store on Canal Street—two and a half months after returning from Georgia—Tinh was about to enter his Brooklyn apartment at 1033 Sixty-seventh Street when he saw a patrol car slowly pull up. A uniformed officer got out. Instinctively, Tinh ran. The cop chased him along Sixty-seventh Street, and with two other officers eventually wrestled him to the ground.

The cops had merely wanted to ask Tinh a few questions about who was living with him in the apartment. Now they wrote Tinh up a summons for "resisting," a charge that required a court appearance.

One month later, when Tinh arrived at the Criminal Courts Building on Schermerhorn Street in downtown Brooklyn, he was approached by three detectives from the Sixtieth Precinct out in Coney Island.

"Are you Tinh Ngo?" asked one of the detectives.

"Yes," answered Tinh.

"We're placing you under arrest," he said, "for robbery. You'll have to come with us."

The robbery had taken place months earlier, before the trip to Georgia. At 5:00 A.M. on the morning of September 19, 1990, Tinh and a handful of other gang members had staged a home invasion at 223 Neptune Avenue, the same apartment building where Tinh lived when he first joined the gang. It turned violent when Richie Huyhn, one of the robbers, began pistol-whipping the lady of the house, a Cambodian woman in her forties.

Now, six months later, Tinh was in trouble. The detectives drove him through Brooklyn to the Coney Island precinct, where he was placed in a lineup with five other Asian males his age. He was quickly identified as one of the robbers, then taken back to the Criminal Courts Building, where he was made to wait overnight in a holding pen.

Awaiting arraignment the next day, Tinh was approached by a

120

United States marshal who announced, "Tinh Ngo, you have a visitor."

Now what? thought Tinh. *Who could possibly be coming to see me at the Criminal Courts Building in Brooklyn?*

Tinh was taken outside the courtroom, into a hallway, where two white guys he immediately recognized as detectives were waiting. The younger of the two was dressed in a flashy suit and tie. The older detective looked like a professional football player; he was maybe six feet four inches tall, and solid.

"Tinh Ngo, we understand you wanted to talk to the police about crimes, right?" said the younger detective.

Earlier, when Tinh realized he was being arrested for robbery, he had asked one of the detectives at the Coney Island precinct if there was anything he could do to help himself.

"Yeah, sure," said the detective. "You can clear your conscience, tell us everything you know about other crimes you or anyone else might have perpetrated."

Tinh had no response. But apparently the overture had been passed along to these two cops now standing in a hallway outside the arraignment room.

Tinh answered the detective cautiously. "Uh, okay. Maybe I talk with you."

The two detectives signed some papers and took Tinh into custody, driving him to yet another Brooklyn police precinct, the Eighty-fourth, located downtown on Gold Street. Tinh was sat down in a small interview room with bad lighting and bars on the windows. The younger detective introduced himself as William Oldham. The older one was named Alex Sabo.

121

"Okay," said Oldham. "We think maybe you're in a position to help us out. Then maybe we can help you out. We already know more than you probably think we know. But I want to hear it from you."

"Yes, sir," answered Tinh.

"So," asked Oldham, "how long you been with the Ghost Shadows?"

Apparently, the cops didn't know much.

"BTK. I used to be with BTK," answered Tinh, pretending he had dropped out of the gang.

"Okay. Why did you leave BTK?"

"Because I think I want to leave. Like, you know, drugs and stuff like that. I want to go back to school and try to get a job."

It was unnerving talking face-to-face with cops. Tinh wanted to strike a deal that would keep him out of jail but was afraid to tell the cops anything that might get him deeper into trouble with the law. He wasn't sure these men could be trusted.

"I assume the gang has a leader," said Oldham.

"Yes, sir," answered Tinh.

"I know his name. Do you know his name?"

"Yes. It's Thai."

"David Thai?"

"Yes, sir."

"And what do you call David Thai?"

"I call him Big Brother."

Tinh's voice quivered with emotion. *What am I doing here?* he asked himself. It was like an audition, with Tinh playing the role of the pliant ex–gang member. He knew he had to show the cops he had information that was valuable. But the ambivalence he felt sitting in this room with them was causing Tinh to sweat; his stomach was churning, his head pounding.

"Listen," said the detective. "You have to tell us the truth now. Because later we're going to use your words to help you. But if your words are lies, they can't help you. They hurt you, and they hurt us. When they hurt us, they will hurt you. Understand?"

"You got a big brother, we have bosses," chimed in Sabo, the older detective. "If we tell the bosses that you told us this, then two months from now you tell them something else, then they say to us, 'Well, wait a minute.' "

"See," interrupted Oldham. "I want you to tell me the truth. Are you able to do that?"

"The truth?" asked Tinh, a quizzical expression on his face. For a person who had lived the last twenty months of his life in the underworld, it was a strange concept.

Deep in his gut, Tinh desperately wanted to come clean. He needed to unburden himself of the guilt that had been building up inside; he wanted to set himself free from the trap his life had become. But his instincts for survival told him to be careful.

The confusion Tinh was feeling manifested itself in this way: For the next two hours, he talked virtually nonstop. Much of what he said was in a breathless, excitable English that the detectives had trouble understanding. What came through was a blizzard of names and events, a byzantine melding of fact and fiction. He told the detectives about real crimes that had taken place, then gave false names. He passed along street gossip about gang-related crimes in Boston, Pennsylvania, Montreal, and Texas. Mostly, he tried to present himself as a small-time outsider, a guy who ran errands for the big boys. "I used to buy crack for them. They smoke crack. The other stuff, I'm the youngest one, so they usually don't need me that much."

As the afternoon wore on, Tinh edged closer and closer to the truth. The more he talked, the more he divulged. He gave the detectives an accurate account of his first armed robbery at the massage parlor on Chrystie Street, the one he committed with Blackeyes. He gave them names. At one point he even gave them David Thai's beeper number.

The detectives were taping the conversation on a small cassette recorder and writing down bits of information. Occasionally, they glanced at each other in disbelief. What's with this kid? they asked themselves. Not only was he unusually talkative, but not once had he posed the question all potential informants usually begin with: What's in it for me? This kid seemed more interested in talking than he did in striking a deal.

At one point, Tinh came perilously close to telling the detectives more than he wanted to about recent events in the state of Georgia. "David Thai, he get his guns in Georgia," offered Tinh.

"He goes to Georgia?" asked Sabo.

"Georgia," repeated Tinh.

"Where in Georgia?" asked Oldham.

"Grandview, Granville, something like this," answered Tinh, unable to remember the exact name of the town where they had stayed.

"Did you ever go with them?" asked Oldham.

"Uh, yeah, I went there once."

"When was this?"

"That's a long time ago."

"One year, two years, three years?"

"Yeah."

"Well, you tell me."

Hesitantly, Tinh claimed that about a year ago he had gone to Georgia with some gang members to buy guns. The detectives sensed that there was more, that he was leading them to Georgia for a reason. He seemed to have something he wanted to say. They prodded him with more questions about the trip. Who did the BTK buy the guns from? Did they bring the guns back to New York?

Tinh was sweating heavily now, his words barely discernible. Detective Oldham suggested they take a break. "Are you hungry?" he asked Tinh.

"What have you got?"

"We've got a McDonald's across the street," suggested Sabo.

While Oldham ran out to get some food, Tinh wiped the perspiration from his brow. *What am I doing?* he asked himself again. *Why am I telling these men these things?*

"You so quiet tonight, my husband. What's wrong?" inquired twenty-six-year-old Ying Jing Gan, the wife of Sen Van Ta.

Ta was seated on the edge of the bed in their small, cramped apartment on East Broadway, in Chinatown. He had been lost in thought, and his wife's question startled him.

"Is it something with the store?"

Ta sighed. He could no longer keep the troublesome events of the last few weeks from his wife. "Yes," he answered. "There been some problems at the store."

Usually, Ying Jing Gan knew better than to ask too many questions of her husband. She was Chinese, and Chinese tradition dictated that a wife not meddle in her husband's affairs, especially when it pertained to his job. But Gan sensed something was wrong. Ever since the robbery, her husband had seemed preoccupied and withdrawn.

"You remember the robbery?" Sen Van Ta asked his wife.

Gan was incredulous. "Of course I remember the robbery. What do you think?"

"Well . . ."

Sen Van Ta proceeded to tell his wife about the series of incidents that had occurred since then. She already knew that her husband had picked two of the robbers out of a police lineup. But she did not know about the threatening message he had received in the mail. And she certainly did not know that David Thai, the leader of Chinatown's most notorious criminal gang, had made a personal visit to her husband.

On the surface, Sen Van Ta remained steadfast in his determination to stand up to the BTK. He would not be intimidated, he told his fellow workers. Secretly, though, he was terrified. Ta knew what the BTK were capable of. "They come after me, they come after you. They come after anybody they think friendly with us," he confessed to Ying Jing Gan.

Gan was barely five feet tall, fine-boned and petite even by Chinese standards. Her hair was black and luminous, with bangs that grazed the tips of her eyelashes. Her cheeks were full and rosy, even without makeup. The product of a traditional rural upbringing, she was a reticent person by nature, and had often been told by others that she was naive in the ways of the world. Her innocence and simple decency captivated Sen Van Ta the first day they met.

Now, standing in the doorway of their small bedroom, Ying Jing Gan was disturbed by what her husband was telling her. She had never seen Sen Van Ta express fear before. She turned and walked into the front room of their apartment, to an alcove where she knelt in front of a small shrine dedicated to her and Sen Van Ta's ancestors.

125

Most traditional Chinese and Vietnamese homes have a similar shrine. A small statue of Buddha was adorned with family photographs, flowers, an incense urn, and a few candles. Gan lit the candles and a stick of incense. She bowed her head and prayed not only for herself and her husband, but also for the baby she carried in her womb.

Bathed in flickering candlelight, Gan thought back to the first time she met Sen Van Ta, less than two years ago. It had been in Shanghai, around the time of the infamous Tiananmen Square uprising, an event that sent shock waves through all of China. Gan was from the rural town of Jinhua, in Chekiang Province, and she had traveled to Shanghai to meet Ta, a man she knew only through letters they had written back and forth. Their transcontinental courtship had been arranged by a

cousin, a matchmaking tradition still common in China even after decades of social change.

In Shanghai, Ying Jing Gan was not disappointed when she first
laid eyes on Sen Van Ta, who had traveled all the way from New York
City. Although he was dressed casually, he wore blue jeans, an extrav-
agance by Chinese standards. Gan wore a white shirt buttoned to the
neck, a long blue skirt, and red high heels.

There wasn't much they could do that first day in Shanghai, what
with military vehicles patrolling the city and police checkpoints everywhere. They strolled across the street from Gan's aunt's house to a small
park, where they walked and talked and rested in the shade. Given the
chaotic events unfolding in China, they knew there wasn't much time.

The very next day, Ta, Gan, and Gan's cousin took a twelve-hour
boat ride back to Chekiang Province, where Ta met Gan's parents.

Ta and Gan had briefly discussed marriage, but Gan was surprised
when Ta came right out and boldly asked her parents, "I would like to
have permission to marry your daughter."

"We consent, if she consents," replied Gan's father.

Everyone looked at Gan. "Of course," she answered, her head
spinning with a dizzying combination of joy and humility.

The following afternoon, Ta and Gan went to the township hall,
registered, and were proclaimed husband and wife.

Sen Van Ta returned to New York. It would be another year before
he was able to secure the necessary immigration papers and retrieve
his wife.

Ying Jing Gan arrived in the States in the spring of 1990, a frightened, innocent bride living for the first time with a husband she hardly
knew. She grew to love Sen Van Ta, but she was also lonely. She missed
her family back in Chekiang Province. She would rather have been
living in China. But she knew she could not go back. Chinese tradition
declared that if you were married to a chicken, you must follow the
chicken; if you married a dog, you must follow the dog's step.

When a Chinatown physician told her in December 1990 that she
was pregnant, Ying Jing Gan was overjoyed. Now, while her husband
worked, she would finally have a companion with whom she could pass
the days. She would not be so lonely after all.

Gan could not believe how hard her husband and other Chinese people worked in the States. Yes, there was prosperity to be had—but the price was high. Sen Van Ta worked seven days a week, from 9:30 A.M. to 7:30 P.M. Gan felt their life together lacked a certain spiritual quality that she associated with rural life in Chekiang. In Chinatown, she and Sen Van Ta saw each other only at night, and often her husband was exhausted.

Gan first heard about the Born to Kill gang not long after she arrived in New York City. There was plenty of neighborhood gossip about robberies. Sometimes, she even heard gunshots and the sound of wailing sirens as police cars raced through the neighborhood. Only later, after her husband's commercial space was robbed and he was beaten, did she become fully aware of the dangers involved in running a business in Chinatown.

Ying Jing Gan said one last prayer to Buddha, then extinguished the incense sticks and blew out the candles on the altar. When she climbed into bed, her husband was still awake.

"I don't know," she said to Sen Van Ta. "Maybe you should just give these people what they want. Life is more important."

"No," her husband insisted. "They ask time and time again. We cannot afford to keep paying money. Besides, it's not right. They should work for a living just like everybody else. Now they rob the store. They beat me over the head. No way I cooperate with these people."

Ta could see that his wife was troubled, and he regretted telling her about his problems. "Look," he said. "I report all of this to the police. They know about the letter. They know about this man Thai. I trust they will not let anything bad happen. I trust they will protect us. Get these people in jail, where they belong."

Sen Van Ta was trying to put a good face on things, but Ying Jing Gan was not so sure. Where she came from, the police were not somebody you turned to in times of trouble. In the People's Republic of China, the police were instruments of the state; it paid to be suspicious of their authority.

Though doubtful, Ying Jing Gan decided to keep her concerns to herself. "Okay," she conceded reluctantly. "Please, let's go to sleep."

Everything Gan had been taught led her to conclude that the course her husband had chosen would only make matters worse, but she was the wife, and he was the husband. If Sen Van Ta believed the

127

police had their best interests in mind, she had no choice but to accept his wishes.

After all, the United States was an unfamiliar place. Ying Jing Gan was still a stranger in Chinatown.

Presumably, her husband knew best.

Chapter 8

With Tinh Ngo, detectives Bill Oldham and Alex Sabo knew they had a ringer. Unless the kid was bullshitting them across the board, which seemed unlikely given his situation, he definitely had inside knowledge about the workings of the BTK. In fact, during the interview at the Eighty-fourth Precinct, Tinh had thrown so many names and events at the detectives they really didn't know where to begin.

Oldham and Sabo were both from the Major Case Squad, a unit with citywide jurisdiction that dealt mainly with robberies and kidnappings—types of crime commonly practiced by Asian street gangs. But neither detective was an expert on organized crime in Chinatown. Oldham had spent most of his time on the force in Narcotics; Sabo was considered one of the department's best-informed detectives on the subject of art theft. When it came to Asian crime, their knowledge was mostly a mishmash of rumors and other information culled from individual robbery investigations.

They knew enough, however, to know that the

BTK was probably the hottest thing going in Chinatown right now. Not only had the gang arrived on the local scene in a big way over the last year and a half, but the NYPD was constantly getting desperate calls from cops in other cities asking for help, explaining, "We just arrested half a dozen Vietnamese males on a local home invasion. We don't know a thing about 'em, except they got BTK tattoos on their arms and New York City addresses."

The most recent example of the gang's far-flung influence involved an arrest that had taken place on Canal Street, just six days before Oldham and Sabo spoke with Tinh Ngo. In the middle of the afternoon, detectives from Toronto, with the help of local cops from the Fifth Precinct, surrounded Sonny Long, a twenty-eight-year-old BTK member wanted for murder. Two months earlier, Long and two other hitmen had sauntered into the Kim Bo Restaurant, a bustling establishment in Toronto's Chinatown. "Don't fuck with my *dai low*," Long exclaimed to a table full of Vietnamese males, just before he and the others opened fire in the crowded restaurant. Two people were killed. One of the victims was shot six times.

At first, Canadian police believed the double homicide was a revenge hit for the shooting at the cemetery in Linden, New Jersey. The motive was never firmly established. Nonetheless, with this shocking midday hit Canadian police were becoming aware they had a sizable Vietnamese gang problem in their two biggest cities, Toronto and Montreal. More than a few of the young gangsters they were arresting—including Sonny Long—had tattoos with the letters BTK underlining the gang's insignia: a coffin accompanied by three lit candles.

Canada wasn't the only place with an emerging BTK problem. In Stockton, California, police arrested Lam Trang, the gang member who had gunned down two young Flying Dragons on Canal Street at David Thai's behest sixteen months earlier. After that well-known double homicide, Trang fled to Stockton, where he founded his own group of BTK gangsters. Before arriving, however, he had stopped in Port Arthur, Texas, where he was suspected of having played a part in at least one and possibly three murders.

The mobility of Lam Trang and other BTK members like him made it seem as if the gang was everywhere. Vietnamese gang members with BTK tattoos were now being arrested routinely in dozens of jurisdictions.

Of course, just because a young Vietnamese gangster had a coffin or a dragon or some other BTK tattoo on his arm didn't mean he was directly affiliated with David Thai. Some of these gangs were made up of renegade New York members on the run. Some were merely local gangs that had appropriated the name. Either way, the BTK's reputation had become so exalted throughout the Asian underworld that gangsters everywhere were attempting to capitalize on the mystique.

The fact that Vietnamese gangs had become something of a national and even international phenomenon was both exciting and daunting to Oldham and Sabo. For starters, they knew they could probably use Tinh Ngo to make local arrests, maybe build a few robbery and even homicide cases. But they also knew this kid was potentially more valuable than that. If even half of what Tinh Ngo had thrown at them proved true, they had the makings of a solid racketeering case. They were also well aware that to build such a case would take more than the efforts of two detectives from the NYPD's Major Case Squad. They would need help from the Feds.

Just two weeks after their initial meeting with Tinh, the detectives made the connection they needed. As is often the case in law enforcement, it did not come about because of some directive from high up the federal chain of command. Instead, an industrious mid-level agent took it upon himself to establish contact with a rank-and-file detective, providing the impetus for an important investigation to begin taking shape.

Joe Greco, an agent with the Bureau of Alcohol, Tobacco and Firearms (ATF), had been working a gun-trafficking case involving a network of Vietnamese gangsters based in Jersey City. The investigation had gotten under way the previous month, in January 1991. Greco and a handful of investigators with the Hudson County prosecutor's office had learned that their main player, an unassuming Vietnamese immigrant named Hoa Tran, had strong BTK ties. Tran had a booth on Canal Street where he sold counterfeit watches. Joe Greco believed that Hoa Tran was also a significant supplier of weapons to David Thai's BTK.

When Greco heard there were a couple of detectives with the NYPD's Major Case Squad looking to build a case against the BTK, he immediately called Bill Oldham, who agreed to meet with him. Greco was already up to his neck in the Jersey City gun case. So while he could serve as a liaison with the NYPD, he probably wouldn't be able

131

to serve as case agent in a major investigation. As a result, Dan Kumor, an agent based in the bureau's Manhattan office, was assigned to the case as well.

Kumor was young—just thirty years old—and he had been with ATF less than three years. Like many people in federal law enforcement, he had yet to familiarize himself with the workings of the Vietnamese underworld.

"BTK? What's that?" he had responded when first told he would be working the case.

"BTK," his supervisor repeated. "Born to Kill. The Vietnamese gang. Based in Chinatown."

That rang a bell. "Oh, yeah, right," said Kumor. "The shootout at the cemetery in Jersey. I remember that."

Kumor called Greco at his office in Newark to ask about his dealings so far with the NYPD.

"Well," said Greco, "there's really not a lot for me to tell you just yet. I've only spoken with Oldham briefly. He thinks he's got the beginnings of a good case."

"What's this about a possible confidential informant?" asked Kumor.

"Yeah. In fact," Greco told Kumor, "I'm going out to Brooklyn later this week to meet the C.I. myself. Why don't you come along?"

"Definitely," Kumor replied.

Starting an investigation with a confidential informant already in place was certainly a plus, but both Greco and Kumor knew better than to get overly excited. In the underworld, there are no shortage of low-level crooks looking to cut deals with the government by supplying information. Whether these crooks ever proved to have anything useful, and whether they had the stamina needed to sustain dangerous and complex criminal cases over the long haul, was a different matter altogether.

Before Kumor met face-to-face with Bill Oldham or anyone else, he knew he had some homework to do. The most recent case he'd worked was a Jamaican drug investigation involving a cocaine and crack posse based uptown, on Edgecombe Avenue in Harlem. It had taken months for Kumor to learn the nuances of heavy Jamaican accents laced with an impenetrable patois rarely understood outside the shantytowns of Kingston. Now he had to learn about a whole new underworld, one peopled by criminals with names and habits that were, to him, equally strange and exotic.

The logical place to start was the case file on Joe Greco's gun-trafficking investigation in Jersey City. In that case, investigators had managed to penetrate a small ring of gun merchants by using an undercover agent posing as a Jamaican posse member. Kumor appreciated the investigators' ingenuity; no Vietnamese gangster would ever suspect that someone who looked and sounded like a Jamaican "rude boy" was a cop.

Already, the investigators had learned that the Vietnamese gangsters were getting most of their weapons from gun shops in Kentucky and Virginia, smuggling them into the New York-New Jersey area, and selling them through a network spread up and down the East Coast.

Along with familiarizing himself with Greco's case, Kumor began delving into ATF intelligence files. Though little had been done with them over the years, the files on Asian organized crime were voluminous, made up mostly of government reports and assorted documents stamped CONFIDENTIAL. Reading the reports, Kumor learned for the first time about triads and tongs and how they interacted with traditional Chinatown gangs like the Flying Dragons and the Ghost Shadows. He read old files on Eddie Chan, Uncle Benny Ong, and other renowned figures in Chinatown.

Despite the abundant background data, there was little current, specific information on the Vietnamese underworld. For this, Kumor thumbed through back issues of the International Association of Asian Crime Investigators quarterly newsletter. He was amazed not only by the geographic breadth of criminal activity associated with Vietnamese gangsters, but by the level of violence. As far as Kumor could tell, what distinguished Vietnamese gangsters from the Italians, Jamaicans, Dominicans, and other organized hoodlums currently thriving in America's vast criminal marketplace was the high levels of recklessness and desperation their actions seemed to reveal.

The other thing Kumor noticed was how tight-lipped they were. In all the IAACI newsletters and government reports, he could not find a single example of a case against Vietnamese underworld figures where a gang member had been "flipped"—the law enforcement term for getting a criminal to join the other side.

All of which made Agent Kumor doubly curious about this so-called confidential informant the NYPD would be introducing him to in Brooklyn.

At 302 Canal Street, in front of Sen Van Ta's store, the sidewalk was packed with the usual human slipstream: a nonstop procession of shoppers, street merchants, and Chinatown residents. Small curbside tables had been set up for peddlers to hawk children's toys, road atlases, and other miscellaneous items, leaving only a narrow walkway for pedestrians.

Inside the entrance to Ta's store, only slightly removed from the hubbub of the street, Ying Jing Gan stared at her husband in disbelief. "You did what!?" she asked incredulously, her voice rising with each syllable.

"I had no choice," her husband defensively responded. "The police came to me. They said, 'Mr. Ta, we know you can make the identification. You must come with us.' *I had no choice!*"

Gan was so stunned by what her husband was telling her that she asked him to repeat the entire story again.

A few days earlier, on the afternoon of February 13, 1991, Sen Van Ta had been working in his store when three BTK gang members came in demanding money. It was just a few days before the culmination of the New Year's season, a time when gang members traditionally increase their extortionate demands for "lucky money."

Sen Van Ta was fed up. First, the gangsters rob him and smack him in the head. Then they harass and threaten him. Now they come looking for money.

"How you expect us to pay money?" Ta admonished the lead gangster. "You already rob this store. Now we have nothing."

Ta continued shouting at the gangsters, telling them he and his fellow workers had nothing left to give. The three BTK hoodlums scowled and left the store.

One hour later, they returned along with two other gang members, holding their hands inside their jackets as if they were packing concealed guns. Sen Van Ta recognized the one who seemed to be their leader; he was named LV Hong.

Like most BTK gang members, Hong was *Viet-Ching*. Nearly six feet tall and slightly older than the others, he had a mole on his cheek with a few hairs growing out of it, a distinguishing feature that made his face easy to remember. It was rumored among local merchants that LV Hong had been personally selected by David Thai and flown in from Texas to replace Amigo as the new Canal Street *dai low*.

"Don't ever raise your voice with these boys," LV Hong warned Sen Van Ta, asking, "Don't you know about respect?" Once again the gangsters demanded money, and once again Ta said he had no money to give. Angrily, LV Hong and the others left the store.

Now Sen Van Ta was really irate. He pictured the gangsters coming back every day, demanding money and threatening his employees. So Ta did the unthinkable: He picked up the phone and called the cops.

One hour later, around five o'clock, two uniformed officers from the local precinct arrived at the store. Ta was still steaming. He told the policemen about the gangsters coming into the store not once, but twice. They seemed to be carrying weapons and they demanded money.

"Could you identify these guys?" one of the cops asked Ta.

"I know who they are," answered Ta. "Everybody know who they are. They gather right across the street from here at two-seven-one Canal Street mall."

"Well," explained the cop, "we can arrest these people on a charge of aggravated harassment. But you have to make an identification. It's called probable cause. If you don't ID them, there's nothing we can do."

Standing inside his store three days later, Ta was still uncomfortable about what happened next. He told Ying Jing Gan that he was none too excited by the prospect of identifying these gangsters right in the middle of a crowded Canal Street mall. He told the police he would be willing to file a complaint, and maybe even pick the gangsters out of a lineup at a later date.

"Nah," the cop replied. "The only way anything is gonna get done is if you finger this bad guy right now."

Reluctantly, Sen Van Ta got into a police car with the two officers.

They drove around the block and pulled up directly in front of the mini-mall at 271 Canal Street. Ta and the cops entered the mall and walked to the Pho Hanoi restaurant in the back. All around them, merchants and customers froze in their tracks.

LV Hong was seated at a table against the restaurant's rear wall talking with three or four other gang members. With the two cops standing behind him, Sen Van Ta walked into the small luncheonette and pointed at LV Hong. "That's the guy right there," he declared.

"Okay," said one of the cops to LV Hong. "Let's go, pal. You're coming with us." They slapped a set of handcuffs on LV and led him through the mall and out onto the street. "Watch your head," one of the cops cautioned LV, as he was lowered into the backseat of the police car.

Standing on Canal Street, the other gangsters looked mostly shocked. From the backseat, LV Hong glared at Ta with an expression of pure, unmitigated disgust.

Hearing the details of LV Hong's arrest, a wave of fear shuddered through Ying Jing Gan's small, bird-boned frame. She may have been naive, but she knew full well the possible consequences of openly crossing a Chinatown gang.

When Gan first arrived in Chinatown, one of the most-talked-about recent events was a retribution murder that had taken place in February 1990. A pretty twenty-two-year-old named Tina Sham had testified at a murder trial against two members of the Green Dragons, a gang based in the growing Asian community of Flushing, Queens. One year later, Sham and her boyfriend had been abducted coming out of the Crown Palace, a restaurant in Queens. They were driven to a secluded area on Long Island and shot multiple times in the head and body. Their partially decayed corpses were found one month later.

The killing of Tina Sham and her boyfriend had been a cruel reminder to people in Chinatown what could happen if they openly cooperated with the law. Ying Jing Gan had been riveted by the story of the vile double homicide; she needed no other reminder of how vengeful the gangs could be.

"You don't respect your own life," Ying Jing Gan scolded her husband.

Ta pleaded with his wife, trying to make her understand that he had not willingly identified LV Hong in public. "Don't you think I would rather go into the police station, where I make identification from behind glass? Do you think I want so these people know who I am?"

Gan could see that her husband was just as distressed by what had happened as she was. She had guessed from his behavior the last few days that something was amiss; he seemed skittish, always looking over his shoulder.

"Well," said Gan, trying not to sound too alarmed, "all we can do now is be careful." She shook her head. "But please, listen to me. Do not talk with these policemen anymore. Do not get us into more trouble than we already are. Please."

Throughout February and into March, Sen Van Ta and his wife lived their lives like frightened mice, scurrying around in the shadows of Chinatown. Each evening, Ying Jing Gan met her husband at his store on Canal Street just before closing time. Each evening, they would take a different route to their home on East Broadway, far on the other side of the neighborhood. They stayed off the main thoroughfares, especially Canal Street.

At home, they locked their windows and kept the door bolted at all times. Idlers standing outside their apartment building—especially those loitering across the street in shabby Seward Park—were viewed with suspicion.

Ying Jing Gan loved her husband, but she was starting to feel resentful. She admired the fact that Sen Van Ta was a righteous man who had the courage to do what he believed was right by standing up to the BTK. But they had to think of more than themselves now. "Feel my stomach," she would say. "Soon you have a child. Maybe seven months, you have a family. What are we supposed to do if something bad happen to you?"

Ta tried to reassure his wife, telling her time and time again that the police would make sure nothing bad happened to him. But Gan remained uneasy. She trembled each time the phone rang, fearing that maybe this would be the call informing her that her husband had been kidnapped in broad daylight, or gunned down on Canal Street.

Not surprisingly, their marriage suffered. Sen Van Ta rarely showed physical affection toward his wife anymore. At night, he lay in bed staring at the ceiling. Ying Jing Gan tried to transport herself. On

137

nights when she could sleep, she dreamed of her rural childhood in Chekiang Province, of the red sky at twilight in the hills west of her tiny village, and the familiar sounds of squabbling chickens, quacking ducks, and the soothing, early morning low of the water buffalo.

Anything to take her mind off the nagging sense of dread that had become an irrevocable part of their daily life in Chinatown.

To the federal agents and police officers who had begun to entertain the idea of bringing criminal charges against the BTK, Sen Van Ta's dispute with the gang was, at most, a distant echo. Detectives Oldham and Sabo were vaguely aware that a robbery had taken place at 302 Canal Street. They had asked Tinh Ngo during the interview at the Eighty-fourth Precinct if he knew anything about the robbery. Tinh told them, yes, he knew David Thai had planned the heist and supplied the weapons. But that incident was just one amid dozens of disconnected names, dates, and other information Tinh had passed along to the cops that day. It wasn't likely they were going to appreciate the severity of Sen Van Ta's predicament until their budding investigation came into focus.

Not long after Ta fingered LV Hong at the Pho Hanoi luncheonette, ATF agents Dan Kumor and Joe Greco drove across the Brooklyn Bridge to the King's County District Attorney's Office for their meeting with the cops—and Tinh Ngo.

Kumor, the youngest of the investigators, viewed the meeting with considerable apprehension. Not only would he likely be entering into a relationship with a confidential informant—an undertaking fraught with potential problems—but he would also be inaugurating a partnership with two of "New York's finest."

In his brief tenure with ATF, it had been Kumor's experience that officers of the NYPD were sometimes more trouble than they were worth. Kumor himself was a middle-class kid from northeast Philadelphia who'd grown up with five brothers and one sister. His father was an attorney who had served two years as a municipal court judge. Coming from a large family, Kumor intuitively understood the value of cooperation, of making concessions for the good of the whole. But that philosophy seemed to be anathema to many detectives with the NYPD.

On the massive Jamaican posse investigation Kumor had recently completed, he often found himself in the middle of ugly jurisdictional battles between the ATF agents and local cops assigned to the case. As the youngest and least jaded investigator involved, Kumor wound up playing the role of mediator. In the end, the case was successfully prosecuted, but most of the agents and cops had divided into hostile factions, with many of the lawmen refusing to even speak to one another.

Kumor found the experience aggravating and counterproductive, and he wasn't looking forward to the prospect of waging similar battles over the next six or seven months.

It was a blustery spring day when Kumor and Greco arrived at the D.A.'s office, located at Cadman Plaza, across from the Brooklyn Criminal Courts Building. The assistant district attorney who was handling Tinh Ngo's robbery charge introduced Kumor and Greco to Detective Oldham. The three investigators were led to a small conference room, where they were soon joined by Tinh, who had been brought from his temporary residence at Rikers Island.

Kumor and Greco took a backseat to Oldham, who by now had met with Tinh on a couple of occasions. This time Oldham was toting a book of mug shots, hoping that Tinh would be able to identify gang members and participants in various crimes he had already talked about. Occasionally, Greco interjected a question. Kumor sat quietly and took notes, observing both the informant and the detective with whom he would be spending most of his waking hours during the course of the investigation.

139

Watching Oldham, Kumor immediately heard alarm bells clamoring inside his head. For one thing, Oldham was dressed in a trendy, tailored suit that looked to have cost about $2,000 more than the discount attire favored by most detectives. With his neatly coiffed hair and GQ apparel, he looked like a Hollywood version of a New York City cop. His manner was cocky, to put it mildly, and he seemed to Kumor like the kind of guy who felt federal agents were a burden that he, a street-smart New York detective, was occasionally forced to endure.

Although he was snooty and dismissive toward Greco and himself, Kumor could see that Oldham knew his job. He may have thought he was the cat's ass, but he also seemed to be intelligent. He handled Tinh well, applying just the right degrees of forcefulness and patience in his inquiries.

As far as Kumor could tell, Oldham's relationship with the informant was still in the developmental stage. The kid was forthcoming, but there was no way of knowing yet just how truthful his answers were. Many of the names he was throwing out seemed to mean more to Oldham than they did to Kumor or Greco, but the detective was definitely still probing. Using information Tinh had given him during previous interviews, Oldham was cross-checking names, dates, and other data, trying to catch the informant contradicting himself.

Kumor was impressed with Tinh Ngo. He had been told the kid had a good memory, but he had not been prepared for how focused Tinh would be. He also seemed to have an excellent attitude. Kumor was used to informants being cagey and manipulative; they usually wanted to know what the government was going to do for them before they offered anything of value. But Tinh seemed amazingly guileless.

He didn't look anything like a gang kid, either. There wasn't the spiky hair or that hungry, haunted look that characterized most of the Asian gangsters Kumor had seen. He knew from Tinh's rap sheet that the kid was about to turn nineteen, but he looked maybe three or four years younger than that. Moreover, he seemed to have the kind of innocence that couldn't be faked. He was also exceedingly polite. Kumor couldn't tell if this was because Tinh was terrified, or if he was just being respectful.

140

The ATF agent looked around the cramped government conference room, with overflowing file cabinets and maps of the city on the wall. It wouldn't surprise him if Tinh was intimidated. There wasn't much precedent for an Asian gang kid entering into a pact with the law. Surrounded by the prosecutorial trappings of the district attorney's office and three sizable Caucasian lawmen, Tinh must be wondering what he'd gotten himself into.

After forty-five minutes or so, the informant was allowed to go. "The kid sounds good," offered Joe Greco after he was gone.

"He's got a lot of information, that's for sure," replied Oldham. "We're still checking a lot of this stuff out. But even if only half of what he's telling us is true, that's a lot to go on."

The ATF agents concurred.

"So, you think your people are gonna want to come on board?" asked Oldham.

Oldham hadn't tried to hide his distaste for federal agents, but he could certainly use their pocketbooks. If the investigation blossomed to the point where travel was involved, or a lot of surveillance, or expensive drug and gun buys, the NYPD would not be able to keep up. Perennially constrained by financial woes, the cops were not equipped to take on a gang the size of the BTK by themselves.

"Well," answered Kumor. "The way I heard it, we already are on board. It's just a question of making it official on paper."

Oldham nodded his approval, and the investigators said their good-byes for now.

Driving back toward the ATF office in lower Manhattan, Kumor twisted slightly in his seat. As he and Greco crossed the stately Brooklyn Bridge, Kumor peered through the enveloping web of iron cable toward the twinkling lights of New York Harbor, with the Statue of Liberty glistening in the distance. Once again he was about to embark on a complicated joint-task-force operation involving his agency and the NYPD—a state of affairs that had his stomach churning with the usual mixture of excitement, anticipation, and trepidation.

At Rikers Island, lying on the well-worn mattress in his cell, Tinh Ngo considered his options for what seemed like the millionth time. Already, he was in much deeper than he ever imagined he would be. He had started by thinking he would tell the investigators only about crimes committed by others, implicating only gang members who were already in prison. But Detective Oldham told him that wasn't good enough.

"I have to know if you are being honest with me," the detective had said during a brief meeting in a secluded room at Rikers. "I hear you talking about other people. What I'm interested in is what you've done."

In just a few meetings, Tinh had told the cops almost everything. He told them about how he got started with the gang, robbing waiters of their tip money in the D train subway station on Grand Street. He told them about his early robberies with Blackeyes and the Vu brothers,

141

Kenny and Tommy. He told them about the meeting at the Japanese restaurant in midtown Manhattan where everyone signed the paper pledging allegiance to the BTK. He told them about the hierarchy of the gang, how David Thai was the boss and the various neighborhoods were controlled by *dai lows*, underbosses who supposedly controlled all the gang crimes that took place in their areas.

Tinh buried the investigators with information. But in all his revelations, he said nothing about the robbery in Doraville, Georgia, where the Cambodian jeweler was shot and left for dead.

Tinh wanted to come clean about the Doraville shooting. But he could not. Partly, he was paralyzed with shame by what had happened. But he was also afraid that if he told the investigators about his role in what he believed was a murder, they would lock him up and throw away the key.

The prospect of spending any more time in prison made Tinh nearly sick with depression. Already, his return to Rikers Island reminded him of what a suffocating trap his life had become. He had asked to be placed in general population, but the investigators insisted he stay in P.C.—protective custody. They told Tinh it was for his own safety, which may have been true. But the cops had other motives as well.

P.C. was not unlike solitary confinement. Each day, the prisoner in P.C. surveyed his bleak, numbingly dull surroundings and became more acutely aware of just how limited his options had become. Each day, the prospect of cooperating with the law seemed more and more like a last glimmer of hope.

Of course, Tinh Ngo was already supplying the investigators with information, and probably did not need further encouragement. But the cops had plans for their young informant—plans that required he be thoroughly and completely predisposed to accommodate the wishes of his overseers.

"What we propose is this," Oldham told Tinh one afternoon at the King's County D.A.'s office. "We think it would be a good idea to put you back out on the street and have you reestablish ties with the gang, just like before you got arrested. You supply us with fresh information. Nobody on the street would know anything about it, of course. It would be a secret undercover operation."

Tinh was confused.

"You know," continued Oldham, "like *Twenty-one Jump Street*. You ever see *Twenty-one Jump Street*?"

"Oh yeah," mumbled Tinh, who was beginning to doubt this detective had any idea what it was like being a member of the Vietnamese underworld.

Oldham had his own reasons for wanting to put Tinh back out on the street. "We could go on interviewing Timmy for months," he argued to the other investigators. "The only thing that will come of it is intelligence—intelligence that will go into department files to be used by other detectives to make arrests."

Like most young, aggressive detectives, Oldham was not interested in stockpiling intelligence data for the use and possible glory of others. He wanted to catch criminals on wiretaps and videotape discussing crimes. He wanted the thrill of nailing criminals in the act. He wanted to spearhead an investigation that was unlike anything ever attempted before in Chinatown, an investigation that would make headlines and enhance everyone's careers.

Later, locked inside his lifeless, ten- by twelve-foot cell, Tinh thought about Oldham's offer. The detective had told him he would have to sign some kind of agreement with the D.A.'s office. In exchange for his cooperation, the D.A. would recommend that Tinh be given a "downward departure," which meant he would walk on the robbery charge.

143

To Tinh, the most appealing part of the government's offer was that it would get him out of Rikers Island immediately. In fact, his desire to get out of prison was so overwhelming that he could hardly think of anything else. The likelihood that he would have to wear a recording device and eventually testify against his gang brothers in court never entered Tinh's mind.

A few days after being asked, Tinh Ngo responded to Oldham's offer by saying, "Yes. I think maybe I could do what you ask."

On the surface, the investigators remained composed. They sent Tinh back to Rikers, telling him that it would be days before the agreement papers would be ready for him to sign. In reality, they were ecstatic. For the first time in living memory, the cops would have a gang member operating as an informant from inside an Asian gang. And not just any Asian gang. This informant would take them inside the most violent and notorious gang in Chinatown—maybe in all of New York City.

There was no way of knowing exactly which direction the investigation would go. But the cops and agents were sure of one thing. With an undercover informant supplying info from inside the BTK, it promised to be one hell of a ride.

PART TWO

The Investigation

Inside ourselves lies the root of
good; the heart outweighs all talents
on this earth.

—NGUYEN DU
The Tale of Kieu

Chapter 9

Ying Jing Gan stood with her husband, Sen Van Ta, on the sidewalk in front of Golden Trading Discount, a small Chinatown clothing store managed by Ta's sister. The store was wedged in at 423 Broadway, half a block north of Canal Street, just around the corner from Ta's own jewelry store and clothing outlet. Often, after closing their own store, Gan and Ta would walk over and help Ta's sister close her shop for the day.

It was early on the evening of Sunday, March 10, 1991. Rain had threatened for most of the afternoon, but business remained brisk. Sundays were traditionally a time when Asians from all over the city came to Chinatown to do their shopping, a day when the malls and shops sometimes sold more merchandise than on all the other days of the week combined.

Gan and Ta began the tedious task of retrieving handbags, scarfs, jackets, and assorted other merchandise from display counters outside Golden Trading Discount. Around them, the day's steady flow of pedestrian traffic was thinning out. Dusk had come and gone, and the sky above the tenements and storefronts along lower Broadway grew dark. Sen Van Ta disappeared inside the store with an armful of leather jackets while his wife took inventory and separated items on the sidewalk outside.

Nearly two months had passed since Sen Van Ta had been robbed by the BTK, then threatened through the mail and in person by David Thai. It was four weeks since Ta walked into the Pho Hanoi luncheon-ette and identified the leader of the gangsters who had added insult to injury by trying to extort money. The pall that hovered over Ta and his wife since these events unfolded had only recently begun to lift. For the first time in many weeks, Ying Jing Gan saw an occasional smile come to her husband's face. Now four months pregnant, she and Sen Van Ta had begun to make plans for the future. They discussed possible names for their child. They even talked about buying a nice middle-class house, maybe in Queens or out on Long Island.

The fear that once consumed their lives may have receded, but it had not disappeared entirely. Criminal charges were being brought against the four gang members apprehended after the wild post-robbery car chase through the streets of Chinatown. No trial date had been set, but Ta and his wife knew that eventually the police and government prosecutors were going to be coming around again. This time, they would want Ta to take the stand in court and testify against the robbers. Neither Ta nor his wife was looking forward to that ordeal, which they had chosen to deal with by not thinking or talking about it.

While Ta and Gan were helping close the Golden Trading Discount Store, two blocks south, at the corner of Broadway and Walker Street, a black sedan pulled over to the curb and stopped. The car was from a taxi service, the driver a Hispanic male. In the backseat were gang members Lan Ngoc Tran and Kenny Vu, both dressed entirely in black.

They had arrived to do the bidding of Born to Kill.

They had come to assassinate Sen Van Ta.

In the weeks since the robbery at Sen Van Ta's store had ended so disastrously for the BTK, high-ranking gang members had met numerous times to discuss what should be done about the store owner. David Thai was shocked when he learned that the robbery victim had picked the gang members out of a lineup. The BTK leader took this as a personal insult. Thai was even more incensed after he visited the store himself, and still his warning was ignored.

Even though it was Sen Van Ta whom David Thai had spoken with that morning in front of the store, *Anh hai* could not be sure whether it was Ta or one of the store's other managers or employees who was cooperating with the authorities. Later, when Sen Van Ta fingered LV Hong on Canal Street, *Anh hai* had actually been pleased. Now he knew for sure.

"The first person who cooperate with police, this is the first person we kill," David promised LV Hong, who was released on bail the day after his arrest.

One week later, Thai and a handful of gang members met at a BTK safe house in suburban Long Island to discuss how they would handle Sen Van Ta. LV Hong was at the meeting, as were Lan Tran, Black Phu, Danny White Boy, Dung Steven, Hai, and Kenny Vu.

"This store owner have to be taken out," declared *Anh hai*. Turning to the gang member named Hai, he asked, "You think you can handle this job?"

Before Hai even had a chance to answer, Uncle Lan spoke up. "I handle this job," Lan volunteered. "This an important job, *Anh hai*. We don't want any fuck-up."

Normally, David Thai liked to use newer gang members for jobs like this. It was a way for him to test a person's loyalty, to give a young gang member a chance to prove himself. But no one was going to argue with Uncle Lan. If the gang's premier killer wanted to be the one who murdered the store owner, then so be it.

On the afternoon of March 10, Lan drove to one of the gang's many safe-house apartments in Brooklyn, this one at 810 Forty-fifth Street in the Sunset Park section. Kenny Vu was living there with a handful of other gang members. "You come with me," Lan told Kenny. "We go kill this store owner on Canal Street."

Lan did not want to drive into Chinatown in his own car, a beat-up, easily identifiable Datsun 280Z. Lan and Kenny tried to find a car

149

they could use from among the two or three vehicles that circulated among the BTK's Brooklyn crew, but no car was available. "No problem," said Lan. "We call a taxi."

BTK gangsters commonly used car-service drivers as unwitting "wheel men" during crimes. To an outsider, the idea of relying on a complete stranger to unknowingly serve as an accomplice during a major act of lawlessness might seem incredible, even bizarre. But since Chinatown gangsters rarely met resistance when preying on merchants, they could literally mosey away from a crime, secure in the knowledge that it wouldn't even be reported. Moreover, if there did happen to be non-Asian witnesses to the crime, having a Caucasian, black, or Hispanic driver had its advantages. Who would suspect that an anonymous taxi driving through Chinatown with a non-Asian behind the wheel was, in fact, a BTK getaway car?

Seated in the backseat of the taxi near the intersection of Broadway and Walker streets, Uncle Lan checked to make sure his gun was safely tucked inside his waist-length jacket. "You wait here five minutes," Lan said to the driver. "We need you take us back to Brooklyn."

The driver shrugged. "Sure, man. It's your money."

In Vietnamese, Lan told Kenny Vu to sit tight, adding, "This should not take too long." Lan got out of the car and headed north on Broadway.

150

At Golden Trading Discount, Ying Jing Gan was still standing on the sidewalk in front of the store, folding clothes and putting merchandise into boxes. Out of the corner of her eye she noticed somebody entering the store, but thought little of it.

Inside, Sen Van Ta was standing near the cash register, wearing a waist-length charcoal coat and faded green khakis. A female employee was near the back; a few feet away, also standing near the register, was Ta's twelve-year-old nephew, Vinh Tran.

Young Vinh Tran was the only one who noticed what he thought was a customer come into the store. A Southeast Asian male dressed in black, the man had a face that looked strange to Tran. He had pock-marked skin, and he was smiling. Not a mirthful smile. More like a creepy, sinister grin, almost a grimace.

Above: Born to Kill gang members carry a coffin containing the body of Vinh Vu, better known as Amigo. Three days earlier, Amigo had been gunned down by rival gangsters on Canal Street.

U.S ATTORNEY, EASTERN DISTRICT OF N.Y.

Left: BTK Leader David Thai stands beside Amigo's grave at Rosedale Memorial Park Cemetery in Linden, New Jersey.

U.S. ATTORNEY, EASTERN DISTRICT OF N.Y.

Above: Gang members parade a BTK banner on Mulberry Street during Amigo's funeral procession. U.S ATTORNEY, EASTERN DISTRICT OF N.Y.

Below: David Thai (*in foreground at left*) and his gang brothers gather around Amigo's grave just minutes before a fusillade of gunfire rang out, sending everyone scattering. U.S ATTORNEY, EASTERN DISTRICT OF N.Y.

Tinh Ngo, as he looked at age thirteen, standing on the grounds of a refugee camp in Thailand. Tinh had arrived at the camp after a torturous journey on a boat similiar to the one pictured below, where fifty Vietnamese refugees are crowded onto a thirty-foot fishing vessel, part of a mass exodus in the years following the U.S. evacuation of Saigon.

Tho Hoang "David" Thai

LV Hong

Tommy Vu

Hoang "Jungle Man" Ngo

Lam Trang

Eddie Tran

Above: Two Chinatown power brokers in a rare photo together. Eddie Chan (*left*) formerly president of the On Leong tong, now a fugitive from the law, and Benny Ong, adviser-for-life of the Hip Sing tong and believed by many to be the "Godfather" of Chinatown.
CHINATOWN HISTORICAL MUSEUM

Left: A classic photo of an early Hip Sing convention
CHINATOWN HISTORICAL MUSEUM

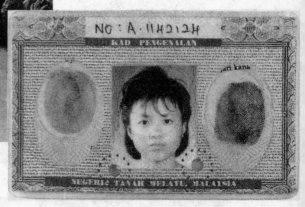

An immigration card belonging to Kim Ngoh Yee, David Thai's second wife, known to BTK gang members as Sophia

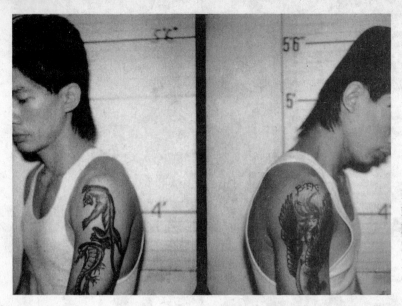

Kenny Vu displays
his tatoos for the
benefit of the
New York Police
Department.

Jewelry store owner Odum Lim,
after a BTK robbery in
Doraville, Georgia,
went awry

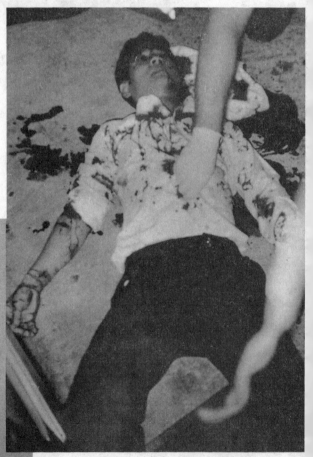

After the bungled robbery in Doraville, it took
the robbers a while to realize that Nicky,
(left) had accidentally been left behind
inside the store.

Sen Van Ta and his Chinese wife, Ying Jing Gan, not long after they were reunited in New York City

Sen Van Ta lies sprawled on the floor of a Chinatown store after beign executed by the Born to Kill gang

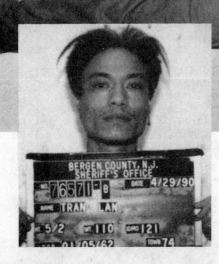

The triggerman, Lan Ngoc Tran

A surveillance photo of confidential informant Tinh Ngo *(left)* meeting on Canal Street with Lan Tran to discuss an upcoming robbery

The team of lawmen that helped put away David Thai and other key BTK gang members. *Above (left to right and below):* Detective Bill Oldham, Special Agent Don Tisdale, Special Agent Dan Kumor and Assistant U.S. Attorney Alan Vinegrad

ANTHONY LOEW

Sen Van Ta bent down to put some merchandise away. As he began to straighten up, he turned his head slightly.

Suddenly, the customer pulled out a gun. Young Vinh Tran's eyes opened wide with astonishment as he watched the man put the gun to his uncle's left temple and pull the trigger.

The gunshot reverberated throughout the small clothing store. Sen Van Ta's face contorted as the single bullet penetrated his skull, pierced through the left and right temporal lobes of his brain and exploded out the other side of his head, behind the right ear. Uncle Lan, the assassin, had turned and was out the door before the body even hit the ground.

Standing outside the store, Ying Jing Gan heard a loud pop! that sounded like a firecracker. When she looked up, a man was hurrying out of the store. He was about five feet two, reedy thin, and Gan would later remember that he had a yellow streak through his otherwise jet-black hair. He turned to his left and quickly headed north on Broadway.

Ying Jing Gan hurried into Golden Trading Discount just as her husband's body was falling to the floor. She saw blood—more blood than she had ever seen in one place in her whole life—gushing from Ta's head. Her young nephew, terrified, had ducked behind the cash register.

Gan felt her entire chest contract violently, as if she herself had been shot through the heart. A sickening wave of nausea engulfed her entire being; her head throbbed and her hands began to flutter uncontrollably. "Noooooooooo!" she cried out, her anguished wail bouncing from ceiling to floor, wall to wall, and out into the street.

Her legs ceased functioning; Gan fell to her knees and struggled to gather her husband in her arms. On the floor around Sen Van Ta's limp body was an expanding pool of blood—blood the color of nuac mam, the dark, amber fish sauce used like soy as a flavoring for traditional Vietnamese foods. Gan wrapped her arms around her husband's body and began to sob hysterically. The blood on her hands turned a deep, shiny black. She could feel the life seeping from her husband's body.

Two blocks away, on Walker Street, Kenny Vu was still sitting in the backseat of the taxi. He waited nervously. After nearly twenty minutes, Lan Tran had still not returned.

Kenny heard police sirens approaching. He saw an ambulance tearing down Canal Street toward Broadway. *Motherfuck!* he mumbled to himself. *Did Uncle Lan complete the job or had something bad happened to him?* With police closing in from all directions, Kenny didn't feel like waiting around to find out.

"I think we go back to Brooklyn now," he told the driver.

An hour after Kenny got back, Lan Tran showed up at the safe house on Forty-fifth Street. "Man, where you go?" Kenny asked him.

Uncle Lan shrugged. "After I do the job, I don't want to cross Canal Street. So I go to Delancey Street and get rid of the gun." From a pay phone, Lan Tran had then called David Thai to let him know that the problem with the store owner on Canal Street had been resolved— execution style.

At the same time Uncle Lan was calling *Anh hai,* a small crowd of Chinatown residents and passersby gathered on the sidewalk in front of Golden Trading Discount. The familiar yellow crime-scene tape had been stretched across the front of the store. Twirling police and ambulance lights cast an eerie, flickering glow on the street and surrounding buildings.

Inside, medics checked Sen Van Ta's vital signs as Ying Jing Gan was led to the rear of the store, where she stood with Ta's sister and nephew, and a few cops. Her face was streaked with tears, her clothing soaked with blood. She felt as if her baby were moving around inside her womb, and asked if someone could find her a chair.

Around 7:20 P.M., fifteen minutes after the shooting occurred, one of the doctors approached to tell Gan what she already knew to be true.

Her husband, Sen Van Ta, no longer existed in this world.

A cold rain swept down on the streets of Chinatown, and it didn't let up for days. The gutters backed up and the street corners began to look like small reservoirs, with puddles of dirty rainwater spraying the street peddlers whenever buses or trucks chugged by. Business dropped off. Darkness fell early. The entire community succumbed to a cloudy, bone-chilling melancholy.

The weather was the least of it. The killing of Sen Van Ta had struck like a dagger rammed deep into the soul of Chinatown. Still, most of the community's residents could not say they were surprised. This was the way the gangs operated. This was the way they had always operated.

On top of everything else, Ta's death reaffirmed an age-old truism in Chinatown: Never, under any circumstances, should an Oriental put his or her faith in the police.

Most merchants and shop owners on Canal Street had been well aware of Ta's dispute with the BTK, but not all were sympathetic. For years, they had studiously avoided confrontations with the gangs by paying whatever was demanded of them. Ta, they felt, was a hothead who had put all their lives in danger by incurring the gang's wrath.

Others secretly admired Ta for standing up to the dreaded BTK. But even these people had been skeptical that anything good could come of cooperating with *low faan*.

The police simply did not understand the true nature of crime in Chinatown, they felt. Take extortion. If a local merchant reported an extortionate act to the police, the cops rarely took it seriously. To them, the amount of money involved—sometimes as little as ten or twenty dollars—was laughable. But merchants in Chinatown knew that the act of extortion was not just about money. Extortion was also about establishing territory, instilling fear, and negotiating the often tricky issue of face.

Studies conducted by community groups showed that the overwhelming majority of merchants doing business in Chinatown—somewhere around ninety percent—paid some form of extortion. Cops in the local precinct sometimes pointed to this fact as an example of how merchants supported and even encouraged gang activity in their areas.

The idea that the police or anyone else might draw a conclusion like this was, to the people of Chinatown, a good example of how non-Asians had come to be called *low faan* in the first place. Fact was, most merchants were not anxious to pay extortion. They paid because they felt they had no choice. They paid because they did not want to wind up like Sen Van Ta.

Ying Jing Gan certainly felt that the extortion demands and other threats made against her husband were not taken seriously enough by the NYPD. The horror of holding a dying Sen Van Ta in her arms would never go away, though her feelings of shock eventually turned to anger.

As far as she knew, the police had never offered to protect her husband, even though they were the ones who had coerced him into making the public identification of LV Hong, the new Canal Street *dai low*. In effect, with that identification Ta had signed his death warrant.

With the help of a passionate young Chinatown attorney named Shiauh-Wei Lin, Ying Jing Gan filed a lawsuit against the NYPD claiming that her husband's death was a direct result of negligence. In response, members of the NYPD claimed in sworn affidavits that they had offered Ta protection, and he turned them down. If so, that revealed an even more saddening fact about life in Chinatown.

Sen Van Ta knew that if he had consented to police protection, he would have been further implicating himself as the person cooperating with the cops. He also knew that the police could not protect him all the time. The gang, on the other hand, was composed of people from the community who could monitor his whereabouts day and night, striking whenever the time was right. It could be a week from now, it could be a year from now.

That was the reality of life in Chinatown: If Sen Van Ta had consented to police protection, he was submitting himself and his wife to a greater degree of danger than if he simply went without.

To the handful of federal agents and cops who were in the process of inaugurating an investigation into the BTK, news of Sen Van Ta's murder hit like a mean, well-placed kick in the groin. Immersed in the process of debriefing their C.I., they had been a few steps removed from Sen Van Ta and his predicament. Now, they were going to have to deal with the consequences of Ta's murder. They were going to have to deal with the intractable fear it was sure to instill in the people of Chinatown—people whose cooperation these investigators were going to need if they hoped to build a case against the BTK.

The best course of action, the agents and cops agreed, was to get Tinh Ngo back on the street as quickly as possible.

On March 13, 1991, three days after Lan Tran silenced Sen Van Ta with a bullet through his brain, Tinh Ngo signed a four-page agreement with the King's County District Attorney's Office. He pleaded guilty to robbery charges, but it was unlikely he would serve time if all went well. His bail, which had been set at $5,000, was waived. In exchange, he agreed to solicit information on the criminal activities of the BTK, which he would then pass on to the authorities.

That afternoon, Tinh was released from custody at the Brooklyn courthouse. Detectives Bill Oldham and Alex Sabo drove Tinh to a motel near La Guardia Airport, in Queens. Oldham handed Tinh $75 in spending money. "Remember what I told you," he cautioned Tinh.

Although the cops were impressed with their young informant so far, it was their natural instinct to think that maybe he was playing them for fools. Oldham had warned Tinh that if he tried to run away after they'd stuck their necks out for him, the NYPD would make his life miserable. Indulging in a bit of standard cop hyperbole, Oldham had told Tinh, "We could get you killed if we wanted to."

Tinh was seated in the back of the unmarked police sedan. The two detectives were in the front, and they were both turned around facing him.

"You don't have to worry," Tinh assured them. "What I say I going to do, that's what I do. I won't run away."

"Good," answered Oldham. "Glad to hear it."

Tinh got out of the car.

Just in case, the two detectives waited and watched as Tinh entered the front door of the motel and checked himself into his room.

All that night, Tinh did what he had been doing a lot of lately: He lay in bed with his eyes wide open, trying to make sense of what he'd gotten himself into.

It *had* crossed his mind to make a run for it after he'd achieved his immediate goal of getting himself out of Rikers Island. He felt sure that if he were to disappear, the authorities would never find him. In virtually any state in the union he could blend into existing Asian communities—communities most American cops could never hope to penetrate.

What good would that do? Tinh asked himself. Sure, he could hide out in Toronto, Bridgeport, Philadelphia, Texas, or any of the other places where Born to Kill had established a beachhead. That was his prerogative as a member of the Vietnamese underworld. In any of these regions, he could live with other gangsters and continue preying on innocent merchants, traumatizing people, and shattering their lives.

None of this appealed to Tinh anymore. He may have been scared and apprehensive about whether cooperating with the cops was the right thing to do, but he knew he did not want to be a gangster anymore. He'd known that ever since the trip to Doraville.

Even before he was arrested one month earlier, Tinh could have drifted away from the gang, maybe gotten a job delivering Chinese food or working in the kitchen of some restaurant. But Tinh never had much faith in himself. If he had submitted to the boredom of a commonplace, low-paying job—the only sort of legitimate employment available to a young, uneducated Vietnamese immigrant like himself—he would most likely have eased his way back into the gang, subconsciously or otherwise.

What he needed was a new life, an opportunity to extricate himself completely from his criminal past. He needed to start over again from the beginning. Tinh still wasn't sure what cooperating with the United States government was going to entail, but he had a feeling it was the key to his future—a future free of the brutal entanglements of his past.

The following morning Tinh took the Number 7 subway train into Manhattan, emerging from the mausoleumlike dimness of Grand Central Station into the bright, bustling cacophony of pedestrian and automobile traffic on Forty-second Street. Indulging a renewed sense of physical freedom, Tinh strolled south through lower Manhattan. As he neared Chinatown, he could feel the energy level increase.

On Canal Street, BTK gang members were out in force. In the days following Sen Van Ta's murder, David Thai had told LV Hong and others in the gang to make themselves more visible than ever at well-known gang meeting places like the Pho Hanoi luncheonette. "We show people we here to stay, they learn to respect BTK," David told his *dai lows.*

One of the reasons the investigators had sprung Tinh Ngo from prison so quickly was to see what he could find out about the murder of Sen Van Ta. Seated at Pho Hanoi with LV Hong and a few other gang brothers, Tinh casually brought up the subject.

Nobody said a word. Clearly, the message had been delivered

along the grapevine that everyone was to keep his mouth shut about the latest BTK atrocity—even among themselves.

Later that afternoon, Tinh took the subway out to Brooklyn. At a pool hall on Eighth Avenue, in Sunset Park, he ran into Kenny Vu and Lan Tran.

"Timmy, how you doing? Where you been, man?" asked Kenny.

Tinh slapped hands with Kenny and Lan. "I been in jail. Rikers Island."

"What they put you in jail for?" asked Uncle Lan.

"Some stupid charge. Robbery, I think."

"Hey," said Lan. "*Anh hai* been asking about you. He wanna know if you still with us."

"Yes," answered Tinh. "Of course I still with you."

Kenny Vu and Lan assured Tinh that David Thai would want to see him right away. "You move in with us, Timmy," said Kenny. "Right down the block—eight-ten Forty-fifth Street. Tonight we go see *Anh hai* in Long Island. He give you some money and put you to work."

That night, Tinh met Kenny Vu again at the pool hall. He climbed into the front seat of Kenny's car, a faded green Buick Regal with Jersey plates.

"We drive to Hicksville," said Kenny, "to David Thai's old house. He got a new place now, but he don't let anybody know where it is."

Tinh nodded. "Who live in Hicksville now?"

"Uncle Lan live there with some other guys. I stay there too, sometimes." David Thai had established a series of safe houses in suburbia to supplement the BTK apartments in the city. In Long Island, Thai would move into a house, live in it for six months or so, and then pass it on to his gang brothers. The lease was usually maintained under an alias, or in the name of Thai's wife or some gang member other than David Thai.

It was a cool, moonless night as Kenny and Tinh drove along the Long Island Expressway toward Hicksville, thirty miles from the city limits. It had been a long time since Kenny first initiated Tinh into the gang, plucking him out of Sheepshead Bay High School and having him move in with them on Neptune Avenue. Tinh still felt affection for Kenny. It was Kenny who taught him how to stand up for himself.

157

"So," asked Tinh, "what about the little brothers who get arrested for that robbery on Canal Street?"

"Oh," answered Kenny, "I think they gonna be okay. There was a witness, a store owner, but we take care of that. We kill this guy. I hear maybe there's another witness. A lady. If we have to, we kill her too."

Tinh nodded solemnly. He knew it would be inappropriate to just come right out and ask who killed Sen Van Ta.

"What David Thai up to these days?" he asked, changing the subject.

Kenny Vu smiled. "David Thai is very crazy. He getting, you know—paranoid. He making bombs in his house."

"What?"

"Yeah," Kenny said. "Bombs. And he make his own silencers. He practicing with his new silencers all the time."

"No," said Tinh, shaking his head in amazement.

"Yeah." Kenny turned to face Tinh. "I think maybe tonight he gonna practice on you."

Tinh grinned nervously and looked at Kenny, who was not smiling. He looked dead serious.

Oh, man, Tinh thought to himself. *Could they know already? How could they know? Did somebody see me talking with the detectives at the courthouse? Did somebody at Rikers Island find out I was meeting with the D.A.?*

Kenny turned his attention back to the expressway. Tinh sat in silence and looked out the window.

"Kenny," said Tinh, finally. "You like to gamble, right?"

"Yes."

"I know a gambling place right near here. We could stop and take a look. Maybe we even want to rob this place sometime later."

"Okay," said Kenny. He veered to the right and got off the expressway at the nearest exit.

Tinh had no intention of gambling, nor did he know of any gambling house in the area. He wanted out of the car—immediately.

Tinh directed Kenny to a house near a gas station. "Let me first check something," he told Kenny. He got out of the car, ducked around a corner for a few minutes, then returned.

"Nah," he said to Kenny. "There's no gambling here tonight. But I'm going to stay with a friend. I see you tomorrow."

"Wait," implored Kenny. "What about *Anh hai?*"

"Tell him I see him tomorrow." Tinh slammed the car door and disappeared around the corner.

For a few minutes, Tinh walked through the strange, placid neighborhood in an attempt to calm himself. His hands were still trembling. Maybe Kenny was just joking. David Thai wanted to use him for target practice. Ha, ha, ha. Tinh made his way back to Brooklyn and cooled out at the safe house.

The next morning, David Thai appeared at the apartment. "Timmy, how you been doing?" he asked Tinh in a friendly tone. He handed Tinh $200. "We got lot of jobs to do, Timmy. I hope you ready to come back with us."

"Okay," answered Tinh. He observed his leader warily, remembering the time *Anh hai* had slapped him around for stealing robbery proceeds. This time Thai seemed calm and relaxed.

Of course, that was *Anh hai*'s way. He was a smart guy. Most of the time, you had no way of knowing what was really going on inside his head. If David knew Tinh was cooperating with the government and wanted to shoot him for it, he was doing an excellent job of keeping it hidden. Tinh could not be sure whether *Anh hai* was once again fulfilling his duties as the gang's kindly overseer, or merely attempting to lull Tinh into a false sense of security, fattening him up to be used as an example of what a horrible fate awaited anyone who even entertained the idea of betraying the ranks of the BTK.

159

"You wanna take a break, Timmy?"

Agent Dan Kumor leaned back in his chair, eyeing Tinh carefully. For the last two hours, he and his young informant had been sitting at his desk, attempting to meticulously re-create many of the crimes in which Tinh had played a role.

"No, Dan. I okay. We can keep going." Tinh took a sip from a can of Pepsi.

Kumor had to marvel at Tinh. Although the agent was hardly a veteran, he'd dealt with more than a few informants in his career and had never come across one like this kid. He kept waiting for Tinh to reveal some dark, manipulative side of his character. But there didn't seem to be one.

In the weeks since Tinh was put back on the street, he had been making semiregular visits to the ATF offices at 90 Church Street, a few blocks north of the twin towers of the World Trade Center in downtown Manhattan. The agents and cops assigned to the BTK investigation had established an informal headquarters there on the tenth floor. Within days, the drab, windowless room had become crowded with overflowing file cabinets, maps of Chinatown, and mug-shot displays. The investigators had begun to categorize the numerous robberies, extortions, and homicides Tinh was telling them about on a series of hand-drawn charts that dominated one wall.

So far, there were only four full-time investigators assigned to the case. Joe Greco, who had been instrumental in getting the investigation started, was busy with his gun-smuggling case in Jersey City and no longer available. Kumor had taken over as the investigation's lead agent; he was backed by Don Tisdale, a veteran ATF agent from the bureau's Manhattan office. Detectives Bill Oldham and Alex Sabo were assigned as representatives of the NYPD's Major Case Squad.

The BTK investigation was certainly more focused than it had been just a few weeks earlier, but there were still many important decisions to be made. Not only was the Vietnamese underworld a vast network with criminal connections that crossed state boundaries, but there was an ominous political dimension that had to be examined.

Since the early 1980s, five Vietnamese journalists had been murdered in the United States, the most recent being Triet Le, a former columnist for *Tien Phong*, a nationally distributed biweekly Vietnamese-language magazine. Although Le's writings were far from supportive of Vietnam's Communist government, the journalist was known as a "caustic voice," whose diatribes never failed to incite emotions on all sides of the political spectrum. In September 1990, Le and his wife were assassinated, shot multiple times while sitting in a car in front of their home in Fairfax County, Virginia.

Triet Le was believed to be the latest victim of a rabidly anti-Communist faction of the Vietnamese exile community, a group not unlike the anti-Castro Cubans displaced by the revolution in that country. There had been some speculation on the part of American journalists and people in law enforcement that Vietnamese street gangs were somehow intertwined with these dissident political forces. Based on what Kumor and his investigators were hearing, Born to Kill had no direct connection with these or any other political killings. Nonetheless, it was an intriguing possibility that bore investigation.

Even among the many crimes that had a definite BTK link, the investigators were going to have to make some hard choices. Tinh was giving them so many names and bits of information, they were never going to get anywhere unless they focused only on those gang members who could be cleanly roped into one neat conspiracy package.

The obvious starting point was David Thai. They knew Thai had plotted many of the gang's crimes, even if he rarely took part in their execution. Thai, it seemed, was much too shrewd for that.

When Tinh Ngo was first released, the investigators told him that one of his primary assignments was to get close to David Thai. Tinh was taken aback. "You want me to meet directly with *Anh hai*?" he asked, astounded by the thought.

Tinh explained that very few rank-and-file gang members ever initiated contact with David Thai. Usually, *Anh hai* preferred to establish communication through his *dai lows,* which was just fine with most gang members.

Especially since the murder of Sen Van Ta, David Thai had been lying low, trying to bolster his mystique by rarely showing his face in public. On those rare occasions when *Anh hai* did speak directly with his young gang members, many were too intimidated to even look him in the face.

"Make him trust you," the investigators encouraged Tinh. "You're a likable guy. You can do it."

Since the ATF offices had been established as the investigation's headquarters, Dan Kumor had been trying to get to know his young C.I. better. He knew he had some catching up to do. Detective Oldham already had a relationship with Tinh. But Kumor was now the lead agent on the case, and he needed to gain Tinh's trust. He didn't want his informant withholding information, or telling things to the detectives that he wasn't willing to tell him first.

Luckily for Kumor, Tinh Ngo was an accommodating person by

nature. Above all else, Tinh liked to be liked. His overriding eagerness to please was part of the reason he had joined the BTK in the first place.

Seated in the ATF headquarters, Tinh approached the task at hand with diligence, poring over mug shots of Vietnamese and Chinese criminals. It had been a long day, with Kumor grilling Tinh over and over about specific details of crimes, a methodical, drawn-out process that would continue off and on over the next eight weeks.

"Hey, Timmy," Kumor finally interjected, "maybe you don't need a break, but I sure as hell do."

Tinh laughed, then sat back and polished off his Pepsi. Kumor left the office to take care of a few errands. When he returned Tinh was still sitting in the same spot, looking distracted.

"Dan," Tinh said, speaking up unexpectedly, "I have a question for you."

"Yes?"

"What would happen if somebody was shot in a robbery I was at?"

"Well," Kumor answered cautiously, "that depends. What do you mean?"

Tinh paused for a moment, struggling to find the words to communicate in a foreign language something that had weighed heavily on his conscience for months. He looked at Kumor, then down at the floor.

In his three or four meetings with Kumor so far, Tinh had come to feel that the young ATF agent was a person he could trust. Perhaps it was because Kumor, at thirty, was closer in age to Tinh than any of the other investigators. But Kumor also seemed to Tinh like someone with a good heart. His sandy-blond hair, blue eyes, and steady, upright posture reminded Tinh of those straight-shooting American cowboys he saw in the old Westerns on late-night television.

"In November," Tinh finally sputtered, "uh, last November, around Thanksgiving. There was a shooting in Georgia. I was there . . . ." Hesitantly, in a disjointed fashion, Tinh proceeded to tell Kumor everything about the robbery of the Sun Wa Fine Jewelry store in Doraville, and the shooting of Odum Lim.

"Jesus," exclaimed Kumor when Tinh had finished.

"Does this mean I gonna be in trouble?" asked Tinh.

Kumor was wondering the same thing. It probably meant that

Tinh's agreement with the King's County District Attorney's Office had just become null and void, since the agreement was predicated on Tinh's having confessed to all criminal activities in which he played a role. Now, it appeared, he had not done so.

"Nah. Listen," Kumor reassured Tinh, "don't worry about it."

Actually, Kumor wasn't feeling that confident. He was going to have to inform his bosses. There were people in the D.A.'s office and elsewhere who would feel this was a clear indication that Tinh Ngo could not be trusted. Some might even want to terminate his services, prosecute him as an accomplice in this new crime, and throw him back into the Rikers Island shark tank.

For his part, Kumor was impressed with Tinh's willingness to finally admit his role in the Georgia shooting. He saw how hard it had been for Tinh to relive this incident, to describe in detail how Lan Tran put the gun to Odum Lim's head and pulled the trigger. The confession clearly represented a turning point.

Tinh had divulged his role in a serious felony.

Now, there was no turning back.

Chapter 10

In 1988, the year Dan Kumor joined ATF, the bureau had just begun to emerge from a long period of obscurity—an obscurity best characterized by a story told in law enforcement watering holes from Maine to California.

The story went like this: A massive task force of state and federal agents from numerous law enforcement agencies had just swept down on a noted drug kingpin in his palatial abode somewhere near Washington, D.C. The dealer looked up from his mounds of cocaine to find himself surrounded by the gun-toting lawmen. "Okay," he remarked, seemingly unsurprised, "you got me."

Each of the agents wore a dark blue windbreaker with bold yellow lettering designating their agency. The bad guy scanned the various jackets. "DEA. Yeah, okay, I expected you guys," he grumbled. He looked at another jacket. "FBI. Yep." He acknowledged lawmen from the U.S. Marshals, the Customs Department, and local Washington, D.C., police.

Then he saw a jacket marked ATF.

"ATF?" he asked incredulously. "Hey, no way. I paid my fuckin' phone bill."

The story may have been apocryphal, but the moral was not. For decades, agents from the Bureau of Alcohol, Tobacco and Firearms had been saddled not only with an unwieldy, slightly ridiculous appellation, but with a mandate that had changed so often in the last two hundred years, even criminals might be confused.

The bureau was first instituted in 1791 as a tax-collection agency. Treasury Secretary Alexander Hamilton had imposed a new tax on "spirits," an unpopular move that led to the great Whiskey Rebellion. More than a century later came Prohibition, and ATF's responsibilities were expanded to include enforcement of the Volstead Act. Agents from the bureau raided bootlegging and moonshining operations, smashed stills, and played a significant role in battling underworld syndicates in Chicago, New York, and elsewhere.

Prohibition proved to be a glorious era for ATF, with the bureau's most famous agent, Eliot Ness, playing a key role in the eventual incarceration of big bad Al Capone. In 1933, passage of the Twenty-first Amendment not only brought about the repeal of Prohibition and a crashing end to the Roaring Twenties, but a diminished role for ATF for many decades to come.

While J. Edgar Hoover's Federal Bureau of Investigation reaped headlines throughout the thirties, forties, and fifties, ATF went about the unglamorous job of enforcing regulations relating to the now-sedate alcohol and tobacco industries. Worse, the agency was denied the status of a full-fledged law enforcement bureau, relegated to a division of the Internal Revenue Service.

The Omnibus Crime Control and Safe Streets Act of 1968 changed all that by establishing an unprecedented federal commitment toward fighting urban crime. The Gun Control Act, also enacted in 1968, created stricter licensing of the firearms industry. For the first time, certain types of bombings and arson were also established as federal crimes, all of which gave ATF a broader mandate and increased profile.

Unfortunately for ATF, its new status happened to coincide with the inauguration of President Richard M. Nixon's so-called War on Drugs, a call to arms later undertaken with great zeal by Presidents Reagan and Bush. By the mid-1980s, drug trafficking had become the most written-about criminal activity since bootlegging. Agents from the Drug Enforcement Administration became the new superheroes of law enforcement, surpassing even the FBI in the number of presidential citations received and lucrative book and movie deals pursued.

By the end of the decade, various arms of the Justice Department had staked out their territory. Most high-profile crime investigations involving *Cosa Nostra* were handled by the FBI. The DEA took on the Colombian drug cartels and major Latin American syndicates operating in the United States. This left a large segment of organized crime—a category people in law enforcement lumped under the heading "emerging crime groups"—open to any agency with the mandate and fortitude to make it its own.

When Dan Kumor first got involved in the Harlem-based Jamaican posse investigation in 1989, ATF had already established itself as *the* lead agency in the area of Jamaican gangs. A number of major federal cases were under way in Miami and New York against drug organizations run by Jamaican nationals, all of which had been initiated or augmented by ATF. Partly, this was due to the posses' abundant affection for guns, which brought them under the purview of the firearms agency. But mostly it was because no other federal agency seemed to care. In the Jamaican underworld, there was no John Gotti or Manuel Noriega, superstar criminals whose prosecution and conviction could make an FBI or DEA agent's career.

The same opportunities that allowed ATF to take the lead on Jamaican organized crime paved the way for its current involvement in the BTK investigation. Like the Jamaicans, the Vietnamese were relatively low on the criminal food chain. The fact that ATF had developed a new identity for itself as an agency willing to take on so-called underworld "fringe" groups meant that the BTK investigation would get high priority.

Dan Kumor was banking on this fact when he approached his bosses to tell them about Tinh Ngo's revelation that he had "aided and abetted" the shooting of a jewelry store owner during a robbery in Georgia.

"Look," Kumor told John Rossero, his supervisor. "So Timmy withheld information. Okay. But it's not like we caught him in a lie. He was the one who came out with it. He was the one who decided, on his own, to tell the truth. I think it means the kid can be trusted."

In another situation, in another agency, Tinh's belated disclosure might have made him seem more trouble than he was worth. But Rossero and others in the chain of command recognized the importance of the investigation. They accepted Kumor's position without argument.

Though Kumor had a surprisingly easy time getting his ATF bosses to back him up, he wasn't about to tell Tinh that. "I really stuck my neck out for you on this one, Timmy," Kumor chided Tinh a few days after his Georgia revelation. "I hope you won't let me down."

Tinh nodded deferentially, eager to please his new masters. "Yes, thank you," he replied. "I not let you down."

They were words similar to those he had used before—with David Thai, the other major authority figure in his life.

As far as Tinh was concerned, it didn't really matter that he had aligned himself with ATF or the NYPD or any other agency from the vast acronym soup of American law enforcement. To a young Vietnamese immigrant in trouble with the powers-that-be, these agencies were virtually indistinguishable. Each was composed mostly of hefty white males with neatly trimmed hair and a jocular, backslapping manner. Tinh liked Dan Kumor; he felt that he could be trusted. But that was not the reason he had decided to come clean about what transpired in Doraville.

187

It was while riding along the Long Island Expressway, when Kenny Vu made the offhand comment about *Anh hai* using him for target practice, that Tinh first came to a sobering realization about his new life as a government informant. Looking back, Tinh knew Kenny had been joking. Still, the incident made it clear that Tinh could not continue to walk the fence, keeping a foot in both camps without ever having to fully commit himself one way or the other. He could not cooperate with the government halfway—the danger of being discovered was too great. He needed a partner he could rely on. For better or for worse, that partner would have to be the United States government.

The thought that he would effectively be cutting himself off from the only social world he knew was troubling to Tinh, but it wasn't long before he got some reassurance he'd made the right decision. On April 18, 1991, just a few days after his last meeting with Agent Kumor, Tinh was privy to a new act of BTK brutality. This time it was orchestrated by none other than David Thai himself.

Tinh was resting in a back bedroom at the BTK safe-house apartment at 810 Forty-fifth Street in Sunset Park when he heard a knock at the door.

"Timmy, come out. *Anh hai* is here," requested a voice Tinh recognized as Shadow Boy's.

Right away, Tinh knew something serious was up. In the four weeks he had been living in the cramped apartment, Thai had rarely made personal appearances.

Tinh walked into the front room, where David Thai was standing with a handful of other gang members. From another bedroom, Tinh could hear the sound of somebody crying. He looked to see LV Hong, the Canal Street *dai low*, hovering over Nigel Jagmohan, an associate of the gang whom Tinh knew only casually. Nigel was sitting in a chair with tears running down his face and blood trickling from his nose and mouth.

LV Hong smacked Nigel hard across the side of his head. "You motherfucker!" screamed LV. "Don't lie to us or we gonna kill you!"

Tinh's eyes opened wide. *Oh shit*, he thought, *it's finally going down.*

Three days earlier, while Tinh was sitting in the apartment with some other gang members watching a Hong Kong action movie, Nigel and Shadow Boy had burst in the door, barely able to contain their excitement. They had just attempted a robbery on Canal Street and things apparently had not gone well.

Earlier that day, Nigel, Shadow Boy, and a third gang member, Johnny Huynh, had driven into Chinatown in a brown Chevy Impala. Johnny Huynh was the leader. He selected the jewelry store they were going to hit, a small stall near the back of the shopping mall at 263 Canal Street. Because the jewelry store was smack-dab in the middle of BTK territory and the robbery had not been authorized by any *dai low*, Johnny did not want any of them to be recognized. He told the robbers they would need to wear masks.

Around two o'clock in the afternoon, the three robbers, along with

a girlfriend of Johnny's named Cindy, stopped the car near the intersection of Howard and Crosby streets, directly behind the mall. Shadow
Boy waited behind the wheel with the motor running. Cindy also stayed
in the car.

Nigel Jagmohan and Johnny got out of the Impala and walked
across the street to the rear entrance of the mall. Just inside a swinging
glass door, they pulled nylon stockings over their heads. Johnny Huynh
took a 9mm handgun out of his jacket pocket. "Let's do it," he said to
Nigel.

The two bandits stormed into the shopping mall. The stall with
the jewelry was near the back entrance, so they didn't have far to run.

"Get out of the way," Johnny shouted at the middle-aged Chinese
shop owner, who was the only person guarding the jewelry display.

From that point on, almost everything went wrong. Nigel hopped
over the glass counter and began scooping the jewelry into a black
canvas bag. He looked up to see the store owner wrestling with Johnny,
trying to get at his gun.

Bam! the gun sounded, echoing loudly throughout the mall.

Customers dove for cover. The bullet struck the store owner in his
right index finger, but he kept tussling with Johnny. Nigel jumped back
over the counter and ran for the rear door. Johnny broke free and
followed.

Outside, Nigel and Johnny pulled off the nylon stockings and hustled into the car. Johnny jumped in the front with Shadow Boy, Nigel
in the back with Cindy. Shadow Boy stepped on the gas and the Impala
sped north on Crosby Street.

They had traveled barely one block when Shadow Boy swerved to
miss an oncoming car and smashed head-on into a utility pole. The car
wasn't traveling fast enough to seriously injure the passengers, but
everyone was rattled. From the street and sidewalk, stunned pedestrians
looked on as Nigel, Shadow Boy, and Cindy stumbled out of the car
into the afternoon sunlight.

An off-duty prison guard from Rikers Island happened to be driving by. He stopped, got out of his car, and approached the crippled
Impala. Instinctively, Shadow Boy pointed his 9mm at the guard, and
they began wrestling over the gun. Cindy disappeared. Nigel ran and
flagged down a taxi. Shadow Boy dropped the gun and also ran. Johnny,

meanwhile, had been pinned inside the car when it collided with the pole. He was arrested by cops arriving on the scene.

Since the robbery had taken place on Canal Street in the middle of BTK territory, word spread fast. Both David Thai and LV Hong were livid. Not only had neither of them authorized this half-assed attempted robbery, but the black canvas bag full of jewelry was never recovered. Apparently, somebody had absconded with the loot!

When Tinh Ngo first heard about the incident, he knew there was going to be trouble. The day after the robbery, Tinh and two members from the Brooklyn faction of the BTK ran into LV Hong on Canal Street.

"Where's the gold?" LV asked Tinh and the others. At the time, Nigel Jagmohan was also living at the small apartment on Forty-fifth Street.

"Nigel say he leave the gold behind," answered Tinh. "Maybe the police got it."

The answer didn't seem to satisfy LV Hong, who was clearly upset that his authority had been disregarded. Not only had an unauthorized robbery taken place in his territory, but he knew the owner of the jewelry store. "This thing make me look bad," he complained.

Tinh and the others knew that few gang members respected LV Hong. Unlike Amigo, his predecessor, LV was the strong-arm type, often threatening other gang members to keep them in line. Some felt he had been flown in from Texas by David Thai precisely for that reason.

Now, two days later, LV Hong was mercilessly whacking the hell out of Nigel.

"No, please," Nigel pleaded between blows to the head, "I don't have the gold. I didn't take it."

There were nearly a dozen gang members in the apartment at the time. Everyone sat or stood, awkwardly silent, avoiding eye contact.

LV picked up a clock radio from a nearby dresser, raised it high in the air and brought it crashing down on Nigel's head. The radio shattered, sending pieces of plastic shooting across the bedroom floor.

Nigel still insisted, "I don't have the gold." This angered David Thai even more. Without warning, he stormed into the bedroom and began kicking Nigel, who had fallen to his knees on the floor.

"You lie, motherfuck! You lie!" screamed David, his reedy voice cracking with emotion. He kept pummeling Nigel, whose shirt was torn, his hair matted with blood.

Finally, a couple of gang members pulled *Anh hai* off. "No, *Anh hai,* we take care a this," advised Shadow Boy. David Thai walked back into the front room where Tinh Ngo stood transfixed by the mayhem.

"Sit down," David ordered Tinh.

Tinh sat.

"You know why we beat this guy?" David asked.

"Why?"

" 'Cause yesterday I go to Canal Street and I almost get arrested. I almost get arrested 'cause this guy rob the jewelry store and he don't let anybody know."

While David Thai fumed, LV Hong stomped into the kitchen and returned to the bedroom holding a wooden cutting board. He began beating Nigel with the solid cedar board, smacking him again and again.

Tinh winced each time the cutting board slammed into Nigel's skull with a loud *whuuump!*

"I know this motherfucker couldn't be trusted," David Thai said to Tinh. "I know he couldn't be trusted 'cause he not one of us, okay? He not Vietnamese."

Tinh nodded. Initially, he wondered why David Thai was making such a grand display of this beating. Now it was clear.

To the BTK, Nigel was an outsider. He'd been born and raised on the Caribbean island of Trinidad, though his parents were originally from India. In 1988, when Nigel was just fifteen years old, his family emigrated to New York City. The Jagmohans initially lived in Brooklyn, then moved to the Bronx, where Nigel began hanging out with a group of Vietnamese and Cambodian teenagers he met at Skate Key, a local roller-skating rink. Soon Nigel was making trips to Canal Street to scheme and commit crimes with his newfound friends.

Nigel wasn't the only non-Vietnamese youth to become associated with the BTK. The gang was a loose enough confederation that almost anyone who took part in crimes with gang members on a semi-regular basis could call himself BTK. There were Cambodians in the gang, and a few Chinese. There were many Amerasians, some partly of African American descent. There were even a few Puerto Rican and Dominican teenagers who helped out with BTK crimes in the Bronx.

Non-Vietnamese members were allowed to join in robberies and home invasions. They may even have been allowed to associate themselves publicly with the gang. (Nigel, for instance, had attended Amigo's funeral and was present during the cemetery shootout in Linden, New Jersey.) But for those gang members who could not speak Vietnamese, the gang's inner sanctums would always be beyond their reach. And as outsiders, they were the first to come under suspicion when things went wrong.

If David Thai had beaten and pummeled a fellow Vietnamese the way he and his Canal Street *dai low* were presently punishing Nigel, Thai would have risked alienating some members of the gang. But Nigel was lanky, his East Indian skin the color of mocha; he spoke English with a curious accent, a mixture of his parents' Indian roots and his own Trinidadian upbringing. Clearly, he was not one of them. This made him expendable in the eyes of *Anh hai*.

"Tell me!" shouted LV Hong. "Tell me where is the gold!"

By now, Nigel had been beaten so badly he was unable to respond.

"Get this motherfuck outta here," David Thai proclaimed disdainfully. "Let him go."

Nigel was helped to his feet by a couple of gang members and led to the front door of the apartment, which opened onto Forty-fifth Street. The door was opened and he was pushed out onto the sidewalk, his face badly mangled, his body bruised. He would spend the next three days and nights in a hospital with severe internal hemorrhaging, cracked ribs, and a fractured skull.

Inside the apartment, the gang members remained silent. Eventually, David Thai stood. "Anyone steal from the gang, anyone lie to the gang, this is what happen to them."

Anh hai checked to make sure no blood had splattered on his clothes, then added, "This motherfucker, he lucky he still alive."

Nigel Jagmohan's righteous ass-whupping frustrated Dan Kumor, Bill Oldham, and others involved in the BTK investigation. Tinh Ngo had paged Oldham not long after the incident and told him all about it, but there was nothing the investigators could do.

Not that they would have squandered the entire investigation by bursting in and making arrests over one beating, however bloody it might have been. The investigators were committed to stockpiling enough information and evidence to put a slew of gang members away on multiple counts. The problem was, individual crimes like this hellacious beating would continue to go unpunished unless they found a way of securing more compelling evidence. As of now, all they had on the beating was Tinh's partial eyewitness account, with no corroboration.

From the beginning of the investigation, Kumor and the others had discussed the idea of having Tinh wear a secret recording device. For agents and prosecutors, incriminating conversations captured live on tape are the ultimate form of evidence in court. In this case, however, the investigators had first broached the subject more as a fantasy than an actual strategy.

For one thing, it seemed unlikely that Tinh would ever be in a position to illicit incriminating dialogue directly from David Thai. Thai seemed to respect Tinh. Maybe he even trusted Tinh more than the average *sai low* now that Tinh had been with the gang for almost two full years. Nonetheless, Tinh had rarely been privy to the detailed planning of the gang's criminal acts in the past. Like most everyone else, he was kept in the dark until the time came to actually do the crime.

There were also obvious dangers involved in having Tinh wear a recorder. Under any circumstances, asking a C.I. to circulate among fellow criminals wearing a hidden recording device is no small request. With the BTK, nobody had any doubt that if Tinh was discovered with a recorder strapped to his body, he would be killed instantly. In short, the benefits to be gained by wiring Tinh had to be carefully weighed against the risks involved.

By early May, a few weeks after the beating of Nigel, Kumor, Oldham, and the other investigators were inclined to take whatever risks were necessary. They had recently begun almost daily surveillance of some of the gang's key members, tailing Lan Tran and others as they drove from BTK safe houses in Long Island and Brooklyn to Canal Street. So far, the best evidence of a criminal conspiracy was surveillance photos of gang members hanging out in front of restaurants and pool halls—photos they hoped would eventually substantiate the relationships that existed among the various subjects of the investigation.

To bolster this newly accumulated evidence, they needed voices, intimate conversations between members of the gang discussing crimes past and present.

On the morning of May 8, 1991, Kumor and Oldham arranged to meet with Tinh at the Municipal Building, where they had rendezvoused a couple of times before. A short walk from City Hall, near the base of the Brooklyn Bridge, the building was a downtown landmark.

It was around 3:00 P.M. when Tinh crossed under the building's historic Corinthian colonnade. He liked the hustle and bustle that engulfed the Municipal Building daily, with numerous subways spilling passengers into the station in the basement of the building. And there were always plenty of lovers, young and old, making their way to the marriage license bureau on the second floor.

Tinh took an elevator to the fourth floor and walked down the cavernous marble hallway to a small deserted office where Kumor and Oldham were waiting. After pleasantries were exchanged, Kumor got right to business.

"Timmy," he asked, "what do you hear about upcoming jobs— you know, robberies, home invasions, anything like that?"

"Yes," replied Tinh, "there's a big job I hear about. More than one robbery. In Philadelphia."

"BTK in Philly are gonna do a robbery?" asked Oldham.

"No. Some of us drive down there to do the robbery. David Thai plan all this himself. I don't know much about it yet."

Tinh told the two investigators that he had heard through Uncle Lan that a handful of gang members, including Tinh, Lan, *Anh hai,* and others, would be driving in two cars to Philadelphia, much as they had on their Connecticut and Georgia excursions. They would be staying at a BTK safe house somewhere in the city, and were supposed to be leaving within the next few days.

"Wow," Kumor responded. "That soon?"

"Yes," said Tinh. "This is what they tell me."

Kumor glanced at Oldham, who shrugged and nodded his head as if to say, "Now's as good a time as any."

"Listen, Timmy," began Kumor, "we have something we want you to do. We want you to carry a tape recorder, a mini-cassette. We want you to try to tape some conversations. Conversations with David Thai,

Lan Tran, anybody you can." Kumor took a small Sony recorder out of his pocket. "Lemme show you how to strap this on."

Tinh looked at the recorder in Kumor's hands as if it were a loaded gun being pointed in his direction. "You want me to carry this recorder?" he asked, trying not to sound too startled. "You want me to record people's voices?"

"That's right," Oldham answered. "We want to use these recordings as evidence in court. We need this to bring charges against David Thai."

The idea of secretly recording conversations was so imponderable to Tinh that he couldn't even think of anything to say. Besides, Kumor and Oldham were not asking him if he wanted to wear the recorder. They were *telling* him that this was what they needed him to do.

"The best way," offered Kumor, "is to hold it in the waistband of your pants. Run the microphone wire up your side. We can tape it. Poke a hole on the inside of your breast pocket, the pocket of your shirt. Nobody will see the mike inside your pocket."

The recording method Kumor was suggesting might have seemed remarkably unsophisticated, but he and Oldham had actually given considerable thought to the subject. They could have used a Nagra recorder, the device normally employed by law enforcement personnel for secret recording operations. Or they could have outfitted Tinh with a Kel transmitter, another commonly used device that allows conversations to be transmitted to another location, where they are taped on a reel-to-reel recorder.

In Tinh's case, neither of these methods seemed suitable. The Nagra, which was about five inches long, four inches wide, and an inch deep, was too big. The Kels came in two varieties—one that fit on a person's waist like a beeper but was somewhat unreliable, and another that fit into a shoulder holster, a method that was cumbersome and sometimes easily detectable.

The Sony microcassette was not designed for undercover police work. Chances were, the quality of the recordings would not be as good with the Sony as they would be with the Nagra. But the Sony microcassette was smaller and, the investigators felt, more suitable for what they had in mind for Tinh.

"You want me to use this right now? Today?" asked Tinh, still trying to fathom exactly what it was he was being asked to do.

"We're gonna be nearby in a car," reassured Kumor. "You got our beeper numbers. We're never gonna be more than a block or two away. Okay?"

"Yes," answered Tinh, sounding none too convinced.

Later that evening and throughout the next day, Tinh attempted a few trial runs with the recorder. As Kumor had suggested, he stuck it in his pants, ran the microphone wire up his abdomen, and concealed the mike in his breast pocket. While on the street, he moved the recorder to his jacket pocket. At another point he slipped it into the breast pocket of his shirt, trying to find a location that seemed comfortable, a place where the recorder could be turned off and on without anyone noticing what he was up to.

Two days later, Tinh was sitting in the front room of the safe-house apartment in Sunset Park. It was a Friday night, and a number of gang members had gathered, including Shadow Boy, Minh Do, and Tam Thanh Do, a gang member better known as "Son."

Among the crimes Tinh had been instructed to try to elicit information about was the accidental shooting of gang member Cuong Pham during the produce warehouse robbery the previous summer. Tinh had already been told a version of this killing by another gang member at Maria's Bakery, just a few days after the shooting occurred. It was one of the stories he had passed on to the investigators, but they told him they needed "corroboration"—a strange word with many syllables that Tinh would be hearing often in the months ahead.

Tinh knew that Son had participated in the robbery at W. C. Produce. Son had watched as Jimmy Nguyen, a gang member sometimes known as "Hong," attempted to shoot the elderly Chinese store owner, instead hitting Cuong Pham in the back of the head and killing him instantly.

As Son began to explain what happened, Tinh felt inside his waistband to make sure the recorder was on.

"That motherfucker," Son said of Hong. "He was sweating, his hands were shaking. [The gun] fired and made a 'bang' noise in the basement."

"Motherfuck," interjected Tinh, using the standard BTK modifier.

"At that time," continued Son, "Hong thought Cuong shot the Chinese guy. But Cuong held his gun at the Chinese guy's head and the Chinese guy, he push the hand away and the gun went off. Hong started shaking then."

Tinh was confused. "Oh. Cuong pointed the gun at the owner's head?"

"Yeah, at the owner. So the owner pushed it away and it went off."

"Then who died? Hong died?"

"No, Cuong died. Hong pointed the gun at the head."

"Whose head was he pointing at?"

Son was starting to get exasperated with all the explaining. "He was pointing it at the Chinese's guy's head. At that time, Cuong was tying up the Chinese guy."

"Oh, oh, okay. And what were you doing?"

"Motherfucker," answered Son, with a wicked chuckle. "We were robbing the place. There was a lot of gold and money. Then the gun made a big noise in the basement. We ran away."

"At that time," Tinh added encouragingly, trying to get Son to verbally identify the participants, "who was there? Hong, Be, you . . ."

"One hour later," Son went on, ignoring Tinh's question, "[I] go to the bus station and drive to California. Stay for three days and three nights."

"Motherfuck," exclaimed Tinh. "Who told you to do that?"

"Anh hai."

By now, a few more gang members had entered the room and were seated on the floor and couch in front of the TV. Chopsticks in hand, some were eating Chinese take-out from white cartons while watching a Hong Kong gangster movie on the VCR.

"Hey," Minh Do cautioned Tinh and Son, "tomorrow we going to rob. Talking about these things is bad."

"Yes," remembered Son. "Tomorrow we are going to cock the gun."

"Cock the gun" had become a favored BTK saying. It meant undertaking a major crime with loaded guns, with a good possibility that somebody—gang member or merchant—might wind up getting shot.

Son and Minh Do turned their attention to the TV. Shadow Boy, seated on the floor in front of the couch, looked at Tinh. "Hey, Timmy, what's that by your shirt? Your shirt is burning."

Tinh immediately flinched. He didn't have to look down to see that Shadow Boy was pointing to where the tape recorder was concealed.

"What?" Tinh asked innocently.

Shadow Boy pointed again. "There. Right there. Your shirt on fire or something."

Tinh looked down. The red indicator light from the recorder was showing through his cotton T-shirt. "Motherfuck," Tinh murmured, "what the fuck is this?" He stood up quickly, walked to the bathroom and closed the door.

Tinh could feel a bead of sweat running down the side of his face. "Motherfuck," he mumbled, grabbing the recorder from inside his waistband. He pulled out the microphone wire, wrapped it around the recorder, then stuck it in his pants pocket.

Tinh's head was swimming; he sat down on the edge of the bathtub to steady himself. *Damn!* The first night he tries to use the recorder to gather information, and already he's been discovered!? Or has he?

A worst-case scenario flickered inside Tinh's head like a bad horror movie: Shadow Boy sees the red light. "What's that?" he asks Tinh. Shadow Boy walks over and lifts up Tinh's shirt, exposing the recorder and the wire microphone. Somebody pulls out a gun and the gang members swarm around him like zombies from *Night of the Living Dead*.

Through the bathroom door, Tinh could hear the TV droning away. Maybe he should crawl out the bathroom window. Then what? He started free-associating, remembering every damn trap he'd ever gotten himself into: the refugee camps, prison, the gang.

"Motherfuck," he mumbled one more time, wiping the perspiration from his brow. Afraid that the gang members would get even more suspicious if he stayed in the bathroom too long, he splashed some cold water on his face and returned to the front room.

Everyone seemed to be engrossed in the movie. Shadow Boy glanced at Tinh. "It was just my beeper," Tinh offered, trying to sound casual. "The light come on when the battery get low."

Shadow Boy nodded and turned his attention back to the TV. Tinh sat down on the couch and stared straight ahead.

The room's overhead lights had been turned off; the only illumination in the room was from the television. On screen, elegantly dressed Chinese gangsters were shooting it out. Gunfire raged and bodies writhed in slow motion, with blood spurting from bullet wounds like lava exploding from a volcano.

It seemed to Tinh like ten minutes passed before he took his first breath. *Man,* he asked himself, as he had been more and more often since signing on with Kumor, Oldham, and the other government investigators. *How on earth did I get myself into this?*

Chapter 11

Kumor, Oldham, and the others were not indifferent to the risks Tinh faced by carrying the hidden tape recorder. They had vowed to have at least one member of the investigative team within the city limits, available to Tinh at all times should he need to beep someone immediately. They tried to talk Tinh through potentially dangerous encounters, and they told him they would be there when he needed to come down from the emotional anxiety of secretly taping conversations.

The thing was, the investigators were distracted most of the time. They had their own problems to worry about.

The beating of Nigel Jagmohan had raised a question that Dan Kumor had been asking himself ever since the day it occurred. What if Tinh had actually been able to inform them about the beating before it took place? Would he and the other investigators have been able to stop it?

The question had become even more pertinent in the last few days, since Tinh first informed them about an upcoming BTK robbery that was supposed to take place in Philadelphia. The very next day, Tinh informed them that the robbery was off. But for a while there, they'd had the gang under constant surveillance, waiting for the robbery plans to develop. It had been tense and even exciting, but Kumor had told himself afterward, I hope next time we have more information. I hope next time we aren't driving around blind, wondering exactly where and when the gang is going to strike.

Kumor was pondering these and other issues when he arrived at his apartment in suburban New Jersey around four o'clock on Saturday afternoon, the day after Tinh had almost been discovered with the tape recorder by his fellow gang members. Kumor was still carrying his gym bag after a badly needed workout. Ever since the BTK investigation began, he'd barely had time to sleep, much less stay in shape—a fact his girlfriend had reminded him of on more than one occasion. This was the first Saturday in a month he hadn't gone into the office; he was thinking about a movie or maybe a nice dinner at home. Maybe pizza.

Then the phone rang.

"It's going down," said Oldham, on the other end of the line.

Kumor was standing in the kitchen. "What do you mean it's going down?"

"The robbery. It's on. Lan Tran, Timmy, the rest of 'em—they're getting ready to go do the job right now."

"The robbery in Philly?"

"Well, yeah, but it's not in Philly. It's in Rochester."

Now Kumor was thoroughly confused. Two days ago, late on Thursday, May 9, Tinh definitely told them the robbery in Philadelphia was canceled. ATF had reassigned most of the agents who'd been helping out with the surveillance, and everyone had gone home thinking it was going to be a relatively peaceful weekend. Now the robbery was back on—not in Philadelphia, as originally planned, but three hundred and twenty miles to the north, in Rochester, New York.

"Timmy just called," Oldham explained. "He says he and two other gang members are on their way to pick up Lan Tran at Fifty-first Street and Eighth Avenue. Two cars, a light green Buick Regal and a maroon Cadillac with Jersey plates. Seems David Thai and his girlfriend are already in Rochester. Timmy and the others are supposed to arrive up there tonight."

"Where exactly?"

"Timmy doesn't know. Apparently, Lan Tran is calling the shots. I think we better try to stop them before they leave the city. Why don't you meet me at Fifty-first and Eighth as soon as you can. We'll use some pretense to pull them over. I'm not sure what."

"That's Brooklyn or Manhattan?" asked Kumor.

"Brooklyn, Brooklyn."

Kumor hung up and tried to get his thoughts together. Dinner was out of the question. So was the movie. He tossed aside his gym bag, went back out the front door, and climbed into his ATF-issue Mustang.

It took less than twenty minutes to zip through Staten Island to Sunset Park, Brooklyn—a drive that, if Kumor had been paying any attention to the speed limit, would have taken twice that long. When he arrived at the intersection of Fifty-first Street and Eighth Avenue, Kumor found Oldham waiting in an unmarked police sedan.

"The kid's not here," Oldham said, looking worried. "He said he was gonna be here."

The two agents waited fifteen minutes, then drove their cars by the BTK apartment at 810 Forty-fifth Street. There was no sign of either the Buick or the maroon Cadillac.

"Shit," scowled Oldham. "We better beep him."

Oldham spent the next forty-five minutes calling Tinh's pager number from his cellular phone while the two investigators combed the neighborhood, looking for some sign of the BTK contingent. Finally, Oldham's phone rang.

"Where the hell are you?" barked Oldham when he heard Tinh's voice.

Kumor sat in the driver's seat of his car, parked alongside Oldham's sedan in the parking lot of a fast-food joint on Eighth Avenue, and waited patiently while Oldham got an explanation from Tinh.

"Well," said Oldham, putting the phone down after a steady ten minutes of conversation, "I guess we missed 'em."

"So where the hell are they?"

"Timmy was calling from a service station in Jersey, somewhere on Interstate 80. Says he doesn't really know what route they're taking to Rochester. Lan Tran's doing the driving, with the other car following. I told him to beep me once they arrive at their final destination in Rochester. In the meantime, we better put in a call to the state police. Tell them we got two carloads of Vietnamese, armed and dangerous, heading upstate to do a job."

"Yeah," agreed Kumor. "But what about Fifty-first and Eighth Avenue? How come they never met out here like they were supposed to?"

Oldham squirmed in his seat. "Uh, I guess that was Fifty-first Street and Eighth Avenue in Manhattan, not Brooklyn."

Despite the gravity of the situation, Kumor had to chuckle. Billy Oldham, he knew, was the kind of guy who did not like to admit his mistakes. Oldham had assumed Tinh meant Brooklyn when he meant Manhattan—and cops were supposed to know that you never *assumed* anything.

In the five or six weeks Kumor had been working around the clock with Oldham, he'd actually grown to like him. Most of his initial impressions still held true. Oldham was arrogant, condescending, and had a knack for rubbing people the wrong way. He had especially angered Detective Alex Sabo, who was supposed to be his partner, and ATF Agent Don Tisdale. They felt Oldham was deliberately keeping them in the dark about important details of the investigation and denying them access to the C.I.

Kumor knew all this, but he still had to admire Oldham's chutzpah. Though only in his late thirties, which was still relatively young for a detective, Oldham had the self-confidence of a twenty-year veteran. Within the police department he was a renegade and a loner who did things his way. Kumor was the exact opposite, a conscientious federal employee trained to do everything by the book. He took a certain vicarious pleasure in the way Oldham circumvented red tape by taking matters into his own hands, though he could see now that Oldham was just as prone as the next guy to make a rookie mistake.

"Okay," said Kumor, doing Oldham a favor by ignoring his screwup. "I'm gonna go to headquarters and make some calls. Keep in touch. Lemme know if you hear anything new."

This was the predicament they'd known was bound to present itself sooner or later. The challenge was to prevent the crime from happening without tipping their hand to the gang members and blowing the larger investigation. If they moved in and arrested the robbers without giving it some thought, they risked exposing their informant, possibly getting him killed. If they didn't move fast enough and the robbery did take place, the investigators might wind up with a dead Asian merchant on their hands.

Kumor called the state highway patrol on the outside chance they might spot the two-car caravan heading north. It wasn't likely, considering the trip to Rochester might take the BTK crew through three different states on a half dozen different highways, depending on which route they took. After two or three hours at the ATF office waiting to hear from someone, Kumor left, driving through the Holland Tunnel back to his apartment in New Jersey. He knew it was a good six-hour drive from Manhattan to Rochester. All he and Oldham could do was wait; hopefully they would hear from Tinh as soon as he arrived.

By the time 2:00 A.M. rolled around, Kumor had begun to think about bed. Then the phone rang.

"Okay," said Oldham. "You got a pen?"

"Yeah."

"I got beeped about five minutes ago. There was a phone number, followed by Timmy's code—three-zero-zero. When I called the number, I got a receptionist at the EconoLodge motel on Jefferson Road, just outside Rochester. He said a group of Asian males checked in half an hour earlier."

Kumor wrote down the address and phone number. "Okay. I've already called the nearest ATF office up there, in Buffalo. They can set up a surveillance, pick up Tinh and the others as soon as they get outta bed. Also, I'm gonna go up there myself—catch a flight first thing in the morning."

"I hope those guys up there know what they're doing and don't expose Timmy somehow by mistake," Oldham said.

"That's why I'm goin' up there," Kumor assured him. " 'Cause we don't wanna take that chance. Hopefully, I can get there before the agents have to make a move."

It was 3:00 A.M. by the time Kumor got off the phone. A few hours later, after a brief cat nap, he was on a commercial airliner high over New York State, headed north toward Rochester.

Earlier that morning, around 1:00 A.M., Tinh Ngo and the others had arrived at the outskirts of Rochester, a gray, industrial city on the banks of Lake Ontario, forty miles from the Canadian border. Tinh was bleary-eyed from the long drive along dark back roads through densely forested stretches of the Empire State.

First, they had gone to the Holiday Inn at 1111 Jefferson Road, where David Thai had told them to ask for "Alan Yee," his alias. The gang members found *Anh hai* with his girlfriend, Sophia, in room 312.

Tinh, Uncle Lan, Son, and Minh Do took seats in the cramped room. Sophia, who did not speak Vietnamese, sat in bed filing her nails and watching television while *Anh hai* explained what he had planned for the following morning. Tinh marveled at how Thai had fine-tuned his method of withholding specific details until the last minute. Even the exact city had been kept secret until earlier that day, which was why Tinh had been unable to notify his police contacts until it was almost too late.

"This robbery should be very simple," David assured his gang brothers. The Ming Jewelry Store, a retail outlet located in an outdoor shopping mall five minutes away, was just waiting to be taken. Thai had checked the place out. There were only two employees, a husband and wife. The husband was usually in the back doing repair work while his wife tended to the customers.

David suggested that Uncle Lan and Son go in first; one minute later, Minh Do and Tinh should follow. Uncle Lan and Son would both have guns, Minh Do a knife. It would be Tinh's responsibility to break the glass counter and steal the jewelry, just like he had in Doraville.

"If the owner fight with you, just put the gun to his head and pull the trigger," *Anh hai* counseled Son, his voice firm but calm.

The gang members nodded solemnly.

Lan Tran had a suggestion. "Listen," he said, "if anybody need to shoot, let me. I have the three-eighty. It won't make so much noise like Son's forty-five."

185

It was agreed that if any killing needed to be done, Uncle Lan would take care of it, using the smaller, quieter .380.

Tinh, Minh Do, Son, and Lan left David Thai's room around 1:30 A.M.. They drove a quarter of a mile down Jefferson Road and checked into the EconoLodge motel, using Lan Tran's Texas driver's license for identification.

Well into the predawn hours, Tinh lay in bed worrying whether the investigators would be able to do anything to prevent the robbery. He had been able to call Oldham's beeper when the other gang members were in the bathroom, but there was no telling what the consequences of that might be. Would the local authorities be notified and attempt to stop the gang members? If so, would Lan and the others resist? And what if the cops weren't notified in time?

This last possibility scared Tinh the most. If the robbery went ahead as planned, how was this going to affect his standing with the government? And what if someone got killed, just like during the dark, disastrous heist in Doraville?

Tinh thrashed around in bed until the morning sunlight began to peep through the cheap motel-room curtains. Around 8:00 A.M., he got up and stepped into the shower, just a few minutes before Lan Tran, Son, and Minh Do also arose.

"Okay," said Uncle Lan when they had all gathered in the front room, "Timmy and me go get *Anh hai*. Minh and Son, you take the Buick and follow us, okay?"

While Minh Do and Son waited in the Buick near the EconoLodge, Uncle Lan and Tinh drove the short distance to the Holiday Inn and knocked on the door of room 312.

"Good morning, little brothers," said David Thai, opening the door and greeting them sleepily. Tinh and Lan waited as David and Sophia quickly showered and dressed.

When all four of them left twenty minutes later, Tinh frantically scanned the parking lot for some sign of Oldham or any other cop. There was none. *Now what?* thought Tinh. *Am I supposed to just go along on this robbery? Am I supposed to stand by idly while Uncle Lan shoots another innocent store owner!?*

The synapses in Tinh's brain snapped like a string of holiday firecrackers. In fact, he was so skittish he hadn't looked closely enough. Earlier that morning, an ATF surveillance team had spotted the gangsters' Caddie and Buick at the EconoLodge and had been sitting on the motel ever since. Together with state and local authorities, a contingent of twenty-five lawmen were spread out in twelve different vehicles, parked behind buildings and around corners, linked by two-way radio and ready to pounce.

It was a slightly overcast day, with the sun occasionally peeking out from behind the clouds, then disappearing instantly. David Thai and Sophia got into Thai's gray Jaguar and pulled out onto Jefferson Road. Lan and Tinh followed in the Cadillac. Both cars came to a stop at a red light directly in front of the motel.

Suddenly, from all sides, cars and vans appeared bearing the insignia of the New York State Police, the Immigration and Naturalization Service, and the Monroe County Sheriff's Department. By the time the traffic light turned green, the dozen or so police vehicles had screeched to a halt, surrounding the Caddie. Apparently, no one had told the lawmen anything about a Jaguar. As they forced the Caddie down the road and into the parking lot near the EconoLodge, David and Sophia sped away.

At the EconoLodge, another cortege of vehicles had surrounded Son and Minh Do in the Buick. When the Caddie was brought to a halt alongside, a swarm of agents and cops, many with guns drawn, jumped out of the cars and surrounded the BTK gangsters.

"Out of the car!" an ATF agent commanded. "Out of the car with your hands on your head!"

Meanwhile, Dan Kumor had landed in Buffalo around 7:30 A.M., where he was met by an ATF agent from the local office. They piled into a car and raced toward Rochester.

Kumor was almost as anxious as Tinh had been. The possibility that his informant might be exposed had been gnawing at him ever since he left Jersey. It wasn't hard to imagine the agents on the scene searching Tinh in front of the other gang members, finding his tape recorder, and blowing his cover.

Forty-five minutes later, when Kumor and the agent arrived at the scene, Tinh and the others had just been loaded into the back of

187

the police cars. Kumor flung open his car door and bounded toward the agent in charge.

"Don't worry," the agent informed Kumor after introducing himself, "everything's in control here." Then the agent asked, "By the way, is one of these guys a C.I.?"

Kumor's gnawing suddenly grew worse. "Uh, yeah," he said. "Look, I think you better let me handle this."

Son and Minh were in the backseat of one police vehicle, Lan Tran and Tinh in another. Kumor took them out one at a time to ask questions, so none of the others would be suspicious when he finally approached Tinh.

"Is everything okay?" Kumor asked his informant quietly.

"Yes," answered Tinh, who had never before been so happy to see a friendly, familiar face in a sea of gun-toting lawmen.

"What happened?"

Tinh explained how the gang members were driving off to do the robbery when the cops descended. Kumor was disappointed to hear that David Thai and Sophia had not been stopped.

"Where's your recorder?"

"Oh, I left that back in Brooklyn," answered Tinh, much to Kumor's relief.

Tinh told Kumor where the gang members had hidden their weapons. Sure enough, a few minutes later the agents found two handguns —a Taurus .380 and a Llama .45—under the hood of the Buick, stashed in a bag behind a headlight. Ammunition clips for both guns were later found under the driver's seat.

The guns posed a problem that Kumor had not anticipated. If the gang members were placed under arrest, sooner or later they were going to wonder who had tipped off the police. But if Kumor didn't arrest them, they might wonder why, since they had just been caught with two unregistered handguns.

A little creative fiction was called for.

"You understand why you were stopped, right?" Kumor asked the four gang members once they had been brought out of the police cars and huddled together in the parking lot.

They shook their heads.

"Well," said Kumor, "we thought you guys were drug dealers. We had information you guys were smuggling cocaine and heroin up here. You know what I'm talkin' about?"

Again, all four shook their heads, trying to look like innocent altar boys.

"We know now you guys aren't the ones we were looking for," Kumor continued. "But we found these guns in the car. You know anything about these guns?"

"We don't know," answered Lan Tran. "This car belong to a friend in New York, in Brooklyn."

Kumor nodded. "Okay, well, your friend shouldn't have these guns in the car. You're gonna have to explain this to a judge, all right? I'm gonna have to give you a summons."

The gang members sniffled, coughed, and avoided eye contact with Kumor.

"See, normally we'd arrest you and take you before a judge today. But it's Mother's Day. Judges up here don't sit on Mother's Day. So we're gonna let you go. But you'll be getting a summons in the mail. Don't ignore it or you're gonna be in a lot of trouble. Understand?"

Son, Minh, Lan, and Tinh all nodded their heads, then watched as the nearly two dozen agents and cops piled into their various vehicles and drove off. There was only one thing left for them to do: begin the long trek back toward New York City, where they would commiserate with one another, curse their bad luck, and begin preparations for the next BTK robbery.

On his return flight that afternoon, Kumor looked out the window at a bed of soft, silvery clouds. "Mother's Day!" a couple of agents had exclaimed, laughing on the way to the airport. The only reason Kumor had thought of it was because he had planned to visit his mother that day, until the BTK derailed his plans by suddenly embarking on their upstate foray.

Okay, thought Kumor, so what if it was a lame excuse? It worked. They'd faced their biggest challenge yet and come through with flying colors. They'd gotten away with it.

This time.

Kumor clamped on a set of headphones and reclined in his seat, allowing himself to relax for the first time in the last twenty-four hours.

Back in Manhattan the next day, after questioning Tinh in detail about the events leading up to and including the trip to Rochester, Kumor and the other investigators felt chastened. Yes, they had successfully prevented the robbery without blowing Tinh's cover. But if Kumor had not arrived on Jefferson Road when he did, the entire investigation could have been pissed away. Obviously, they needed to improve communications, not only with Tinh but with the vast coterie of law enforcement people they would need to call on if the gang continued to hatch robbery schemes that took them beyond New York City.

On the positive side, the investigators had accumulated a wealth of evidence pertaining to a serious felony: attempted robbery. They had taped conversations of the crime being discussed by gang members in the Brooklyn safe house. They had confiscated guns, which Kumor brought back on the plane with him. And they had numerous eyewitness accounts of gang members having been in Rochester the day the crime was scheduled to take place. Kumor, for one, felt that if they continued to thwart BTK robberies in this manner, reaping an impressive harvest of evidence each time, they were well on their way to establishing a comprehensive racketeering case.

190

The foiled robbery also proved to be an important catalyst. One week later, Alan Vinegrad, an assistant United States attorney for the Eastern District of New York, paid a visit to the ATF headquarters, where he met the various investigators assigned to the case and their star C.I., Tinh Ngo.

A federal prosecutor was key to the investigators' hopes of being able to nail the BTK by using federal RICO (Racketeer Influenced and Corrupt Organizations) statutes, a sweeping collection of laws that had grown out of the 1968 Omnibus Crime Control and Safe Streets Act. RICO turned out to be the ultimate tool in the United States government's fight against organized crime. Throughout the 1980s, the RICO statutes were used successfully against the Mafia in a number of highly publicized trials. More recently, RICO had also been used against Jamaican posses, Latin drug cartels, and even in some notorious cases of white-collar and corporate malfeasance.

To successfully prosecute a RICO case, you needed mounds of evidence to establish an "ongoing criminal conspiracy" or "racketeering enterprise." You also needed a federal prosecutor to champion your investigation, to shepherd it through the bureaucracy and commit the time, money, and manpower necessary to bring the case to trial.

Alan Vinegrad, just thirty-one years old, had been with the United States Attorney's office less than two years when he was handed the BTK case as a result of another, more experienced prosecutor's taking a leave of absence. Like Kumor, Vinegrad was only vaguely aware of the BTK when the case first came his way. In fact, he drew a blank until his immediate supervisor reminded him, "You know, the shootout in the cemetery. The cemetery in New Jersey."

"Oh, yeah," answered Vinegrad, "of course."

Vinegrad may have been a neophyte when it came to the BTK, but in his relatively brief tenure with the U.S. Attorney's office he had acquired more than his share of expertise on the broader subject of Asian organized crime. Since joining the office in September 1989, he'd spent most of his time with the Eastern District's narcotics bureau working on a massive Chinese heroin case involving what was, at the time, the single biggest seizure of heroin in U.S. history.

That case had begun in October 1989 when an FBI-NYPD task force seized 820 pounds of China White, high-grade heroin from Southeast Asia's Golden Triangle, the infamous poppy-growing region that encompasses parts of Burma, Laos, and Thailand. The heroin had been discovered inside the rubber tires of garden carts, part of a huge shipment delivered to two residences in Queens. Once in New York, the heroin could be "cut," or diluted, and sold primarily to African-American and Dominican distributors. With an estimated street value of roughly $1 billion, the shipment represented staggering profits for the Chinese businessmen and triad members who arranged the cargo's safe passage halfway around the world.

By the time Vinegrad became involved in the case, code-named White Mare, more than forty suspects had been arrested in New York, Thailand, and Hong Kong. For more than a year, a team of prosecutors from the Eastern District set their entire caseload aside to concentrate on various aspects of the investigation. There would be at least two trials, two sentencing hearings, four extradition cases, and dozens of plea bargainings before more than two dozen people were put behind bars on RICO charges.

With White Mare, Vinegrad had been dealing with the upper echelons of Asian organized crime; the defendants were mostly successful businessmen who smuggled dope as if it were a legitimate commodity and then buried the huge profits in real estate, restaurant chains, produce markets, and dummy bank accounts throughout Chinatown, Manhattan, and the rest of the United States. They ran the gamut from high-rolling nightclub types to reputable businessmen with solid family backgrounds, all of whom were seduced by what drug agents and economists were now calling the most profitable cash business in the world.

It didn't take Vinegrad long to realize that his current case was something else entirely. David Thai might have had pretensions of one day sitting high in an office tower atop New York or Hong Kong, but most of his BTK brothers were content with a warm place to sleep and a healthy bowl of *pho*. Throw in a silk shirt, a tailored suit, and a year's supply of stylish black sunglasses and they might even have thought they'd risen above their station. The large-scale trafficking of heroin was far removed from the sort of street-level robberies, extortions, and home invasions that had become the BTK's stock-in-trade.

192

Or was it? Once Vinegrad began sifting through the evidence and other data the ATF investigators were accumulating, he was struck by the ways in which the Asian underworld reinforced its iron grip. In Chinatown, disparate groups within the community's byzantine criminal structure seemed to benefit from one another's activities, whether they were directly involved in those activities or not. Certainly the young ruffians who comprised the BTK were not involved in the underworld's more lucrative rackets, which were controlled by Chinese criminal syndicates spread across the globe. But for major heroin trafficking to take place, the proper climate was required. Asian youth gangs, from the Ghost Shadows to the Flying Dragons to the BTK, were the ones who created and maintained this climate through day-to-day acts of terror and violence.

The way Vinegrad saw it, the BTK investigation presented a rare opportunity to strike at one of the most pernicious aspects of Asian organized crime: the street-level brutality that made it possible for gangsters and racketeers at every level to ply their trade.

When Vinegrad met Tinh Ngo for the first time at the investigators' tenth-floor headquarters, it was not exactly love at first sight. Tinh was there to drop off a couple of mini-cassette tapes he had recorded the day before. Now that he was using the tape recorder on a regular basis and had become responsible for alerting the agents to major crimes the gang might be planning, the intense pressure he was under had begun to show. Tinh's weight had dipped to around one hundred and five pounds, and he seemed increasingly withdrawn and anxious.

Though physically a wreck, Tinh impressed Vinegrad with his intelligence. His command of the English language was better than average. He had an excellent memory for names and dates. Most important of all, he seemed to have an even temperament; he never lost his cool while being questioned on subjects he had probably been grilled about dozens and dozens of times in the last few months.

After speaking with Tinh, Vinegrad was more convinced than ever that much of the case would revolve around his secret recordings. The problem was, nearly all of the tapes were in Vietnamese. Not only would they have to be carefully transcribed, they would need to be sent to a language institute where they could be translated into English—a laborious process that could take weeks, even months.

"Until I see some of these transcripts," Vinegrad told Kumor and the other investigators, "I won't really know what we have."

"How long's that gonna take?" asked Kumor.

"Maybe I'll have something in a few weeks. We'll meet again then."

In the meantime, the investigators had their informant out on the street, keeping a close eye on his gang brothers. On May 21, 1991, nine days after the aborted robbery in Rochester, Tinh was supposed to take part in another heist. This time the gang's target was a leather-goods store in Copiague, Long Island, forty miles outside of New York City.

David Thai had told Tinh to select two other gang members to commit the robbery with the help of Lan Tran. They were to steal cash, expensive leather jackets, and as much other merchandise as possible, which they could later sell at reduced prices to Chinatown merchants.

The day the robbery was supposed to take place, Tinh phoned the BTK safe house in Hicksville, Long Island, where he was scheduled to meet Lan Tran and David Thai.

"Where are you?" Lan Tran asked Tinh angrily.

Tinh played dumb, his mini-recorder pressed against the earpiece on the phone. "I don't know where to meet *Anh hai*."

Lan was exasperated. "Huh? Oh, God. I'm waiting for you. *Anh hai* just went out to the store, the store we rob, to wait for you guys."

"Now, I can't," Tinh replied. "The car has no gas. I thought you were coming here to Brooklyn, to get us."

"Wow, Timmy, you say one thing and you do another. You fucking kill me. . . . Yesterday, *Anh hai* said he'd wait here at twelve o'clock for you guys to call."

"Oh" was all Tinh could think to say.

Uncle Lan let loose a long, weary sigh. "And now you don't have gas to come here. And you don't have any money?"

"No," answered Tinh, "not even one dollar. Right now I'm calling collect to *Anh hai*, to you. I can only make collect calls."

"Wow," replied Lan, sighing again. "You guys really kill me."

By making himself unavailable, Tinh had successfully scrambled the robbery plans that day. But he had also run out of excuses. The following afternoon, he could stall no longer. He and two other gang members took the gang's green Buick and headed out to meet Lan Tran and David Thai in Copiague.

At least this time Tinh had been able to give the investigators some advance warning. On their way to meet Uncle Lan and *Anh hai*, Tinh and his companions were pulled over by Detective Oldham and ATF agent Don Tisdale. They told Tinh he had run a stop sign. When none of the occupants of the car was able to produce identification, they were handcuffed and taken to a nearby police station. There they were held for a few hours until the robbery plans were once again effectively derailed.

Back at ATF headquarters, the investigators slapped themselves on the back for having prevented another BTK crime. But it didn't take long for the euphoria to wane. They may have stopped the robbery and netted more damaging evidence against the gang, but an obvious question was beginning to loom:

How much longer could they continue to make miraculous appearances just as BTK gangsters were about to go do a job before someone in the gang got wise, putting their C.I. in even more serious jeopardy than he already was?

Chapter 12

"**W**ho want to betray the gang?" asked Lan Tran, glowering at his BTK brothers. "You! You want to betray the gang?" Uncle Lan pointed an accusing finger at Son.

"No, Uncle Lan. No way," answered Son. "I don't betray the gang."

Lan was swaying from too much beer and *ma tuy*, marijuana. He had shown up unexpectedly at the safe house on Forty-fifth Street in Sunset Park, and he was in a foul mood.

Usually, Lan Tran was remarkably even-tempered. He may have been a killer, but he was a cool-headed killer who rarely showed his emotions. Only when he had too much to drink did his mood turn dark and surly.

"What about you? You betray the gang?" Lan demanded as he staggered around the front room of the apartment, indiscriminately pointing at gang members. There were seven or eight people in the room at the time. They'd been watching TV when Lan burst in.

Minh Do, one of the gang members who'd gone on the trip to Rochester, was seated on the couch. Known as Fat Minh to most of the gang, Minh Do sank in his seat as Uncle Lan approached; he tried to avoid eye contact with *anh ba*, the Vietnamese honorific for the second highest brother after *anh hai*.

"You!?" barked Lan Tran. "Would you betray the gang?"

"No, *Anh ba*," Minh Do replied meekly.

Lan reached out and smacked Fat Minh with an open hand. Minh tried to protect himself as Lan slapped him a few more times across the side of the head.

"You all weak now," announced Lan, turning so that everyone in the room could hear him. "BTK used to be the toughest gang in Chinatown. Now, you new gang members, you all chicken!"

Lan Tran had been under a lot of pressure lately, and it was beginning to show. Ever since the murder of Sen Van Ta, he'd become more and more paranoid, especially as Ta's death garnered increasing attention in the mainstream newspapers.

At first, the brazen killing of Sen Van Ta had been reported as just another gang shooting in Chinatown. The NYPD neglected to mention that Ta had been cooperating with the cops in an ongoing robbery and extortion case. Later, Peg Tyre, an enterprising reporter with *Newsday*, discovered that Sen Van Ta had been murdered because, in fact, he was a cooperating government witness who'd been left unprotected. This revelation proved embarrassing to the NYPD, forcing them to give the investigation of Ta's murder high priority.

Though no one in the gang talked openly about it, everyone knew that Lan Tran had been the triggerman. And Lan Tran knew that everyone knew, which was why he had begun to exhibit more pronounced signs of paranoia.

Lan continued reeling around the room, practically stumbling over furniture, until he came face to face with Tinh Ngo, who was standing near the kitchen. Tinh met Lan's gaze head-on. Normally, the subject of betrayal would have made Tinh jumpy. But he was reasonably certain that, this time at least, Lan Tran was just blowing smoke.

Tinh had spoken with both Lan and David Thai on the phone a few days earlier, trying to explain why he and the others were stopped on the way to the robbery in Copiague. "I only drove past the stop sign

197

a little bit," Tinh told David. "I don't know, I'm having really bad luck, *Anh hai*."

David Thai was philosophical. "Yes. This is an unlucky year. It's my birth year."

"How old are you this year, thirty-three?"

"Thirty-five. My birth year. So whatever I do, something always goes wrong. My head tries to think of big things, but . . ."

"I really want to help you, *Anh hai*," Tinh butted in, "but I can't seem to help you."

David sighed. "Everything I've done failed, you know? I can't understand it. Whatever I do fails, it just fails."

Tinh actually felt sorry for *Anh hai* as he listened to him blame himself for the gang's recent botched robbery attempts. The conversation was also reassuring. For the first time, Tinh was convinced that the gang's leader had not even begun to entertain the possibility there might be a traitor in their midst.

Lan Tran had answered the phone that day and was sitting with *Anh hai* when Tinh spoke to him. If Lan had any serious accusations to make about betrayal, he would have done it then. Tinh figured that the big show Lan was putting on now, storming around the room smacking people and getting in their faces, was mostly a warning, a way of instilling fear in the younger gang members who'd not yet seen Lan Tran in action.

Standing before Tinh Ngo, Uncle Lan adopted a more sober posture. "What about you?" he asked, locking eyes with Tinh. "What do you think?"

"Hey, you know me long time," answered Tinh coolly, knowing Lan would have to respect his status as a "veteran" gang member. Lan glared at Tinh a few seconds more, then moved on.

In fact, Tinh had known Uncle Lan for nearly two years, but there was much about the BTK's premier hitman that had remained enigmatic, to Tinh and everyone else. Lan was eight or nine years older than most of the gang members, but he seemed even farther removed than that. Most gang members had a vague knowledge of Lan's self-described history as an operative for the deposed South Vietnamese government. Still, even those who knew nothing of his past could tell that he had been through something dark and troubling. It seemed as if much of

Vietnam's recent history—the residue of the war, the refugee boats, the camps, the swath cut by Vietnamese gangs in the United States—had been captured in Lan's haunted eyes and prematurely aged face.

Lan rarely socialized with the other gang members. Instead, he preferred to spend long hours alone in his room at David Thai's suburban Long Island home, writing in his journal. Few gang members were aware of it, but Uncle Lan had been chronicling his and the gang's exploits for a number of years. Lan always fancied himself something of a poet and scribe. When he entered the United States in 1982, on his immigration papers he listed his occupation as "writer." Since then he'd filled numerous spiral notebooks with neat, compact Vietnamese script.

Mostly, Uncle Lan's writings were an account of the BTK's rise to power as the gang members themselves might have seen it. "In New York," Lan wrote, "there came a gang bearing a terrifying, unbelievable code name . . . [whose] presence has facilitated and benefited the Vietnamese businesses in Chinatown." David Thai was referred to with great veneration as "a model example of a young Vietnamese man. Thai is tall and his body is well proportioned. Girls from rich families, meeting him, could not stop themselves from falling in love with Thai."

Along with giving an "official" version of the gang's history, Lan wrote long, vivid descriptions of his own exploits leading up to his involvement with the BTK. In many of these descriptions Lan portrayed himself as a professional, remorseless assassin.

199

> Known as "Killing Hand," I always observed the rules of the underworld. This time was my first opportunity in America. Me and my gun played the role. Five terrible bullets found the targets. Things were chaotic, patrons ran helter-skelter from the restaurant. Taking advantage of the situation, I ran. The damn car wouldn't go. I was bewildered. . . . It's truly destiny. Holding up the .38, I said thank-you and threw it in the snow-covered bush.

Lan Tran himself would later admit that much of his writing was a melding of fact and fiction, an imaginative rendering of his life filtered through too many Hong Kong gangster movies and further heightened by his own feverish vision of reality. True or not, his writings eloquently expressed the unique combination of romanticism, alienation, and violence that had become a hallmark of young Vietnamese gangsters, from New York to California.

> Tonight, snow has fallen thicker than usual. I wandered the street. Each lonely step, I carried with me my feelings. The wind was blowing one gust after another, burning my face. Life here is always related to the present issues. I have never experienced coldness like this before. . . . Looking down, I see this huge city buried in snow. New York, the infamous city in the underworld which has scared people, has opened itself to me. . . .
>
> As the night progressed, the bar was almost deserted. I was still passionately involved with my newly served beer. All of a sudden, an old white American came to my table. I did not think that patrons here could cause trouble. In reality, this American was standing before me, talking baloney. It turned out that he served in Vietnam, all that baloney. I did not pay attention. Suddenly he pounded his two hands on the table, toppling the beer, sending liquid in all directions. I was mad but didn't answer, bent down to pick up the glass and put it back on the table. He quickly threw the glass to the ground again and insulted me with dirty words. I could not control my temper, felt humiliated when I heard the two words "Viet Nam," and it was too late for people around to stop me. "Crack," my chair landed on the head of the white American. . . .

The point of view conveyed by Uncle Lan in his writings was an accurate reflection of how the others saw him: the alienated loner whose life in the underworld was guided by a strict code of honor. To Tinh Ngo and the other BTK gang members, Lan was a near mythical figure. His reputation was enhanced by the fact he was pure Vietnamese, not *Viet-Ching*, like many of the others. He had been born and raised in

Hue, Vietnam's ancient imperial capital. In the United States, he was a well-traveled criminal who had reputedly given the Born to Kill gang its catchy name. If David Thai was the BTK's mandarin leader, Lan Tran was its dark prince, the highly disciplined, cold-blooded gangster that most of the gang's lesser members could only pretend to be.

Like the others, Tinh started out worshiping Uncle Lan. But his feelings for the elder gangster had gone through an evolutionary process. Now that he had begun to come out from under the dark cloud of the gang, Tinh saw clearly what a trap Lan Tran's life had become. Lan was the most irrefutable kind of killer. He believed he was killing for a cause, in this case the cause of brotherhood. And by setting himself up as the truest and most devoted gang member, he'd sealed his fate. Prison or death were the only avenues left.

Tinh felt sorry for Lan, but his sympathy was tempered by a harsh reality: He knew that Lan was crazy. And he knew that if his betrayal of the BTK ever came to light and somebody had to put a bullet in his head, the triggerman would most assuredly be Uncle Lan, who would no doubt carry out his assignment with the same ardor—and the same literary flair—he'd employed on all the other occasions.

Their confidential informant may not have been overly concerned by Lan's drunken accusations of betrayal, but Dan Kumor and the other investigators were. As far as they knew, this was the first time the issue of betrayal had been brought into the open by one of the gang's ranking members.

Their concerns intensified a few days later when they learned that Lan had barged into the Sunset Park safe house early on a Saturday morning and rustled Tinh out of bed.

"Timmy," said Uncle Lan, "Timmy, wake up. Let's go find some money."

Tinh got up from his mattress on the floor and pulled on some clothes. He had no choice but to go with Uncle Lan as they drove to the gang's safe house in Belmore, Long Island, a thirty-minute drive on the Long Island Expressway. During the drive, Lan told Tinh they were going to rob the same leather-goods store in Copiague they'd missed earlier.

When they arrived at the house in Belmore, Tinh sat at the kitchen table and tried to gather his thoughts. He was barely awake. There was no way he was going to be able to notify Kumor, Oldham, or anybody else. Once again, he was about to embark on a robbery with his fellow gang members. Only this time, there wasn't a damned thing he could do about it.

Fifteen minutes later, David Thai showed up with Sophia. "Forget it," *Anh hai* told Lan, Tinh, and the others. "I just check it out. That store isn't even open today."

Tinh breathed a sigh of relief.

Later, when he told Kumor and Oldham what had happened, they became more worried than ever that David Thai or Lan Tran was suspicious. The gang's leaders had given Tinh very little advance notice of robberies in the past; this time, they'd given him none at all.

And there was more. Later that same day, David Thai had taken Tinh into the apartment's main bedroom to show him a new cache of weapons he'd recently scored. From a suitcase under the bed, *Anh hai* had produced his pride and joy, a brand new Tech-9 semi-automatic machine gun.

"Haven't had a chance to use it yet," said David, "but I'm looking forward to it."

All of which made the investigators very uneasy. Ever since Tinh had gone back out on the street, they'd had to scramble to keep up with the amount of criminal planning his life as a BTK member involved. So far, they'd been lucky. Tinh's status as an informant had not been discovered, nor had he been forced into any crimes that might later compromise his standing as a government witness. But after only nine weeks of working undercover, Tinh had been through a number of close calls, and it seemed only a matter of time until his luck ran out.

For some time, Kumor had known that he and Oldham and probably Tinh were going to have to take a trip to Georgia. Tinh's story of the shooting at the jewelry store in Doraville had given the investigators important leads that needed to be followed up on. They would have to check with the local authorities in Doraville, and also with cops in Chattanooga, Tennessee, where, Tinh informed them, a couple of BTK gangsters had committed an additional violent robbery.

Kumor figured there would never be a better time for the trip to

Georgia than right now. Removing Tinh from the scene would alleviate, if only temporarily, the danger of discovery and the pressure to participate in BTK crimes. Also, by retracing the gang's steps in Georgia—something the investigators were going to have to do eventually anyway—they would be accumulating evidence crucial to securing a federal indictment against the BTK.

Already, Bill Oldham had made a phone call to the Doraville police department. That was when the investigators learned that Odum Lim, the Cambodian jewelry store owner shot in the head and left for dead, had not perished.

Despite three excruciating weeks spent in a Doraville hospital recovering from his wounds, Odum Lim counted himself among the luckiest people on earth. The .38-caliber bullet fired into his head at close range by Lan Tran had entered near his right temple at a slight downward angle, grazed his skull, wormed its way along his right cheek bone, and exited out the side of his face. Lim lay in a pool of blood spilling from twelve stab wounds and a gaping head wound. But he had stubbornly refused to die.

On the phone, Oldham asked a captain with the Doraville police if they'd had any luck with their investigation into the robbery and shooting.

"Well," answered Detective Captain Cliff Edwards, a fourteen-year veteran, "as a matter of fact, yeah."

Edwards had gotten to know Odum Lim well since the day he arrived at the Sun Wa Jewelry Store to find him lying in a pool of blood on the sidewalk. Later, when the local newspaper reported that Lim had survived the shooting, Edwards insisted on putting his hospital room under twenty-four-hour guard. He didn't want any gangsters coming back to finish the job.

The Doraville detective told Oldham that one month after the shooting, the mother of one of his fellow officers had clipped an article out of a Colorado newspaper about a robbery perpetrated by Vietnamese gangsters. According to the story, six armed criminals had stormed into a Catholic church in Wheat Ridge, Colorado, robbing some thirty parishioners during Sunday mass.

When Edwards called Colorado, he was informed that six suspects had been arrested in nearby Colby, Kansas, just across the border.

203

Kansas state police sent Edwards fingerprints and photos of the six Vietnamese males they had in custody. Edwards took the photos over to the Lim's jewelry store, which was located less than a mile from the Doraville police station.

Odum Lim had only recently been released from the hospital and was still angry. Determined to see the people who'd robbed his store, terrorized his family, and shot him in the head brought to justice, he picked out three of the photos.

Detective Edwards did not feel good about the identifications. He had a feeling that, given his zealous desire to see the perpetrators punished, Odum Lim's judgment might have been skewed. Edwards seriously doubted the identifications would stand up in court. But he wasn't about to admit that to some New York City detective who refused to even identify himself by name over the phone.

"We've got the robbers identified," Edwards assured Oldham. "They're in custody out in Colorado right now, and I'm gonna move for an indictment."

"Don't do it," Oldham bluntly warned. "Those are not your people."

Edwards was startled. "Well, who the hell are you? Where you comin' from?"

"Look, that's all I can tell you right now. I'm working a federal case here in New York. I'm NYPD. I'm not bullshitting you. Believe me, those people you're getting ready to indict are not your robbers. I know who your robbers are."

"Oh, yeah?"

"Yeah. Myself and an ATF agent are gonna be down there soon. I'll fill you in when we get there." Then Oldham hung up.

A couple weeks later, on the morning of June 10, 1991, Oldham, Kumor, and Tinh Ngo arrived at Atlanta International Airport after a comfortable ninety-minute flight from New York City. It was a sultry summer day, with temperatures in the high eighties, and the sky was a cloudless, crystalline blue.

It had been nearly eight months since Tinh made the long drive along I-80 with the rest of the BTK road crew into the heart of the Deep South. In that time, Tinh had done his best to repress his recollections of the events surrounding the shooting at the Sun Wa Jewelry store.

Since signing on with Kumor, Oldham, and company, he'd been forced to unearth many of them. But there was much that remained hazy. He remembered that he and the other gang members had stayed in a town called Gainesville, which he knew to be about fifty miles outside of Atlanta. He remembered the drive from Gainesville to the jewelry store where the robbery and shooting took place. But he did not remember the exact location of the store, nor was he certain he could find the precise house in Gainesville where he and the other gangsters had stayed.

On a map the two investigators and their informant picked up at the airport, Tinh was able to pick out the tiny suburb of Doraville, roughly fifteen miles outside the city. Kumor, Oldham, and Tinh piled into a rented Lincoln town car and drove north, through downtown Atlanta, until they arrived at Northwoods Plaza.

The cops were lucky. Tinh recognized the area immediately. The Sun Wa Jewelry Store, though inauspiciously located in the middle of the outdoor mall, was on Doraville's main thoroughfare, at 5081 Buford Highway. Within minutes, Tinh spotted the store where Odum Lim had been stabbed, shot, and left for dead. It was located not far from a neatly painted sign mounted along the highway that must have held a special irony for Odum Lim. It read:

WELCOME TO THE CITY OF DORAVILLE
"A GOOD PLACE TO LIVE"

Once they'd found the store, Kumor and Oldham drove Tinh back to a hotel in Atlanta, where they checked into two adjoining rooms. They had decided not to take Tinh into the jewelry store. There was no telling how Odum Lim might react to having one of the robbers standing before him again. Besides, there was no reason for Tinh to be there anyway.

Tinh stretched out on the hotel bed, watched TV for a while, and then took a nap. Kumor and Oldham, meanwhile, got back in the car and returned to Doraville.

After arriving at the jewelry store and being buzzed inside, the two investigators introduced themselves to Odum Lim and his wife, Kim Lee.

"We were hoping maybe you might be able to help us," Kumor explained to the Lims. "We're police investigators from New York, and we're working on an important investigation into the activities of a Vietnamese gang called Born to Kill. We think they may have been involved in the robbery that took place here last November twenty-sixth. Could you describe for us what happened that day?"

Kumor and Oldham were pleased to hear that the Lims' version of the robbery and assault matched Tinh's in virtually every detail.

Even eight months after the fact, Odum Lim was bitter about what he, his wife, and two children had been forced to endure that day. Lim had a deep scar and indentation on the side of his face, where the bullet from Lan Tran's gun exited. Occasionally, he suffered from severe headaches and upsetting flashbacks. The shooting, he told the two investigators, was almost as traumatic as some of the things he'd experienced during the terrifying reign of the Khmer Rouge.

Kumor and Oldham sat riveted as Lim recounted his years in Cambodia in the late 1970s, a slow descent into hell shared by tens of thousands of other Cambodian refugees.

"It all started in Phnom Penh," said Lim, explaining how he had served in the country's capital city as an interpreter for the U.S. military attaché. When the murderous Khmer Rouge, the Communist regime led by Pol Pot, overran Phnom Penh in April 1975, he and his family were forced into labor camps with other Cambodians. Untold numbers starved to death, or were brutally tortured and slaughtered in the notorious "killing fields" of rural Cambodia.

After three and a half years as prisoners and slaves in their own country, Odum Lim and his wife escaped the work camps and fled on foot toward Thailand. For five agonizing months they endured poisonous leeches and malaria in the rice paddies of western Cambodia, hiding from roaming Khmer Rouge execution squads in search of fleeing refugees. In early 1979, the Lims and a group of fellow refugees finally reached the border, where they were refused entry by Thai government authorities. Forced back into Cambodia, many of the Lims' companions died when they stepped on land mines and were blown to smithereens. Those lucky enough to survive hid in the mountains for four months, then made another run at the Thai border.

This time, Odum and Kim Lee made it into Thailand, where they spent nearly two years in a refugee camp. For a time, Odum Lim served as a camp administrator. In August 1981, the Lims were sponsored by a Catholic church in Atlanta and brought to the United States as political refugees. Odum Lim worked for a while in a factory cleaning fish, then sold jewelry door to door until he'd raised enough money to open his own store in Doraville.

"For so many years," Lim said angrily to Kumor and Oldham, "me and my wife survive the worst the Khmer Rouge have to offer. Then we come to United States and almost die in one day. Shot in the head by Vietnamese gangsters." Lim shook his head in disgust. "The United States have no death sentence, that's the problem. It too easy to commit crimes here."

As sympathetic as Kumor and Oldham may have been to Lim's political sentiments, they had work to do. They'd brought a photo album containing many mug shots, including everyone they believed had taken part in the Doraville robbery. They needed IDs. They were particularly hopeful of getting positive IDs from the Lims' two daughters, since young children make especially appealing and effective witnesses in court.

Both girls were in school. Kumor decided to wait on the photos, and told Odum Lim that he and Oldham would come back later that afternoon. In the meantime, it was time for the two investigators from New York to pay a visit to Detective Captain Cliff Edwards of the Doraville PD.

After the call from Oldham, Captain Edwards had held off on his own investigation, waiting and wondering what cards the boys from New York were holding in their deck. "What can I do for you, gentlemen?" Edwards asked cordially after Kumor and Oldham had taken seats in his modest, wood-paneled office at the Doraville police station.

Oldham did the talking. As always, he seemed intent on getting as much information out of the local authorities as possible without offering anything in return.

"What we thought you might be able to help us with," he told Edwards, "is in locating a local Vietnamese criminal. All we have is a first name—Quang. We believe this guy selected the robbery target here in Doraville and another one in Chattanooga."

"And you want us to help you find Quang?" asked Edwards.

"That's right."

Cliff Edwards was in his early forties, lean, with thinning blond hair and a friendly, unassuming manner. A Georgia native, he was, by nature, an accommodating sort. But there was clearly a lot these two tight-lipped Yankees from north of the Mason-Dixon line weren't saying.

"Look," he offered, "nobody wants to see this crime solved more than I do, if you catch my drift. But y'all gonna have to tell me what the hell this is all about."

It was Kumor who finally filled Edwards in.

"Okay. We've got an informant," explained Kumor. "A kid who took part in the robbery at Odum Lim's store. Not only has this kid been providing us with information about a powerful Vietnamese gang called Born to Kill, he's been working undercover. The investigation is highly sensitive. We were hoping you could help us tie this robbery at the jewelry store into a federal RICO case, put these guys away for a long time. And we were hoping you could do it as quietly as possible."

Captain Edwards smiled. "Well, shit," he replied, "of course we'll help. Why didn't you just tell me all that in the first place?"

"We just wanna make sure," interjected Oldham, "that you understand when the time comes to arrest this guy Quang, if we find him, we're the ones who get credit for the collar."

"Collar?" Edwards asked quizzically. "I got a collar on my shirt. You mean arrest?"

"Yeah, something like that," Oldham retorted.

"Hell, we don't care about that. This is Doraville. There isn't enough crime around here for us to be fighting over who gets credit for arrests."

With Edwards on board, everything seemed to fall into place. Over the next few days, Kumor and Oldham gathered more evidence than they could have hoped for. Quang Van Nguyen, the BTK's Southern contact, was located and quietly taken into custody. Two sets of fingerprints retrieved from a glass counter at the Sun Wa Jewelry store were positively linked to two of the robbers, Tung Lai and Little Cobra. And the Lims' two children, along with Mrs. Lim, were able to pick out photographs of four members of the robbery crew, including the shooter, Lan Tran.

On the fourth day of their stay in Atlanta, Kumor, Oldham, and

Tinh drove to Gainesville. It took the entire afternoon to find the house on Maverick Trail Road where most of the gang had stayed. They spoke with Kathy Ivester, the Southern belle who lived at the house with her Vietnamese boyfriend. They showed Ivester their book of photos, and she was able to identify mug shots of all of the gang members who'd stayed with her the week of the robbery. She especially remembered David Thai. "That boy tied up my phone for hours," noted Ivester.

Across the street from the house, the investigators rummaged around in a wooded marsh, looking for signs of the gang's target-practice session.

"I think we hit pay dirt," Oldham said finally, hunched down in the wet grass near a small pond.

Incredibly, a half dozen shell casings were still scattered in the grass. Later, an ATF ballistics report would link the casings to a Rossi .38 Special, the same gun that was used to shoot Odum Lim in the head.

By the end of the week, Kumor and Oldham could hardly contain their excitement. For the first time, the case was clearly coming into view. They could see the noose tightening around the collective necks of the BTK.

One night during their stay in Atlanta, Dan Kumor noticed that the Philadelphia Phillies were in town. Kumor had grown up on Phillies baseball. When he was a kid, his father would sometimes take him to Philadelphia's old Connie Mack Stadium, where he would gorge on hot dogs and popcorn while reveling in the sights and sounds of the ballpark.

Kumor found Tinh less than enthusiastic when he suggested they take in a game. For Tinh, baseball was an unpleasant reminder of those years when he'd first arrived in the United States and the other kids had ridiculed him about his ignorance of American sports. Baseball, in particular, with its complex rules and slow, subtle pacing, had seemed impenetrable.

Kumor, concerned that Tinh never seemed to have any fun, was adamant. "Look," he said, "all you've been doing is sitting around the hotel room ever since we got here. You're going—period."

While Oldham passed the evening at an Atlanta singles bar, Kumor and Tinh drove the short distance to Fulton County Stadium.

There was a sparse turnout—barely fifteen thousand fans in a stadium built for more than fifty thousand. Kumor and Tinh sat beyond the outfield fence in center field.

It didn't take long for the home team to establish a lead. In the first inning, Braves slugger Jeff Blauser hit a pitch into the bleachers for a three-run homer. Dan Kumor groaned; he and Tinh had just sat down, and already his hometown team had fallen behind.

Over the next few innings, while the Phillies continued to take a beating, Kumor and his prize informant had a chance to talk for the first time about something other than police issues. Up to now, the investigators had been so overwhelmed gathering evidence and keeping up with the gang's robbery plans, no one had taken the time to get to know Tinh on any kind of personal level. On the few occasions Kumor had tried to get Tinh to talk about his feelings, Tinh had been reluctant.

The easy, leisurely atmosphere at the ballpark seemed to loosen him up. As the game progressed, Tinh related the story of his life to Kumor in greater detail than ever before. He told how he'd been put on a refugee boat by his parents and sent out to sea when he was a mere eleven years old; how he'd spent two years in refugee camps in Thailand until he came to the United States. Tinh talked about bouncing from foster family to foster family, feeling lost and lonely in a strange country. Occasionally, his eyes would well up with tears. But he always caught himself, as if he were ashamed to show his Amerian overseer that he had feelings.

Listening to Tinh, Kumor was reminded of his own relationship with his father. A strict Catholic who went to mass every day, Kumor's father had provided him with something Tinh obviously never had—a sense of direction. In his own relationship with Tinh, Kumor could sense the yearning for some sort of wisdom or guidance from a male authority figure that Tinh could trust. No doubt this overriding need was what had made Tinh so susceptible to a master manipulator like David Thai.

Between sips of Coke and assorted ballpark concessions, Tinh asked Kumor questions about his life. The young agent tried to give Tinh a picture of what it had been like growing up in Northeast Phil-

210

adelphia, one of seven children in a fairly typical middle-class American family.

"It was pretty normal," related Kumor, "until late in 1985. That's when it seemed like my whole world fell apart."

One day, not long after his twenty-fourth birthday, Kumor had been driving home when he came across a nasty accident at an intersection near his home. A police car responding to a medical alert had run a red light and totaled somebody's car. Kumor got out of his own car and approached the accident. The car that had been hit looked familiar, but it was so badly mangled he couldn't really be sure. Then he overheard a bystander say, "What a shame. She was such a nice girl. She had six brothers."

It hit Kumor like a roundhouse right to the jaw: the mangled car was his sister's. Kumor found a cop at the scene, told him who he was, and asked what happened. "I'm afraid your sister was killed instantly," said the cop.

Kumor's father never really recovered from losing his only daughter so suddenly. Six months later, he collapsed in his driveway after returning from church one morning. Dan was there and had tried to save his father's life with CPR. It didn't do any good. His father died that day from a massive heart attack.

Tinh was quietly amazed as he listened to Kumor relate the tragedies that had shaped his life. Here he'd assumed this blond-haired, blue-eyed American had lived an easy, pampered life. But he too had experienced loss. He too knew what it meant to be dealt a cruel and crippling blow, to be an innocent victim of fate.

Tinh was jarred from his musing by the roar of the crowd. It was the bottom of the sixth inning and the Braves had just scored another run, increasing their lead to eight to two.

"Jesus," complained Kumor, "this is pathetic. I've seen enough. Let's get the hell outta here."

As they headed for the exit, Tinh gave Kumor a good-natured ribbing about his hometown team. "Dan, what happen? You tell me the Phillies a good team, but they no good. They no good at all."

Tinh kidded Kumor all the way out into the parking lot. "They terrible, Danny. I think maybe they must be the worst team in all baseball."

Kumor smiled. He'd never seen Tinh in such a jocular, carefree mood. The kid actually seemed to be having a good time, just like a nineteen-year-old was supposed to.

"Ha, ha, ha, Timmy," Kumor replied in mock seriousness. "Very funny. Very fuckin' funny."

Chapter 13

By the time Kumor, Oldham, and Tinh returned to New York City, the investigation had definitely kicked into high gear. Not only did the trip to
Georgia net an impressive variety and quantity of evidence, but the backup team of Alex Sabo and ATF
Agent Don Tisdale had also been busy. Working with
information supplied by Tinh, Sabo and Tisdale made
a trip of their own to Bridgeport, Connecticut, retracing the gang's steps there. Accompanied by the local
police, they visited the Bang Kok Health Spa and
the Vientiane Restaurant, situated a couple of miles
from each other on Main Street in downtown Bridgeport.

At both locations, employees who'd been present
during BTK robberies were able to make positive
identifications from the thick book of photos Sabo and
Tisdale brought with them. Everyone seemed to have
an especially vivid recollection of Lan Tran. Even the
heavyset American customer whose "session" at the
Bang Kok massage parlor was rudely interrupted by
the robbery remembered Uncle Lan. He came by the

Bridgeport police station and picked out Lan's photo from an array of more than fifty mug shots.

Also, Tisdale and Kumor secured another important piece of evidence without leaving New York City. In late June, the two ATF agents paid a visit to Nigel Jagmohan, the BTK's unlikely East Indian-Trinidadian gang member. Not surprisingly, Nigel had been trying to distance himself from his Vietnamese brothers since the day he was beaten to a pulp and booted out onto the sidewalk in Sunset Park. Afterward, he stopped hanging out with the gang and took a job at a nursing home in the Bronx where his mother worked.

Kumor and Tisdale found Jagmohan in the dietary department on the third floor of the nursing home. He was taken to the Fiftieth Precinct on Kingsbridge Avenue in the Bronx, where he was given a cup of coffee and seated at a table in the interrogation room.

Just seventeen years old, Nigel was visibly nervous; his leg twitched as if there were a steady electric current running through it. At first, he was reluctant to tell the investigators anything about the vicious beating that had landed him in the hospital with severe internal bleeding and a fractured skull. Afraid of retribution by the BTK if he cooperated with the cops, Nigel also knew that if he were to explain the reasons behind the beating he would have to admit his own involvement in the Canal Street robbery that led up to it.

The only reason Nigel eventually loosened up was because his mother was brought to the precinct.

"You better talk to your son," Kumor suggested to Mrs. Margaret Jagmohan. "We know Nigel was involved with this gang. We even know the reason he got beat up. If he doesn't come clean he's gonna wind up in a lot of trouble."

After considerable prodding from his mother, Nigel finally gave the investigators a detailed description of the beating he'd received.

His description of the robbery was not quite so detailed. Nigel claimed he had only acted as a lookout while Shadow Boy and Johnny Huyhn robbed the jewelry store near the rear of the small shopping mall at 263 Canal Street. He was beaten up later, he said, because David Thai and LV Hong believed he'd absconded with the robbery proceeds. According to Nigel, this was a grave injustice.

"When the getaway car ran into the telephone pole," he insisted,

"I tossed the bag of diamonds and gold jewelry under a parked car and ran away. I don't know what happened to it after that." Whether this story was true or not, the jewelry was never recovered, and David Thai held Nigel personally responsible.

The statement from Nigel Jagmohan—which implicated LV Hong and Thai in the crime of felonious assault—gave the investigators another piece of evidence they would need if they hoped to convey to a jury the full magnitude of the BTK's crimes. In court, all the circumstantial evidence in the world was nowhere near as effective as the eyewitness testimony of one simple victim. Nigel Jagmohan was no saint; he had knowingly and willingly joined the gang. Moreover, he was a bit of a punk, with a modest rap sheet that included arrests for robbery and criminal possession of a loaded gun. But his testimony—coupled with that of the Lim family, the robbery victims in Bridgeport, and other victims the investigators were still tracking down—would put a human face on the BTK's campaign of terror and intimidation.

The investigation may have been going well, but by July 1991, the same could not be said for the small team of lawmen who were spending most of their working hours gathering evidence, conducting surveillances, and monitoring Tinh's whereabouts day and night. In fact, a few of the group could hardly stand the sight of each other—a development that Dan Kumor had dreaded since the day the investigation began.

To Sabo, Tisdale, and several ATF agents working the case on a part-time basis, the problem was simple: Bill Oldham. Kumor could not say he was surprised. The irony was that Kumor himself was able to see something in the prickly detective that nobody else did, and the two young lawmen had become inseparable.

Sabo and Tisdale, on the other hand, were both old-school veterans with their own ideas about how investigations should be conducted. Al Sabo had come out of the police academy and joined the NYPD in 1963, when Bill Oldham was barely ten years old. Tisdale was a convivial Irishman, a twenty-year veteran who'd become an ATF agent at a time when the bureau was still thought of as the bastard child of the Internal Revenue Service. Both Sabo and Tisdale had little time for the new breed of hotshot lawmen who, they felt, had been weaned on too many TV cop shows.

Oldham, usually clad in Armani-style suits and a cashmere overcoat, was a classic example. "Billy's biggest problem," Sabo once said to Tisdale in a moment of exasperation, "is that he can't decide who he wants to be: Don Johnson or Bruce Willis."

Personality conflicts are not uncommon in law enforcement. Human nature dictates that when a group of strangers are thrown together, especially in an intense, demanding situation like the evolving BTK investigation, problems can and usually will arise. Most of the time, a sense of professionalism wins out. Supervisors step in, or the agents and cops themselves set aside their differences for the overall good of the investigation.

For the most part, the BTK investigators were able to keep their personal feelings under wraps. But not always. Once, after hearing that Oldham had gone to their boss and tried to have him removed from the case, Sabo went ballistic. "Just who the hell do you think you are!" the veteran detective challenged Oldham, standing in the hallway outside the offices of the Major Case Squad. At six feet four and built like a longshoreman, Sabo towered menacingly over Oldham before he finally calmed down.

Sabo was from a generation of cops who believed that if you were having problems with your partner, you took it up with him, not his superior. Oldham was from a different generation.

"Gee, Al," Don Tisdale later said to Sabo, "it's a good thing you didn't hit him. He probably would have had you arrested."

Dan Kumor may have been the youngest of the officers assigned to the investigation, but he was also the agent in charge. As such, he was responsible for seeing that things ran smoothly. Kumor believed the current clash of personalities stemmed mostly from the heavy workload everyone was under. "What we need," Kumor told his supervisor during their regular Monday morning powwow at ATF headquarters, "is more manpower. How about having another agent assigned full time to the case? Better yet, how about having a full-time agent who speaks Vietnamese?"

The fact that no Asian agents were working the case on a regular basis had begun to emerge as something of a hindrance, especially now that the investigators were attempting to enlist the cooperation of Chinese, Vietnamese, Cambodian, Laotian, and Korean victims of the gang.

So far, language had not been a major problem. But Kumor had a feeling it would be later on.

Kumor's most immediate "cultural concern" had to do with his confidential informant. For some time now, he'd been worried that Tinh Ngo was becoming isolated from the investigative team, with whom he had little in common. If nothing else, a Vietnamese-speaking agent would give Tinh someone to talk to in his own language.

In early July, roughly one month after Kumor, Oldham, and Tinh returned from their trip to Georgia, Kumor got his wish. It had not been easy. Of the three thousand ATF agents stationed in regional offices throughout the United States, there were only a half dozen who spoke Vietnamese—as a native language or otherwise.

Huyen "Albert" Trinh arrived at ATF headquarters at 90 Church Street wearing a conservative summer suit, a tie, and hair so short it conformed to the contours of his head. At five feet eleven, he was tall for a Vietnamese; his broad, brawny physique was a marked contrast to the lean, bony frames of most BTK gang members.

Trinh was fresh off the plane from Los Angeles, where he lived and only recently had begun work as an ATF agent. Like Kumor, he was young—just twenty-five years old. The fact that two such relatively young agents would be playing significant roles in a major criminal investigation was, in many ways, unique to the Bureau of Alcohol, Tobacco and Firearms. The agency was smaller and, in the eyes of many, less prestigious than the FBI or DEA, which meant it had a less stringent pecking order.

Meeting Albert Trinh for the first time, Kumor was taken aback by the young agent's formal, highly polished demeanor. For the last four months, Kumor had been following around a group of scruffy, poorly educated Vietnamese refugees. He'd never met a Vietnamese person like Albert Trinh, who came across as part Ivy League honor student, part Trappist monk.

"How long you been with the bureau?" asked Kumor once they'd sat down and begun to chat.

"Just thirteen months," replied Albert. "In fact, I've still got some training to complete down at Glynco." The ATF training academy, attended by all aspiring agents, was located in Glynco, Georgia.

217

"You've still got training to complete?" Kumor asked, trying not to sound too startled.

"Yes," answered Trinh.

Kumor grimaced. "Geez, you're licensed to carry a gun, aren't you?"

"Well, not exactly." Albert explained how a leg injury during training had kept him from getting his gun permit.

Kumor rolled his eyes. He'd asked for an agent who spoke Vietnamese, and they'd given him one—an agent so green he wasn't even licensed to carry a weapon.

"All right," grumbled Kumor, making his dissatisfaction apparent. "Do me a favor, will ya?" He grabbed the thick BTK photo book off the top of his desk and dropped it into Trinh's lap. "Look these mug shots over. Get a feel for the players. Then we can talk."

As Albert Trinh flipped through page after page of BTK mug shots, the first thought that entered his head was "These guys don't look like any Vietnamese I've ever seen before." Trinh was struck by the hungry, haunted look on most of the faces. These young criminals appeared crude and unworldly, the epitome of what more established exiles referred to as FOBs, immigrants who were "fresh off the boat."

Most of the Vietnamese males pictured in the BTK photo book were not much younger than Albert, but they could hardly have been farther removed. As a well-educated child of diligent, hardworking parents, Trinh was one of the lucky ones. Born in Saigon in 1965, he'd grown up in a household that was middle-class by Vietnamese standards. His father worked as a civil servant, and his mother was a nurse.

Though he was a toddler during some of the worst years of the war, Albert, the third of seven children, was largely insulated from the turmoil that engulfed his country. Even the American military checkpoints situated throughout Saigon were simply part of the landscape, in place from the day he was born. At the age of five, Albert was sent to an exclusive private grade school where he learned to speak French. As a child, his evenings were spent watching the government-run television station, which showed *Bonanza, Star Trek, The Mickey Mouse Club*, and other popular American programs.

Although Albert's early childhood involved copious input from his country's most recent colonial rulers, his parents both saw themselves as true Vietnamese. The surname Trinh was historically Chinese, but the family bloodline was deeply rooted in the cultural traditions of Vietnam. Albert's parents objected to the philosophy of Ho Chi Minh and his Communist followers not so much for ideological reasons but because of the financial chaos they felt would surely follow if United States forces were defeated and the South Vietnamese government toppled.

When the inevitable finally came to pass in April 1975, eleven-year-old Albert and the rest of his family stood jammed in a massive airplane hangar with thousands of other Vietnamese waiting to be processed. Albert's mother had given each of her children a small packet which she told them was "spending money." But Albert knew that it was more like survival money, in case he and his family were separated during the hectic evacuation.

In the early morning hours of April 27, 1975, the Trinh family was loaded onto a cargo plane along with several hundred other frightened refugees and airlifted to a U.S. army base in the Philippines. From there they were shipped to Guantánamo Bay in Cuba, where they were quarantined and then flown to the United States.

During the chaotic months immediately following the American evacuation of Saigon, Vietnamese refugees were brought to one of two places: Fort Chaffee, in Arkansas, or Camp Pendleton, seventy miles south of Los Angeles. The Trinhs chose California, where they were eventually sponsored for foster care by a Baptist church near Los Angeles. Albert, his parents, and his siblings were dispersed throughout the community, wherever there was room. Albert wound up living at the Baptist minister's house, where the first word he learned in English was "thirsty."

For Albert Trinh, leaving Vietnam and resettling in the United States was an adventure more exciting than traumatic. Because he was so young, he had not established deep-rooted emotional ties to the country he was leaving behind. For his parents, it was another story. They'd left behind a life-style and social standing attained through years of achievement that, given their age and the broad cultural gulf they now faced, they would probably never be able to reproduce in the States.

Success in America, they knew, would come through their children, and they instilled in young Albert a strong determination to become a worthy American citizen.

"Master the language," Albert's father told him time and time again. "Become an American. You will probably never be returning to Vietnam."

Albert took his father's advice to heart. He was an exceptional student in grade school, high school, and at the University of California at Irvine, where he graduated with a degree in social ecology. He took some postgraduate law courses, served for a time as an orderly at a hospital in San Antonio, then spent three months working for the Orange County Public Defender's office. When Albert decided to pursue a career in law enforcement, his parents were supportive, though it was an unusual choice for a young Vietnamese-American male.

As a Los Angeles resident, Albert knew all about Vietnamese gangs. As a student in college he had conducted a research study on gangs in the Los Angeles area. He was surprised to learn that, although local police estimated there were as many as fifty different Vietnamese gangs in Orange County alone, the gang members were not all starving refugees from failed foster families. In fact, many of Southern California's Vietnamese gang kids were from middle- or lower-middle-class families. They joined gangs for the same reason most Chicano, Chinese, and African American youths had—protection, power, and self-respect.

In the faces of the young gangsters who comprised New York City's Born to Kill gang, Albert Trinh saw something else. These were the kids he had wondered about years ago when video footage of Vietnam's "boat people" was first beamed around the world. Like everyone else, Albert had been riveted by the images of destitute refugees hanging from flimsy boats, risking everything for freedom and a new life in the United States. It had made him feel fortunate to be among the first wave of refugees who'd escaped by air with their families relatively intact. The mug shots that Albert perused now were those who had not been so lucky, the lost souls he'd heard more established Vietnamese refugees sometimes refer to as *bui doi*, "the dust of life."

Trinh was not given much time to ponder the hapless fate of his fellow refugees. Before he'd even finished flipping through the entire

BTK photo book, Kumor tapped him on the shoulder. "Hey, we need you to come with us," he said. "We've got an arrest going down in Brooklyn. It'll give you a chance to get your feet wet."

Thirty minutes later, Albert found himself sitting with Kumor in an ATF sedan, parked on a side street in Sunset Park, lying in wait to arrest Tuan Tran, otherwise known as Blackeyes. Nobody had bothered to tell Albert who Blackeyes was, but he could tell from the placement of more than a dozen arresting agents around Blackeyes' apartment building that he was something more than a petty parole violator.

In the more than two years since Blackeyes first initiated young Tinh Ngo into the ranks of the BTK, he'd led something of a charmed life in the Vietnamese underworld. When Tinh first met him, Blackeyes was considered the gang's Brooklyn *dai low*. He led Tinh, Kenny, and Tommy Vu on numerous robberies, including Tinh's first, the massage parlor at 59 Chrystie Street in Chinatown. Tinh and the others had always looked up to the charismatic gangster with "Buddhist ears," who was the epitome of what they hoped to become. Blackeyes dressed sharp, ate American food, and he was popular with Chinese and even some of the American girls who hung out at the pool halls and skating rinks frequented by Chinatown gangsters.

In fact, Blackeyes was so popular with the little brothers of the BTK that David Thai soon began to see him as something of a rival. In the summer of 1990, when Blackeyes branched off from the gang and declared he was no longer a member of the BTK, rumors began to circulate that *Anh hai* had put out a contract on his life. For a short time, Blackeyes operated freely as an independent operator, a posture virtually unheard of in Asian crime circles. But rumors about young BTK hitmen looking to make a name for themselves by taking him out soon got Blackeyes packing. He fled New York City and was rumored to have formed his own small gang, a group that roamed the eastern seaboard committing home invasions and other crimes.

On the afternoon of the Fourth of July—just one week before Albert Trinh arrived in New York—Blackeyes committed his most audacious crime. Far from the streets of New York, in St. Petersburg, Florida, Blackeyes and six other gangsters burst into the Jabil Circuit Company, located on Roosevelt Avenue. Ten employees were tied up

221

with duct tape and held at gunpoint while the gangsters fleeced the company's warehouse, stealing approximately one million dollars' worth of computer chips.

It must have seemed like the heist of a lifetime, but it didn't take long to turn sour. A few days after the robbery, two suspects surrendered to authorities in Wilkesbarre, Pennsylvania, and implicated Blackeyes.

When Kumor and the other investigators heard from Tinh that Blackeyes was back in the New York City area looking to sell a shipment of Intel-series computer chips, they immediately volunteered to make the arrest. They knew all about Blackeyes' adversarial relationship with David Thai and were hoping that maybe, before Blackeyes was shipped off to authorities in Florida, he could be talked into cutting a deal.

Now, waiting in the car less than a block from Blackeyes' apartment on Forty-sixth Street, Albert Trinh could feel the excitement. He had never been to New York City before and was amazed at how much it looked like countless photographs and movies and TV shows. The old Brooklyn tenements were musty and run-down; across the street a handful of children were playing in the torrent of an open fire hydrant, trying to take the edge off the sweltering July heat. The avenue was alive with people of all ages talking and hanging out, teeming with a neighborhood atmosphere unlike anything Albert knew in Los Angeles.

Blackeyes finally ambled out the front door of his apartment building, dressed casually in jeans and a T-shirt. Within seconds, the team of agents swooped down.

"Let's make this easy, Blackeyes," advised the arresting agent.

Blackeyes appeared only mildly startled, and he surrendered with no resistance.

At a local police precinct, Kumor and Tisdale sat Blackeyes down in a small, windowless room and tried to talk him into giving them some useful information. They got nowhere.

"Let me try," Albert suggested to Kumor. "I can speak to him in Vietnamese."

Alone with Blackeyes inside the stuffy interrogation room, Albert tried the nice-guy approach. "You and me," he reassured Blackeyes, "we're both Vietnamese. I understand where you're coming from. If you can help me out, maybe there's something I can do for you."

Blackeyes eyed Albert curiously. He asked where exactly Albert was from, and how he wound up being a federal agent. But it was soon apparent that Blackeyes had no intention of divulging information of any value about anyone, especially David Thai.

The other agents took one last shot. Trinh watched through a glass partition as Kumor, Tisdale, Oldham, and Sabo all hovered over the young Vietnamese gangster, who had begun to slink down in his chair. They stuck their faces in his, gesticulating angrily. One of the agents waved around a photograph of Blackeyes' girlfriend that they'd found in his wallet.

Albert was fascinated. Here he was, a spanking new agent from six thousand miles away. He was still finishing ATF training, where they spent hours teaching the proper arrest and interview techniques according to the strictest interpretations of the law—most of which were being flagrantly ignored by the group of investigators haranguing Blackeyes in a gamy interrogation room in the middle of a humid afternoon in the heart of Brooklyn.

Albert had to smile. If he needed a reminder that he'd arrived in the Big City, this was definitely it.

Dan Kumor hadn't really expected to get anything out of Blackeyes, but he figured it was worth a try. After all, David Thai had been attempting to claim a portion of the proceeds from the Florida computer-chip robbery, for no reason other than the fact that he was the leader of the BTK. Lan Tran had even suggested to Tinh in a taped phone conversation that, on behalf of David Thai, they kidnap Blackeyes. In the interrogation room, Kumor tried to persuade Blackeyes that there was no reason to protect a person who would probably have him killed if he could. But Blackeyes remained stone-faced.

Nothing gained, nothing lost. The BTK investigation was such that minor disappointments were quickly subsumed by newer events. By the time Blackeyes was shipped off to Florida to face the music there, Kumor and the other investigators were already deeply engrossed in yet another BTK robbery plot involving Tinh and their two primary targets, David Thai and Lan Tran.

It began on the afternoon of Saturday, July 20, 1991, when Tinh

223

was eating lunch at Pho Bang, a popular Vietnamese restaurant on Mott Street in Chinatown. Around 2:00 P.M., his beeper sounded. *Anh hai* was trying to reach him. Tinh got up from the large circular table where he was seated with three or four other gang members, went to a pay phone, and called Thai's beeper, leaving the number on the pay phone at Pho Bang.

Thai called back immediately. "Timmy, where are you guys? I've been looking for you."

Tinh explained that he and the others living in the Forty-fifth Street apartment in Sunset Park had been kicked out by the landlord. They hadn't paid their rent in months, and what with the gunfire and occasional beatings of gang members like Nigel Jagmohan, they'd been making a lot of noise. Now that Blackeyes was no longer using his apartment just around the corner at Forty-sixth Street and Eighth Avenue, Tinh and a handful of others had moved in over there. But they still needed money for rent.

"Don't worry about rent money," *Anh hai* assured him. "I take care of that."

David Thai then told Tinh he had a "job" coming up, and would need Tinh's assistance. He instructed Tinh to pick out two more gang members to help out.

"Of course, *Anh hai*," Tinh answered dutifully.

The fact that David Thai was delegating Tinh to line up accomplices for BTK robberies was something new, though not unexpected. Tinh had been a *sai low* for more than two years now, an old-timer by BTK standards. Thai had come to trust Tinh and was giving him more responsibilities, a sign of respect.

For a person who was once afraid to even look *Anh hai* in the eyes, Tinh had come a long way. He was dealing directly with David Thai now, without going through a *dai low* or any other intermediary. In fact, Thai was treating Tinh as if *he* were the Brooklyn *dai low*, giving him duties that David had entrusted to a string of others before Tinh —most of whom were now either dead or in prison.

That night Tinh returned to the apartment in Brooklyn and tried to talk two gang members into going along on the robbery, which Thai told him was scheduled for early Monday morning. But the responsibility of being a *dai low* was not so easy. Dat Nguyen, a light-skinned

Amerasian known as "Hawaii Dat" because he had only recently arrived in New York from Honolulu, was decidedly unenthusiastic. Tinh also asked Eddie Tran, the veteran gang member who, almost two years earlier, had signaled the arrival of the BTK in Chinatown by throwing a homemade bomb into a police van on Elizabeth Street.

"Timmy," Eddie told Tinh, "I just get out from prison after one year. I'm still on parole. Please, no robberies."

Exasperated, Tinh later spoke on the phone with Lan Tran about the difficult time he was having finding willing gang members.

"Forget them," Uncle Lan told Tinh. "We don't need them. Me and you, we do the robbery with *Anh hai.*"

The next day, on Sunday afternoon, Tinh sneaked over to Detective Oldham's office at One Police Plaza in downtown Manhattan and told him about the robbery scheduled to take place the following morning. As yet, Tinh had no idea what store they were going to hit.

Oldham had a suggestion. "Timmy, we gotta find out where this store is so we can stop this robbery from happening. Call David Thai. Try to get as many details as you can."

Tinh balked; he was afraid that if he kept calling Thai to press him for information, *Anh hai* would grow suspicious. "I don't think this is such a good idea," he told Oldham.

"Hey, Timmy," the detective countered. "I'm not asking you, I'm telling you."

Tinh beeped David Thai, who called him back on a private line at the offices of the Major Case Squad.

"*Anh hai,*" said Tinh, "I'm on Canal Street right now, at a pay phone. What you want me to do about tomorrow?"

David explained that Tinh still needed to line up another gang member to serve as a getaway driver. "Me and Lan gonna drive there together from my place," he told Tinh, "but you need someone to drive you from Brooklyn." Thai also instructed Tinh to buy some "nice clothes." Tinh was probably going to be the first person to enter the store, and David Thai wanted him to look as much like a normal, respectable customer as possible.

Tinh was not able to get any details from David Thai about the location of the robbery. But later that afternoon, when he met Lan Tran in front of the Asian Shopping Mall in Chinatown, he was finally told they would be robbing a jewelry store on Fourteenth Street, a bustling commercial thoroughfare on the northern edge of Greenwich Village.

Tinh was somewhat surprised that the target was a store outside the city's traditional Asian enclaves. Apparently, David Thai had developed a new philosophy. The BTK was no longer indiscriminately robbing stores, tea rooms, and gambling dens in rival gang territory. On Canal Street, they were running out of stores to rob. The time had come to look elsewhere.

Their geographic range within the city may have been expanding, but the homogeneous ethnicity of their victims remained steadfast. The jewelry store on Fourteenth Street, Uncle Lan told Tinh, was owned and run by Asians; in this case, Koreans. David Thai had been tipped off about the place by a Vietnamese peddler whom the Koreans allowed to sell counterfeit watches from a table in front of the store.

That evening, after Tinh told him what he had learned, Bill Oldham drove the entire length of Fourteenth Street, from one side of Manhattan to the other. Currently under major construction, the street was more chaotic than usual, with gaping holes in the pavement and barriers restricting the flow of traffic, all underscored by the constant clamor of jackhammers. Despite the noise, the cut-rate clothing stores, toy shops, and electronics outlets packed side by side were still doing a brisk business. For two hours, Oldham kept looking until he located two jewelry stores run by Asians—one at Second Avenue on the east side of town, another at Sixth Avenue, four wide crosstown blocks to the west.

The following morning, a couple of hours before the robbery's scheduled 9:00 A.M. start, Oldham and the rest of the investigative team moved into action. Virtually every ATF agent Kumor had at his disposal was ready. Two agents sat in a car outside David Thai's home in Long Island, waiting to trail Thai and Lan Tran into the city. Another surveillance team was set up outside the safe-house apartment on Forty-sixth Street in Brooklyn, where Tinh emerged with Hawaii Dat, who had finally agreed to come along as his getaway driver.

Even though the investigators were reasonably certain that the gang's target was the jewelry store on Sixth Avenue, just in case, ATF agents Kumor and Tisdale set up surveillance on the other jewelry store,

226

the one on Second Avenue. The Sixth Avenue store was covered by Oldham himself.

Early that morning Oldham had arisen and pulled his old police uniform out of the closet. He hadn't worn it since making detective four years earlier. The pants were a little tight around the waist, but all in all it was not a bad fit. It would serve nicely for what Oldham had in mind, a scheme that perhaps only he would have had the audacity to attempt.

After donning his uniform, Oldham drove to Fourteenth Street and stood in front of the Eldorado Jewelry Store at Sixth Avenue, waiting patiently for the BTK crew to arrive.

Around 9:00 A.M., David Thai's gray Jaguar crept by. When it stopped at a red light, Oldham could see Lan Tran lean back in the passenger seat and look him directly in the eyes. Oldham tried to look oblivious, like a neighborhood cop patroling his beat.

Uncle Lan cursed under his breath. The light turned green and Thai's Jaguar continued up Sixth Avenue, then circled the block a couple of times. Each time it came past the store, Oldham was standing there like a lazy patrolman with nothing better to do. The BTK gangsters drove off angrily.

Later, the investigators learned from Tinh what happened. "David and Lan see Billy there, they say they can't do it. Mess everything up. Lan, he curse about it, say, 'BTK have nothing but bad luck.' "

In the days that followed, Tinh paid close attention to David Thai's reaction to this latest failed BTK robbery. This was the third or fourth robbery that had fallen apart at the last minute, and by now Tinh was certain that somebody would be suspicious. But every time he brought up the subject around *Anh hai* or Uncle Lan, he got the same response. The gang was jinxed, they would say. They were having a bad year. The sun, the moon, and the stars were not properly aligned. Somebody's karma was off.

To Tinh, *Anh hai*'s inability to figure out why the gang's robbery plans kept getting derailed was nothing short of astounding. From the day he'd first met David Thai at the Asian Shopping Mall on Canal Street, Tinh had believed the BTK leader to be infallible. To a man, Thai's followers regarded him as all-seeing, all-knowing. His superior intelligence and sophistication was something Tinh and the other gang members not only took for granted—it was something they had built their lives around, a truism that served as a clarion call to young Vietnamese males throughout the United States.

The possibility that David Thai might be just some run-of-the-mill gang leader with money in the bank and a nice conservative haircut was more than dismaying to Tinh; it was a realization that, once it began to sink in, turned his entire world upside down.

"You sure this guy doesn't suspect anything?" Kumor asked Tinh every time he came by ATF headquarters in the days following the thwarted robbery on Fourteenth Street.

Tinh shook his head, more amazed than any of them. "No. David Thai, he don't suspect nothing. He don't know anything."

Then, uttering the unthinkable, Tinh added, "In fact, I think maybe David Thai—he not so smart. He not so smart after all."

Chapter 14

Throughout the summer of 1991, as the BTK investigation continued to gain momentum, events far beyond Chinatown added an air of urgency to the efforts of Kumor's team. Across the United States, the subject of gang violence was becoming a hot topic, with the inevitable panel discussions on national TV talk shows like *Geraldo* and *Donahue*.

Street gangs in America had come a long way since the days when the Sharks and the Jets danced their way into the national imagination in *West Side Story*. Uzis, Tech-9s, and other automatic assault guns long ago replaced brass knuckles and switchblades as the weapons of choice in most gang altercations. Nearly ever major city and many mid-sized cities had experienced their share of drive-by shootings, with children and other innocent bystanders falling prey to a spasm of urban violence unlike anything ever seen in the United States before.

Many people blamed drugs, though the reason for the country's burgeoning gang problem was actually far more complex than that. In the West, the Crips and the Bloods had become the primary source of ego gratification for an entire generation of youths who might have been born within the boundaries of the continental United States but who were as far removed from any realistic hope of economic achievement as the lowliest immigrant. In Los Angeles and in smaller cities like Tacoma, Omaha, and St. Louis, gang colors had replaced school colors as a primary statement of identification for a staggering number of teenagers.

In Southern California, Chicano gangs had existed in *el barrio* since at least the late-1950s and had by now become deeply entrenched in the state prison system. On the street, the traditional Latino gangs were now vying for turf with newer, younger gangs made up of recent immigrants from Central America. In the southwestern states and in Texas, gang violence had claimed the lives of American Latinos in dozens of cities, particularly those in close proximity to the U.S.-Mexico border.

As for Chinese and Vietnamese gangs, the phenomenon was not restricted by regional boundaries. In Los Angeles, San Francisco, and elsewhere, long-standing gangs had regenerated, and brand-new gangs were proliferating. As the country in general became more violent, so did the gangs' criminal activities, with garden-variety robberies and extortions often ending in pointless homicides, brought about by the widespread availability of guns, guns, and more guns.

When it came to the country's growing, multiethnic gang problem, New York City, ironically, had always been something of an exception. In New York, youth gangs were something a wayward kid might join in his early teens before moving on to a more serious, market-driven brand of criminal activity. Groups of people who gathered together to commit crimes in New York usually had some connection to a larger social framework, either within their own community or, in the case of the Mafia, the city at large. Because of the city's population density, criminal activity for profit was stringently organized. Thus, New York City didn't have a "gang" problem. It had an organized-crime problem.

The one part of the city where street gangs had been a significant factor was Chinatown. But even in Chinatown the gangs had always been part of a larger criminal structure. Gang activity, as violent as it may have been, was usually predicated on a move for turf or power based on a clear-cut profit motive. In that sense, gang activity seemed to be engineered by forces that were readily understood—at least to the people of Chinatown.

What had terrified everyone so much about the emergence of the BTK was that it appeared to represent a more anarchistic style of gang behavior, one that had the potential to overtake the area's traditional patterns, establishing a senseless, 1990s style, where innocent bystanders would fall prey to random, disorganized bloodletting.

In July 1991—three weeks before the BTK's foiled robbery attempt on Fourteenth Street—an incident occurred that stoked these fears. At one of Chinatown's busiest intersections, a tourist was accidentally shot and killed during a gang dispute.

Rhona Lantin, a twenty-six-year-old bride-to-be from Silver Spring, Maryland, had been out for dinner with a group of friends. Around 11:30 P.M., she was sitting in the passenger seat of a Ford Explorer driving north on Mulberry Street. As the vehicle crossed Bayard Street, there was a sudden *pop, pop* that sounded so much like exploding firecrackers few pedestrians seemed to notice. The Explorer rolled to a halt as Rhona Lantin slumped over in her seat, shot through the head with a .38-caliber bullet.

It was the night before the Fourth of July holiday and the streets had been swamped with revelers, but no witnesses came forward. Bayard Street ran through the heart of Ghost Shadows territory, and the word on the street was that the shooting stemmed from a power struggle between rival members within the gang. Rhona Lantin, a popular graduate student at the University of Maryland, had simply been in the wrong place at the wrong time.

Among other things, innocent bystanders getting shot while dining or shopping in the neighborhood was not conducive to a brisk, profitable commercial trade. Once again, gang activity was threatening Chinatown's "life's blood," a state of affairs that brought about the inevitable loud demands from politicians and business leaders for swift police action against the gangs.

As if the unpredictable antics of Chinatown's many gang members weren't trouble enough, Dan Kumor and the BTK investigators were feeling the heat from other quarters as well. Though few people were aware of it at the time, a major FBI investigation was under way against the Green Dragons, a gang centered in Flushing, Queens, New York City's second Chinatown. A team of investigators more than twice the size of Kumor's ATF squad had been gathering evidence for months and was rumored to be on the brink of announcing a RICO indictment against the gang.

Like the BTK, the Green Dragons were relatively new on the scene. Comprised mostly of recent immigrants from Fukien Province on China's southeastern coast, the gang had been founded in 1987 by Paul Wong, better known as Foochow Paul. In June of 1989, rival gangsters ambushed Foochow Paul outside a private house in Flushing, filling him with four bullets. While he was recuperating, Green Dragon gang members, on the pretext of being relatives, guarded Paul Wong around the clock, using handguns that had been smuggled into Wong's hospital room in the hollowed-out core of a Yellow Pages.

Foochow Paul survived the assassination attempt, then fled the United States to China. Although he remained the gang's overseer, the Green Dragons' daily operations were subsequently controlled by Chen I. Chung, a skinny twenty-year-old Taiwanese American.

Chen I. Chung presided over a gang of some forty members that robbed and extorted money from restaurants, nightclubs, and pool halls throughout Flushing and the nearby neighborhood of Elmhurst, Queens.

Along with the BTK, the Green Dragons had initiated a criminal reign of terror that obliterated Chinatown's traditional borders and balance of power. The more deeply entrenched gangs of the 1970s and 1980s—the Ghost Shadows and the Flying Dragons—had given way to a new generation, of which the Green Dragons were a prime example. They preyed on merchants in a community more prosperous and slightly more middle-class than the city's older Chinatown. They were not connected to any of the traditional tongs or business associations. And they were extremely violent.

It was the Green Dragons who murdered Tina Sham, the young woman who testified against a member of the gang in court. The horrific killing of Tina Sham and her boyfriend had haunted Ying Jing Gan in the weeks leading up to the death of her husband, Sen Van Ta.

Along with being brutal, the Green Dragons were reckless. Another of their many killings involved a young Korean student gunned down in a drive-by shooting the previous winter. The hitmen had mistaken the student for a member of the BTK, who'd been infringing on Green Dragon territory in Queens at the time.

Cathy Palmer, an assistant United States attorney based in the Eastern District of New York, was handling the federal prosecution of the murderous Green Dragons. A small, bespectacled woman in her thirties, Palmer had played a key role in most of the major Asian-crime cases in recent years. She'd indicted Golden Triangle drug lords, and once received a package at her office with a loaded gun inside, rigged to fire when the packaged was opened. Fortunately for Palmer, the gun was discovered and the assassination attempt foiled. "The Dragon Lady," as she was affectionately known to fellow members of the bar, cops, and newspaper reporters, had gone on to become the foremost Asian-crime prosecutor in New York City, if not the entire United States.

Dan Kumor, Bill Oldham, and the other investigators working the BTK case knew that if the FBI's Green Dragon case broke around the same time as their BTK indictments, they could expect little coverage in the local press. Kumor and Oldham, in particular, had no intention of spending a year of their lives investigating the BTK, delivering the case gift-wrapped to a prosecutor, then having it overshadowed by an FBI case. As a result, Kumor and Oldham began pestering their own assistant United States attorney, Alan Vinegrad, to at least begin the process of moving toward an indictment.

Vinegrad was adamant. "We're just not there yet," he told the investigators. "We need more incriminating conversations on tape. We need more circumstantial evidence. We need more potential witnesses."

Kumor and Oldham mumbled something under their breath about Vinegrad being unnecessarily cautious, but secretly they knew he was right. If they moved the case to trial prematurely, they would only wind up looking bad in the long run. Of course, if they waited too long, the next innocent civilian fatality might be from a BTK bullet, and how was that going to make them look?

Kumor, Oldham, and the other investigators continued pressing

233

forward, trying as best they could to ignore the considerable pressures mounting around them.

Inside the investigation's tenth-floor headquarters at the ATF building on Church Street, agent Albert Trinh hunched over a small tape recorder, a set of headphones clamped to his ears. He listened carefully for a moment, then clicked off the recorder. "Okay, Timmy," said Trinh, taking off the headphones, "this part here where Son says to the merchant, 'I want to get paid.' And the merchant says, 'I paid before.' And Son replies, 'I want more. I want twenty dollars, that's it.'"

"Yes," remarked Tinh.

"You're sure he said 'want' and not 'need'? Because legally, there's a big difference between 'want' and 'need.' One implies coercion."

"*Coercion?*" Tinh repeated the word quizzically, trying to enunciate the many syllables without tripping over his tongue.

Albert Trinh smiled. "Coercion," he repeated. "It means pressuring somebody into doing something they don't want to do."

In the three weeks since Albert Trinh and Tinh first met, they'd spent a couple of hours almost every day going over Tinh's secret recordings and the transcripts of those recordings. In many cases, the recordings were extremely difficult to understand. Some had been made in clamorous restaurants or on busy street corners, and the incidental background noises sometimes overwhelmed the conversations. Working with Tinh, Albert Trinh was attempting to fine-tune the transcripts, as well as transcribe and translate more recently recorded tapes.

The tape Albert and Tinh were currently working on was one Tinh had made two days earlier, on Saturday, July 27, 1991. During a surveillance on Canal Street in the middle of a busy afternoon, Tinh had circulated with a handful of gang members collecting extortion money. The gang members themselves referred to the process as collecting "tax money."

Though the money collected from individual store managers and street peddlers was sometimes as little as twenty dollars, the gang's weekly extortion rounds were the backbone of their entire operation. By the end of a typical day, the gang members could have collected as much as $2,000, which was usually distributed to various *dai lows* to

234

buy food for the gang's rank and file. More important than the money, however, was the fact that by continuously reasserting its presence, the gang was making it clear to area merchants who was boss on Canal Street.

The July 27 surveillance was the second time investigators had wired Tinh while he and the others collected tax money. One month earlier, on June 29, they'd set up a team of ATF agents across the street from the Asian Shopping Mall, at 271 Canal Street. From the first floor of a bank that was closed for the day, the investigators monitored the gang with video and still cameras. They did the same thing again on July 27, recording a group of BTK members led by Minh Do, who made his rounds wearing a T-shirt that spelled out the BTK philosophy. Across the front of Fat Minh's T-shirt, in English, was printed, "Money talks, bullshit walks."

Albert Trinh resumed following the group on tape. "Hey, Mr. Owner, help us out," he heard Fat Minh demanding of a merchant.

"Help what?" the merchant asked.

"Money, what else you think?" answered Fat Minh. "Think you'll help us some other way? Only money."

Trinh remembered this conversation; in fact, he witnessed it. Because he was Vietnamese, it was possible for Albert to circulate in the area without being noticed. Dressed casually in shorts and a T-shirt, he could supplement the electronic surveillance by following the gang on their rounds, staying within a few feet of Tinh, Fat Minh, and others, eavesdropping while they moved from store to store.

Albert was mildly surprised that Fat Minh and the others rarely had to resort to intimidation or even raise their voices as they made their collections. In the past, when the gang first began to make its presence felt on Canal Street back in 1989, "muscle" had been needed. Merchants were sometimes slapped around, street peddlers were chased off the block, store windows broken. In stubborn cases like Sen Van Ta, more drastic measures were taken.

By now, everyone pretty much got the picture.

Seated at ATF headquarters, Albert pulled off the headphones, picked up a pen, and continued transcribing bits of conversations. First, he wrote down the conversation in Vietnamese; later, it would be translated into English.

Even for someone who knew the language, it was painstaking work. Vietnamese is a tonal language, spoken with differing regional accents and pronunciations. In Vietnamese, the words spoken are important, but just as important is the way in which those words are spoken—whether a person's voice goes up or down, whether the intonation comes from the throat or is given a flat nasal twang. Simple variations of pronunciation can drastically alter the meaning of a word or phrase. A common word like *ma* could have two dozen different meanings. With a slight tonal variation, a phrase like "May Vietnam live for ten thousand years" might easily come out as "The sunburned duck is lying down."

That, plus the fact that the tapes had been recorded under such noisy, difficult conditions, made transcribing them a numbing, meticulous task. Even a normally focused worker like Tinh got bored easily. Albert, a hard taskmaster, had to stay on him.

In the weeks since Tinh and Albert first met, they'd gotten to know and like each other, though it seemed an unlikely match at first. Albert was so clean-cut and his English so fluent that at first, Tinh could hardly believe he was a fellow countryman. Immediately after they met, Tinh asked Dan Kumor, "What is this guy, Japanese or something?"—an observation that was not meant as a compliment.

But once they began working on the tapes together, they developed an easy, respectful rapport. Tinh had never met anyone like Albert— an educated, well-adjusted Vietnamese American around the same age as himself. To break the monotony of working on the tapes, Tinh would ask Albert endless questions about growing up in the United States, where he got his education, how he'd become an ATF agent.

Albert, meanwhile, couldn't help but be taken by Tinh's sincerity and his quietly endearing personality. Even the other agents seemed to feel that way. "He's not a bad kid," Kumor told Albert in the beginning. "In fact, he's a good person. I guess he was just easy to manipulate. I guess he got caught up in something that was bigger than he was."

Albert may have been a relative newcomer to the ranks of American law enforcement, but even he knew this was not the way cops and agents usually talked about confidential informants. Maybe to their faces they were friendly and conciliatory, but behind their backs the agents usually referred to the informants they had to deal with as scum, the lowest of the low. The disdain they felt toward their C.I.s often resulted in a kind of pathetic inverse reciprocity, as the informants tried in vain to endear themselves to their new masters.

Tinh Ngo seemed to have won the agents over simply by being himself.

As a refugee fortunate enough to be airlifted out of Vietnam soon after the fall of Saigon, Albert was as curious about Tinh as Tinh was about him. Growing up on the fringe of Southern California's refugee community, Albert had heard many stories about life in Vietnam in the years immediately following the war. He knew all about the refugee boats and the camps. But he'd never had the chance to speak directly with someone who'd taken that route to the underworld.

"Why?" Albert asked Tinh. "Why would someone as bright as you become involved with criminals? How could someone like David Thai manipulate you so easily?"

Even in his native language, these were not easy questions for Tinh to answer. "Ever since I come to the United States," he told Albert, "these are the people I know. These are the people I eat with, sleep with, hang out with. David Thai, he the only person that ever really care for me. At least, I think this person a good person. I think, *Anh hai*, he look out for Vietnamese people."

Albert recognized much of what Tinh was saying. In East Asian cultures in general, but even more so with the Vietnamese, if a person takes care of you financially, you become almost spiritually indebted to that person. To Tinh and the others, David Thai's willingness to pay their bills and give them pocket money was a matter not only of benevolence but of some greatness in his personality. In return, the ranks of the BTK felt they owed David Thai respect, loyalty, obedience.

That was clear on the tapes, in the language the gang members used to underscore their subservience to *Anh hai*. When referring to themselves, individual gang members always used *em*, a Vietnamese word used like the pronoun *I* when speaking with someone older and wiser. It connotes a deference based partly on age, but is also used to show respect for a person's power, financial wealth, or superior intelligence.

David Thai certainly had been successful in getting his BTK minions to view him as *cao so*, a man who was "highly destined." But Albert knew that Thai's appeal went even deeper than that.

237

Long before the U.S. military created a generation of refugees by first ravaging and then abandoning Vietnam in 1975, the Vietnamese people had come to see themselves as the inevitable victims of a cruel fate. Over the ages, the history of Vietnam had been marked by turbulence and torment, by terrible natural and human forces unleashed against helpless individuals. Many times, typhoons had devastated the densely populated delta and coastal regions of north and central Vietnam. Just as often, the people were victimized by military regimes who inflicted misfortune on the populace in the name of ideology.

After conquest and despite numerous rebellions, the Chinese, the French, and the Americans lorded over the country for one thousand years. With few exceptions, native rulers were also tyrants, adopting and maintaining a Chinese-style system designed more for repression and suppression than to deliver justice to the people.

In the face of such a tortured history, the Vietnamese have come to see themselves as the victims of an evil karma, an identity most eloquently encapsulated in an epic poem written two hundred years ago, known to Vietnamese throughout the world as *The Tale of Kieu*.

Written by Nguyen Du, a poet and Confucian scholar, *The Tale of Kieu* is the story of a young woman cast adrift by her family who is compelled to endure many hardships, including being forced into prostitution. Central to Kieu's tumultuous journey through life is the concept of *oan*, a word for which the nearest equivalent in English is "wronged." Throughout the poem, Kieu is forced into submission by circumstances beyond her control. Ultimately, she prevails because she is able to endure.

For many Vietnamese, *The Tale of Kieu* has served as a cultural Bible and window to their soul from the time it was published in the late eighteenth century. The poem is still taught in Vietnamese schools and many of its 3,254 verses have been memorized by young and old, peasant and scholar. For refugees living in exile in various parts of the globe, the poem holds a special significance. The very term *Viet-Kieu*, used to describe itinerant Vietnamese scattered throughout the world, was derived from Nguyen Du's masterpiece.

For those who have felt the sting of abandonment, *The Tale of Kieu* contains a powerful unifying message. Whether they see themselves as victims or survivors, all Vietnamese refugees have been severed from the land of their ancestors. Like Kieu, they have been compelled to serve false masters, to do things they otherwise might not have done were it not for the cruel demands of fate. To face horrible odds, to suffer, to toil in misery—these are all essential aspects of the Vietnamese refugee experience.

From what he had heard from Tinh and seen for himself, Albert Trinh knew that David Thai was a man who understood the power of mythology. When he first gathered his BTK brothers at the Japanese restaurant more than two years ago, he'd used the phrase *Con kien cong con vua*—"By sticking together, the tiny ants can carry the elephant." The ant was a powerful metaphor to most Vietnamese, many of whom viewed themselves as tiny, insignificant entities in a large, uncaring cosmos.

Certainly, Thai was promising his BTK brothers strength in numbers, an opportunity to forge an identity for themselves in the midst of a hostile environment. But he was also promising something more— much more.

At the gang's first big sit-down, *Anh hai* referred to their mission as being part of a larger "journey." By doing so, he was knowingly evoking the mythology of *The Tale of Kieu.* A generation older than his followers, Thai recognized that Tinh Ngo and *his* generation had no roots. Severed from all sense of country, culture, or family, they yearned for something—*anything*—to reconnect them with the culture that had shaped their lives, but one they had hardly any tangible relationship with beyond the sweet, hazy memories of childhood. By calling on his young BTK brothers to join him on a journey through perilous waters, David Thai was offering them a chance to reconnect. He was giving them something that seemingly no one else could: an opportunity to fulfill their destiny as Vietnamese.

In the weeks since he'd gotten to know Tinh, Albert Trinh had come to feel that it was his mission to offer his young Vietnamese brother a counter-myth to the one offered by David Thai. When transcribing the tapes, Albert deliberately worked Tinh hard, hoping to show him the value of diligent, sustained labor. When they walked around the ATF offices or stepped outside to get lunch, Albert noticed that Tinh slunk around with his head down, like a timid mouse.

"Timmy, you walk like a defeated person," Albert pointed out. He

239

admonished Tinh, telling him, "Stand up straight. When you speak with a person—I don't care who—look them in the eye."

Later, Albert offered more words of advice, simple words that were, nonetheless, a revelation to Tinh. "Be proud of who you are," Albert told the young refugee. "You're as much a citizen of this country as anybody else."

Even though Tinh liked and respected Kumor, Oldham, and the other investigators, they could not offer Tinh what Albert did. As their relationship developed, Tinh was able to express his fears to Albert about carrying the tape recorder. He was able to relax with Albert in a way he never could with his American overseers, no matter how friendly or understanding they might be.

In turn, the relationship was good for the investigation. Throughout July, as Tinh and Albert labored over the tapes, Tinh took a greater interest in the case, asking Albert and the others pertinent questions about arcane matters of law. He began alerting the investigators about upcoming events and conversations that he knew would be crucial.

"You know, Albert, I glad to be working with someone like you," Tinh said out of the blue one afternoon.

Albert did not ask Tinh to elaborate, but he took the phrase "someone like you" to mean a Vietnamese brother, one who possessed something Tinh had found to be so elusive since coming to the United States: a sense of self-worth.

240

Once, Albert accompanied Tinh to midtown Manhattan's boisterous Penn Station, the railway hub located underneath Madison Square Garden. To explain his hours away from the gang, Tinh had constructed a fake cousin who supposedly lived outside the city. On this particular morning, Tinh had told his gang brothers he would be visiting his "cousin" when, in fact, the investigators had made arrangements for him to stay at a house in New Jersey for a few days as a brief respite from the pressures of gang life. Tinh purchased his ticket, then sat inside the station with Albert, waiting for his train to board.

Frenzied commuters hustled up and down escalators and across the terminal's expansive linoleum floor. Over a loudspeaker, a voice bellowed departure notices and a long litany of obscure towns where the trains would disembark.

Albert and Tinh sat quietly, enjoying their moment of calm isolation amid the swirl of activity; enjoying each other's company in a way that made conversation unnecessary.

Seated under bright fluorescent lights deep in the bowels of Penn Station, Albert was struck by the irony. The United States government had flown him all the way from Los Angeles so that Tinh Ngo would have someone with whom he could speak Vietnamese. And yet, the times he and Tinh felt the most comfortable was when they sat together peacefully as *Viet-Kieu*, saying absolutely nothing.

"You know what I think?" Eddie Tran asked his gang brothers, seated at a large circular table at Kinh Do, a crowded Vietnamese restaurant. "I think the way *Anh hai* talks to me is very short-tempered. I don't know why."

Tran was keeping his voice low. David Thai and his wife, Sophia, were seated at a table not far away.

"I don't know about you guys," Eddie continued, "but that's the way he is with me. And I don't fucking know what the fuck I did. I don't fucking know."

From his seat across the table from Eddie, Tinh Ngo leaned closer, trying to adjust the microphone in his breast pocket without anyone noticing. "Who? Mr. Thai?" Tinh asked Eddie Tran.

"Yeah," Eddie answered.

"No," replied Tinh. "He don't say nothing bad about you. There's nothing."

Tinh and Eddie were seated with three other gang members, Hawaii Dat, Lam Truong, and Mui Pham, a gang member known as "Number Ten." It was early in the afternoon, and the BTK brothers were seated among the restaurant's usual patrons, a collection of middle-class Asians and well-heeled white folks.

The Kinh Do restaurant was located just beyond Chinatown's traditional boundaries, in the trendy Manhattan neighborhood of SoHo. Behind a wood facade with large front windows, the restaurant's interior was bathed in a pastoral greenish blue. There were plenty of mirrors, and dominating one whole wall was a mural of a typical, palm-tree–laden beach somewhere along the coast of Vietnam. Slightly more upscale than most Chinatown establishments, Kinh Do was famous for its

Vietnamese "summer rolls," a tasty concoction of vermicelli, shrimp, chopped onions, and lettuce in a rice-paper wrapping.

The restaurant hadn't been open more than a few months before the gang made its first business call. Kinh Do's owner initially balked at paying tax money. Then a BTK gang member got hold of his home phone number and made a threatening personal call, which seemed to do the trick. More recently, the gang had adopted Kinh Do as a sort of new headquarters, one certainly more appealing than Pho Hanoi, the tiny, sweaty luncheonette in the rear of the shopping mall where they used to meet.

"So that's *Anh hai*'s chick?" Eddie Tran asked, nodding toward Sophia. Since Eddie had just gotten out of prison recently, he was somewhat out of touch.

"It's *Anh hai*'s chick," Lam Truong answered, stating the obvious.

Eddie Tran smiled. "You know, when I come out of jail, she look so smooth."

"Maybe you misunderstood," Tinh observed. "Did you want to court her?"

The others laughed at the idea of Eddie Tran mistakenly putting the moves on David Thai's wife.

"Well," Eddie answered, "I said *before* she was smooth. Now, because he used her too much . . ." Eddie left the sentence hanging and laughed out loud.

Just then, David Thai approached, and the gang members all quieted down. Standing at the table, just over Tinh's shoulder, *Anh hai* said hello and asked his gang brothers if anyone had court dates pending.

"No," Tinh answered firmly. "No court date yet." He could feel his heart pounding faster. Tinh had secretly recorded conversations with David Thai before, but they were always over the phone, never in person.

"I still have to go to court," Eddie Tran butted in.

"Oh?" asked Thai. "When you are booked, you use a false name, right?" The use of bogus Vietnamese names to fool the police was a standard gang practice.

"I used a false name but it didn't work. After three minutes, they discover my identity."

Tinh forced out a laugh. "One time," he offered, "the computer showed me with something like eight names. Eight false names came out."

David Thai chuckled and the others laughed.

For another few minutes, the gang members continued chatting amiably. Lam Truong noted that quite a few veteran gang brothers were scheduled to be getting out of prison over the next few weeks, an occurrence David Thai welcomed.

"These new Canal Boys now are so shy," lamented Thai. "Very timid. No one train them. I tell them to leap to the other side, they walk slowly, slowly, slowly."

Tinh Ngo, Eddie Tran, and the other "veteran" gang members nodded knowingly.

"We must act to strengthen our group," *Anh hai* continued. "We must revive our economy."

There were more eager nods of agreement all around.

"You guys know how it is, you've been living at this so many years. All I ask, if you are going to [do a job], then hit a big one, you know? Be visionary a little bit. That's all—be visionary."

While David Thai was regaling his minions with words of encouragement and inspiration, across the street from the restaurant, Detective Bill Oldham stood on the sidewalk. Positioned on the far side of a small lot filled with shrubs, flowers, and other inventory from a nearby plant store, Oldham waited patiently for the BTK gangsters to emerge, a 35mm camera in hand.

Thirty minutes passed before David Thai, Sophia, Tinh Ngo, and the others walked out of the restaurant and stood for a few minutes near Thai's silver Jaguar, which was parked at the curb. As traffic zoomed by, Oldham raised his camera and snapped a dozen photos.

He watched Tinh Ngo walk to a nearby street corner and pretend to use a pay phone. After a few minutes, Tinh returned to the group.

Ten minutes later, after the BTK gangsters had split up and gone their separate ways, Oldham strolled across the avenue and stopped at the pay phone. There, resting on top of the phone box, the detective found what he was looking for: a near-empty pack of Marlboro cigarettes with a mini-cassette tape inside, just as he and Tinh had planned. Oldham marked the tape "8-2-91: Kinh Do restaurant." Later, he would drop it off at ATF headquarters, where it would be placed in the bureau's evidence vault with the twenty or so other mini-cassette recordings Tinh had made.

In recent days, Oldham and the other investigators were paying even closer attention to the gang than usual. They'd gotten wind of at least two major crimes the BTK had in the works, and they were digging for more details. The investigators first learned about one of the crimes five days earlier, during their July 27 surveillance of the gang on Canal Street.

While the other gang members were making extortion collections, Lan Tran had pulled Tinh aside in front of the Asian Shopping Mall. "We are preparing for something different," Uncle Lan told Tinh, "something profitable. We are preparing to rob a big watch company. We're waiting for the Italians, so we can collaborate. We let them act like police officers, then we follow them and steal the goods."

"Oh, oh, oh. You mean, they pretend to be FBI?" Tinh asked Lan excitedly.

"Yeah. You and me be together in one group. They got two companies for us to rob at once. But don't let anyone know at all. Just hang out for now and say nothing."

The investigators were intrigued by this strange robbery plan Uncle Lan had mentioned, though they weren't quite sure what to make of it. Was Lan Tran really suggesting that the BTK was going to collaborate on a robbery with a group of Italians? "Italians" as in *Cosa Nostra*?

While the investigators were still scratching their heads in wonderment, Tinh Ngo received a phone call from David Thai initiating another intriguing crime. At first, *Anh hai* told Tinh little, other than that he was planning a "job" in Chinatown, and he wanted Tinh to select two apprentice gang members to help.

There wasn't much the investigators could do except encourage Tinh to solicit more details. In the meantime, they followed the gang members everywhere—to David Thai's new suburban home in Melville, Long Island, to Canal Street, and to the gang's new headquarters, the Kinh Do restaurant.

On August 3, 1991, the day after detective Oldham snapped pictures of the gang in front of the restaurant, the investigators heard more.

"Dan, you know that job I tell you about?" Tinh asked Agent Kumor over the phone that afternoon.

"Yeah," answered Kumor.

"It's a bombing."

"A bombing!" Kumor repeated, startled by the prospect.

Tinh still hadn't been told much. Following his usual pattern of telling Tinh only what he needed to know at the time, David Thai had said simply that the BTK would be delivering a bomb to a restaurant in Chinatown.

The investigators were concerned. Very concerned. There had already been a bombing in Chinatown a few days earlier, near the front entrance of a Chinese restaurant on Mott Street. A small explosive device had been detonated, shattering glass and damaging a wall. Luckily, no one was nearby at the time.

There had been no warning beforehand. Neither the restaurant owners nor the local cops had any idea what the bomb was about. When Dan Kumor asked Tinh, he didn't know either, though it sounded a lot like something David Thai might have planned.

The investigators were beginning to worry. Was this the beginning of a terrible new extortion technique on the part of the BTK?

Kumor told Tinh to keep them posted. Again, there was little they could do except keep key members of the gang under constant surveillance.

Two days later, on the evening of August 5, Kumor was beeped by Tinh. When he called back, Tinh uttered in hushed tones, "Dan, I can't talk on the phone. Maybe you come meet me."

Thirty minutes later, Kumor and Oldham picked up Tinh on a street corner in Sunset Park and drove to a stretch of Third Avenue near Red Hook, a burned-out Brooklyn neighborhood of deserted warehouses and empty, rubble-strewn lots. They turned onto a side street and parked. Even in the middle of nowhere, Tinh slumped down in the backseat so he couldn't be seen.

He had startling news: "This morning David Thai come by and give me the bomb."

"What kind of bomb?" Kumor asked.

A homemade bomb, Tinh said, one that Thai claimed to have

assembled himself. Inside a glass jar, Thai had wrapped what looked to Tinh like a stick of dynamite in foil. Packed tightly around the dynamite were hundreds of small nails.

Tinh told the investigators that he'd found two volunteers to deliver the bomb. The target was Pho Bang—an appropriately named restaurant under the circumstances—located right next door to the Chinese restaurant where the other bomb had been detonated.

"When's this supposed to happen?" asked Oldham.

"Right now," said Tinh. "Soon as I get back to the apartment. Two gang brothers waiting for me."

"Jesus," Kumor exclaimed, trying to get his thoughts together. "Okay, look, here's what we're going to do . . ."

Kumor told Tinh to stall as long as he could. In the meantime, Kumor and Oldham were going to hightail it over to Chinatown, and try to get Tisdale and Sabo there as a backup team.

"When I beep you, bring these guys over to do the job. But drop them off a few blocks from the restaurant, on Centre Street, where we'll be waiting. We'll stop them on the street before they get to Pho Bang." That way, Kumor figured, he and Oldham could arrest the bombers without implicating Tinh.

"I don't know," Tinh answered, a trace of uneasiness in his voice. "They ready to go now. I don't think I can delay much longer."

"Just do what you can," replied Kumor.

The investigators dropped Tinh off a few blocks from the apartment in Sunset Park and headed for Chinatown. On the way, they stopped at a pay phone. Kumor called Tisdale at ATF headquarters and told him to meet them in front of E-5 Communications, the beeper store on Centre Street where the BTK maintained an open tab.

By the time Kumor and Oldham arrived in the area, it was around 9:00 P.M. Dusk had settled and automobile traffic was sparse. But the streets were still alive with pedestrians, many of whom had come to Chinatown to eat dinner, some probably at Pho Bang.

Oldham double-parked on Centre Street. Kumor got out of the car and ambled toward a pay phone. With Tinh not due to arrive in Chinatown until he was summoned, Kumor figured he had plenty of time.

The agent kicked an empty beer can out of the way and was about to drop in a quarter when he spotted a car parked down the block that he immediately recognized as the BTK's green Buick. His heart sank.

Kumor dropped the phone receiver and walked toward the car. There were two people in the front seat. As he got closer, he recognized the passenger as gang member Lam Truong. Tinh was in the driver's seat. The two young bombers were nowhere in sight. For a brief second, Kumor's and Tinh's eyes met. Tinh looked slightly panicked and seemed to nod his head in the direction of Pho Bang.

Holy shit! thought Kumor. He raced back to the ATF car and shouted through the open window on the driver's side, "Hey, Bill, Tinh's here already! He dropped the bombers off!"

Oldham snapped into action. "We better get over there," he warned, starting the car and gunning the engine.

Kumor had already disappeared down the block, running as fast as he could in the direction of the Pho Bang restaurant.

Chapter 15

Racing east along Hester Street, a typically narrow downtown lane lined with parked cars, Kumor dodged pedestrians and garbage bins overflowing with debris. His legs and arms churning, he sped past produce markets, an Italian-American social club, a Catholic church. He darted out into the middle of one intersection, narrowly missing oncoming traffic. Horns honked and motorists shouted obscenities.

Goddamnit, Kumor mumbled to himself, *you went too far this time. You finally pushed it too damn far.*

Throughout the investigation, he, Oldham, and the others had been cognizant of the risks. Trying to halt BTK crimes was essentially a high-stakes game of chicken. Each time they successfully thwarted one of the gang's schemes, the dangers intensified. In a way, this was precisely what made the investigation so unusual and exciting to Kumor. In his seven-year career in law enforcement, he'd never been involved in a case even remotely like it, where his duties as a lawman were so inexorably tied into the day-to-day operations of a violent criminal enterprise.

So far, the investigators had met each challenge with a good deal of ingenuity, stopping each crime as it was about to unfold. This time, Kumor was afraid they'd miscalculated. This time, maybe they were finally about to get burned.

The Pho Bang restaurant was three long city blocks from Centre Street, where Kumor had spotted Tinh Ngo *without* the two bombers. As he dashed across Mulberry Street, Kumor almost collided with a woman pushing a baby carriage. He could see pedestrians looking at him like he was a crazy person. So be it. He juked and jived and kept on moving, listening for a sound he did not want to hear, a loud, echoing *ka-boooooooooom!* coming from the direction of the restaurant. At Mott Street, Kumor slowed and made a sharp right.

Pho Bang was nestled in the middle of the block, on the ground floor of a classic turn-of-the-century tenement. Underneath a cast-iron fire escape, a large, garish sign proclaimed the restaurant's name in Chinese, Vietnamese, and English. The block was thick with pedestrians. Old ladies waddled along with bags of groceries. Apartment dwellers walked their dogs. A number of old men were lounging in front of a bakery next door to Pho Bang.

By the time Kumor got to the restaurant, he was sucking wind. He stopped and scanned the area.

Tinh had given him a description of the two young bombers; one was fifteen, the other sixteen. There were a number of teenagers walking by, but none who seemed to fit Tinh's description. Had they already come and gone? Scenes flashed through Kumor's mind of a bomb going off inside the restaurant, sending glass and debris flying out into the street, injuring him and dozens of innocent bystanders.

Night had fallen on Mott Street. Kumor squinted, his eyes adjusting to the streetlights and neon signs, as he looked frantically for the two young bombers. He started slowly down the block past Pho Bang toward Canal Street, thinking perhaps he would catch them coming from that direction. His gaze was fixed so firmly in the distance that he almost missed the two young Vietnamese males as they briskly walked right past him.

Kumor spun around and pulled his ATF shield out from under his shirt, letting it dangle on the chain around his neck. Less than twenty feet from the entrance to Pho Bang, he accosted the two young bombers from behind, shouting, "Hey, up against the wall! Now!"

Whipping out his government-issue 9mm from a hip holster underneath his shirt, Kumor pushed them up against the facade of a Chinese restaurant. One of the bombers was holding a plastic shopping bag, which Kumor quickly grabbed. He peeked inside and spotted the homemade bomb; it was in a glass jar about ten inches long and five inches thick, crudely wrapped in duct tape, with a five-inch fuse.

One of the kids had a lit cigarette in his mouth, presumably to light the fuse. He had a baby face, with thick black hair parted in the middle, and was wearing a T-shirt with *Terminator 2*, the title of the latest Arnold Schwarzenegger opus, emblazoned across the front.

"You know why I'm stopping you guys?" Kumor asked the pair, who were facing the wall with their legs spread wide.

"No," they both mumbled.

Kumor grabbed the cigarette from the mouth of Terminator 2, threw it on the pavement, and stamped it out. "Yeah, you know," Kumor growled at him. "You're wanted, aren't you? There's a fucking warrant out on you."

The kid responded indignantly, "Nah, I don't know what you're talking about."

"Well, I'm gonna find out who you are because I think there's a warrant out." Then Kumor addressed the other bomber. "And you, I don't know who you are. But you're with him, so I'm gonna have to take you in too."

By now, Detective Oldham had pulled up to the curb, hopped out, and was standing alongside Kumor. A small crowd of onlookers gathered, curious about what was going down on this mild summer evening. Oldham and Kumor handcuffed both teenagers, loaded them into the backseat of Oldham's car, and drove them three short blocks to the Fifth Precinct.

In an interrogation room, the two pubescent gangsters stonewalled, claiming they didn't know it was a bomb they'd been carrying in their shopping bag. They were charged with possession of explosives.

By the following afternoon, the investigators had learned most of what they needed to know about the attempted bombing. The NYPD's Bomb Squad examined the bomb—a powerful M-1,000 explosive packed inside a glass jar—and determined it was the same sort of device that had blasted the restaurant next door to Pho Bang one week earlier. That bomb, Kumor learned later through Tinh Ngo, had actually been intended for Pho Bang. The assignment was given to two young gang members who mistakenly threw the bomb into the wrong restaurant!

Furthermore, the investigators were able to piece together a motive. David Thai told Tinh Ngo that he was being paid $10,000 by another person to bomb Pho Bang—a claim neither Tinh nor the investigators believed. A more likely motivating factor was an avowed reluctance on the part of the restaurant's owner to continue making extortion payments. Not only that, but a recent article on gang violence in *The New York Times* had quoted Tang Hai—described as "the operator of the Pho Bang restaurant on Mott Street"—criticizing the BTK. "It is very easy to tell them apart [from members of other gangs]," noted Tang Hai.

Hai's comment, in and of itself, wasn't much of an insult. But coming in the middle of an article that singled out the BTK as the area's most universally disliked gang, it was noteworthy.

According to the unwritten rules known and adhered to by most merchants in Chinatown, those associated with Pho Bang had committed at least two major mistakes.

One, they were quoted in print criticizing a Chinatown gang.

Two—an inexplicable and even more perilous faux pas—they had allowed themselves to be quoted *by name*.

Late on the night of the foiled bombing attempt, Dan Kumor drove home to his apartment in suburban New Jersey, popped open a beer, and put his feet up. After the first satisfying sip, he let loose a steady, sustained sigh of relief.

All the way home, through the Holland Tunnel and on the Jersey Turnpike, Kumor had replayed the incident in his head. Along with the potent M-1,000, David Thai's homemade bomb had been tightly packed with tacks, screws, and nails—shrapnel that would have sprayed the entire restaurant had the device exploded. Pho Bang was a popular spot. Employees from the nearby government buildings ate there. Innocent tourists. Women and children.

Visions of mayhem and carnage haunted Kumor's dreams that night. By the next morning he'd reached a conclusion.

"We've accumulated mounds of evidence," he told Oldham and the other investigators in a meeting at ATF headquarters. "We've got Timmy. I'm sure we can flip a few more of these guys. Give me one good reason we shouldn't dump the whole thing in Vinegrad's lap right now, get warrants, and make the arrests."

The investigators looked at one another. When he thought about it, even Kumor knew the response to that challenge. It could be summed up in two words:

The Italians.

The possibility that David Thai and his BTK brothers were about to attempt a major robbery with some Mafia wiseguys was just too good to pass up. Ever since Kumor and his fellow ATF agents had begun working the "emerging crime groups" beat in the late 1980s, it had been apparent that most of the new gangs preferred to work in isolation. If they did branch out, it was usually to groups of similar ethnicity. A Dominican gang might do business with a Puerto Rican, Panamanian, or Colombian organization. A Jamaican posse might do business with an African American gang. But never had anyone imagined, much less seen, a group of young Vietnamese gangsters join hands with Italian-American *mafiosi*.

For decades, Canal Street had existed as an unofficial borderline between Chinatown and Little Italy. Even though these two communities, among the oldest in New York City, were located side by side, their inhabitants rarely intermingled. It wasn't due to any overt hostility. The gulf between the two neighborhoods was simply a reflection of the broad cultural differences between Southern European Catholics and East Asians, most of whom were Chinese and Buddhist.

In the 1980s, as Chinatown's population grew and the neighborhood's boundaries expanded well north of Canal Street, Little Italy became diluted. As this transformation occurred, local cops sometimes speculated about a possible alliance between the two oldest and largest criminal organizations in the history of New York: the Mafia and the

Asian underworld. It was unlikely that David Thai had anything quite so grandiose in mind. Still, the possibilities were too intriguing to ignore.

The day after the failed bombing attempt, Kumor had Tinh Ngo put in a call to David Thai from ATF headquarters. With the microphone from his tape recorder affixed to the mouthpiece, Tinh explained to *Anh hai* that last night's bombing had been "unsuccessful."

Once again, Thai cursed his bad luck, blaming the two young bombers. "They were told to go individually," he complained. "They go together, they get arrested."

"What do you want to do, *Anh hai*?" Tinh asked.

"Huh?"

"What action are you going to take?"

David Thai sighed—the sound of a beleaguered gang boss stoically shouldering the burdens of his less talented brethren. "Now, we must wait to see what will happen. That's all."

Tinh changed the subject. "*Anh hai,* what about the situation tomorrow?"

"About tomorrow?" Thai repeated the question absently, his mind still mulling over the enormity of his responsibilities as the "oldest and wisest brother."

"Yeah. Tomorrow," repeated Tinh.

Anh hai finally snapped into focus. "Yes, yes. Tomorrow is on. Ten o'clock. I'm coming over to pick you up."

"You'll be over here at ten?" Tinh asked, as if he were calling from the Sunset Park safe-house apartment.

"Yes. If anything comes up, I'll get in contact with you later. If I beep you, answer me right away. Understand?"

Tinh could tell from the tone of David Thai's voice that these were serious plans for a major robbery. "Yes, *Anh hai*. I understand."

After Tinh hung up, Kumor and the other investigators went over their options. They were in a familiar predicament. Once again, they knew of a major BTK crime that was about to go down. But once again, David Thai was revealing little, leading his gang brothers into the robbery while divulging only what they needed to know to move them from one stage to the next.

"I'm prepared to let the robbery plans develop," Kumor said to the others. "Let's see where this leads. But we've got a problem. We gotta stop this robbery before it happens. And there's absolutely no room for error."

This time, the investigators figured, it was unlikely they would be able to prevent the robbery without tipping their hand. There was no ruse they could think of to explain their fortuitous appearance at a robbery involving half a dozen BTK members *and* a couple of Italian-American coconspirators. Using Mother's Day as an excuse or having Bill Oldham stand around in a police uniform was obviously not going to work.

"This is it," declared Kumor. "When we move in to make the arrests this time, it's for keeps."

The investigators worked late into the evening of August 6 mapping out the logistics. Two separate surveillance teams would follow David Thai and Lan Tran from Thai's Long Island home into the city. Another surveillance team would sit on the BTK safe house where Tinh was staying in Brooklyn. Another crew would be responsible for watching the meeting site in Manhattan, wherever that turned out to be. Still more agents would guard the watch factory the gang was planning to rob, once they found out where that was.

Another team of more than a dozen agents and cops would be responsible solely for making the arrests. The assumption was that all the robbers would be armed—although at this stage, the investigators weren't even sure how many robbers there were going to be.

All told, the operation would involve nearly forty cops and agents culled from the NYPD's Major Case Squad and Emergency Service Unit, two local precincts, and ATF.

Early the following morning, by 7:30 A.M., Kumor, Oldham, and two other ATF agents were positioned roughly one block from David Thai's suburban abode, a modest wood-shingled house in a quiet, colorless section of Melville. Clean, smoothly paved streets and green lawns blanketed the area; birds chirped their greetings as a new day dawned. Crowded into Kumor's maroon Mustang with tinted windows, the lawmen sipped from cups of coffee and waited.

Around 8:30 A.M., an entourage emerged from the front door of the house that included David Thai, Sophia, Lan Tran, LV Hong, and Number Ten.

Agent Kumor raised a Kodak video camera and aimed it toward the group. "Okay, boys," he announced. "It's showtime."

The group piled into David Thai's gray Jaguar, parked in the driveway in front of the house. Thai took the wheel, Sophia sat in the front passenger seat, and the other three jammed in the back.

The surveillance team followed Thai's Jaguar through Melville and out onto the Long Island Expressway. Both vehicles crawled through bumper-to-bumper traffic. A pale brown tinge of exhaust hovered along the roadway. Just past the vast expanse of New Calvary Cemetery in Queens, Thai veered to the right and exited onto the Brooklyn-Queens Expressway. The towering skyscrapers of Manhattan glistened from across the East River as Thai continued west to the Manhattan Bridge. With the surveillance car following, the Jaguar exited the expressway and zipped across the bridge into Chinatown.

A few minutes later, at the intersection of Walker Street and Sixth Avenue, the Jaguar pulled over and stopped. Lan Tran, LV Hong, and Number Ten climbed out and headed toward the Kinh Do restaurant, half a block away. David Thai drove on.

From the Mustang, Agent Kumor called a secondary ATF surveillance team on his two-way radio. "Get a video camera and set up on Kinh Do, at Nineteen Sixth Avenue," he ordered.

Kumor and Oldham elected to stay with David Thai. A few blocks to the east, near the corner of Walker and Broadway, the Jaguar again pulled over to the curb, this time alongside a pay phone. The lawmen watched as Thai got out of his car and made a call, then hung up almost immediately. Evidently, he had just paged someone, most likely Tinh Ngo.

At that moment, miles away in the Sunset Park section of Brooklyn, yet another surveillance team was watching 757 Forty-sixth Street, formerly Blackeyes' apartment, now the latest BTK safe house. A few minutes after David Thai hung up the phone in Manhattan, Tinh emerged from the apartment building. From their surveillance vehicle, Agent Don Tisdale and Detective Alex Sabo watched as Tinh walked half a block down Eighth Avenue to the AK&Y Laundromat.

Tinh often used the Laundromat as a private office of sorts. From a pay phone on the wall, he returned beeper calls to those in his life to whom he had become hopelessly beholden—his ATF overseers and David Thai.

Tinh called *Anh hai*. "It's you and Tieu today," David told Tinh. "Tieu" was a nickname they sometimes used for Eddie Tran.

"Okay," Tinh answered.

"Both of you dress up nicely, okay? Wear good clothes. I'm gonna drive to Brooklyn now, be there right away."

With Kumor and Oldham following, David Thai drove out to Sunset Park. Tinh was ready to go, but Eddie Tran, just out of prison and not anxious to take part in BTK robberies, was still in bed.

"Get the fuck up!" ordered *Anh hai*. They waited while Eddie reluctantly got dressed.

David, Tinh, and Eddie headed back to Manhattan. In Thai's Jaguar, they drove north on Sixth Avenue past the Kinh Do restaurant into Greenwich Village. At Sixth Avenue and Third Street, in front of an outdoor basketball court bustling with activity, Thai dropped off Tinh and Eddie Tran. Not long afterward, they were joined by Lan Tran.

From a distance, Kumor and Oldham watched while Uncle Lan, dressed respectably in black pants and a silk shirt buttoned to the collar, stood on the street corner trying to make himself as visible as possible. He was holding a large manila envelope, waiting to meet the Italians.

Meanwhile, David Thai parked his Jaguar in front of a McDonald's on West Third Street, just half a block from where Lan was standing. He, Sophia, and LV Hong got out and disappeared inside the McDonald's.

Forty minutes later, a black Cadillac with New Jersey license plates pulled up slowly in front of the basketball court.

"It's the Italians!" Dan Kumor exclaimed from the front seat of the surveillance car. He watched as two beefy white males got out of the Cadillac. Lan Tran immediately walked over and they began to chat.

"I'm gonna try to find a decent observation post," Kumor told Oldham and the other agents. "You guys stay here."

Kumor jumped out of the Mustang and walked along Sixth Avenue, across the street from the Cadillac. He came to a corner apartment building and began pressing buzzers until a tenant came to the door.

"Look," said Kumor, flashing his ATF badge. "I'm a federal agent.

We've got some police business under way here. I need an apartment that faces Sixth Avenue where I can sit and conduct surveillance for a while."

The man looked skeptical, but he brought Kumor up to his third-floor apartment.

Kumor could hardly believe the view. Directly across the street from the apartment window, Lan Tran was talking with the two Italians. Tinh Ngo and Eddie Tran stood in the background, watching a group of kids playing basketball. Kumor pulled up a chair and hunkered down, this time aiming a 35mm camera with a zoom lens at his subjects.

Short and squat and in their mid-thirties, the two Italians didn't exactly look like high rollers. One was bald on top with black, closely trimmed hair on the sides. The other was slightly taller, with the inflated physique of a habitual steroid user. Both were dressed casually in sleeveless shirts and blue jeans.

Although the investigators didn't know it yet, the robbery was scheduled to take place at Sun Moon Trading Inc., a large watch manufacturer a few miles away. According to the plan, the Italians would go in first, posing as plaincloths cops, using a fake search warrant that Lan Tran had brought along. Then Tinh, Eddie, and Lan would storm the warehouse, steal everything in sight, and bring it down to the street. The Italians had called a couple of accomplices to meet them in a getaway van at the scene. As usual, David Thai would play no role in the actual robbery. Rather, he would lurk in the background waiting to receive the stolen bounty.

257

At one point, Thai did appear on Sixth Avenue to speak briefly with the two Italians, then disappeared once again inside the nearby McDonald's. Moments later, the entire operation almost went up in smoke when a tow truck began hoisting up Thai's Jaguar, which was parked illegally in front of a fire hydrant.

Oldham quickly approached the driver of the tow truck. "Whoa there," he exclaimed, "I need you to leave that Jaguar right where it is." Oldham discreetly flashed his detective's shield.

The Jaguar stayed put.

Eventually, the Italians climbed into the front seat of the black Cadillac, and Lan Tran, Tinh, and Eddie Tran climbed into the back. The car pulled away from the curb and headed north on Sixth Avenue.

Kumor dashed from his observation post to the surveillance car outside. "We better stick with the Caddie," he said to the others, throwing the Mustang into gear.

The morning dew had long since given way to a typically clammy August afternoon, and the streets were thronged with pedestrians. Kumor and the others followed the Cadillac as it crawled slowly through the city streets, carefully obeying all traffic lights and signs. After ten minutes or so, the Caddie pulled over to the curb in front of a nondescript office building, in a part of midtown Manhattan known as the Flatiron District.

"All units, meet in the vicinity of Twentieth Street and Broadway," Kumor announced over his two-way radio.

It was approaching four o'clock, and the narrow midtown streets were bathed in long, creeping shadows cast by the industrial tenement buildings that dominate the Flatiron District. The two Italians and the BTK boys piled out of the Cadillac and stood on the sidewalk in front of a corner deli. Once again they seemed to be stalling for time, waiting idly for another set of accomplices to arrive.

By now, there were nearly two dozen agents and cops dispersed among the seven or eight surveillance vehicles that had converged on the area. Tisdale and Sabo were among the last to arrive, in a black sedan. They pulled over to the curb at the intersection of Broadway and Twenty-first Street and waited for the robbers to make their move.

Less than a block away, the Italians had begun to get restless. The shorter of the two crossed over to the far side of the street and began checking out cars double-parked in the area. The other Italian —the one pumped up like a poor facsimile of Sylvester Stallone— headed north on Broadway in the direction of Tisdale and Sabo.

Because they were seated with their backs to the Italians, Tisdale and Sabo didn't notice the Stallone lookalike until he was right on top of them. For a second, their eyes met. Then the Italian turned and walked back toward the BTK crew. The two watched in the rearview mirror as he threw his hands in the air and said something to Lan Tran.

Uncle Lan looked in the direction of cops.

"Uh-oh," said Tisdale, asking his partner, "Should we bolt?"

"It doesn't matter now," lamented Sabo.

Lan walked up to their car and boldly looked inside. By then, the Italians were already climbing back into their black Cadillac.

"Shit," mumbled Tisdale. He picked up his two-way radio as soon as Lan walked away. "We've been made," he announced over the air to the other agents and cops. "I repeat, we've been made."

Poooooof! Nearly nine hours' worth of careful, methodical surveillance had just gone up in smoke. The Italians drove off. Within minutes, Uncle Lan, Tinh, and Eddie had flagged down a cab, jumped in, and disappeared. The agents had no choice but to return to the ATF offices, dragging their asses behind them.

In the investigation's tenth-floor headquarters, the air was rank with dejected mumbles and curses as the various agents turned in their car keys and two-way radios.

"Who's got the aspirin?" one yelled.

"Better yet, who wants to get a fuckin' drink?" moaned somebody else.

Within a few hours, Dan Kumor felt better. And it had nothing to do with aspirin or alcohol. In reality, the investigation was going well— too well to let one day's turn of events throw everyone into a deep funk.

Granted, the investigators had been close. When the robbers converged on Twentieth Street and Broadway, the agents were five minutes away from swooping down, making the arrests and bringing the entire five-month investigation to a head.

So it didn't happen—so what? thought Kumor. The busted surveillance hadn't been a total loss. For one thing, they were able to glean additional information about the Italians. From the license plate number on the Cadillac the investigators were able to identify the two beefy homeboys as Michael DiRosario and Frank Russo, of West Orange, New Jersey. Both men appeared in the government computers as small-time associates with the Lucchese and Genovese crime families, although there was no evidence that either was a "made man," an official *soldato* in the Mafia.

The BTK had done business with DiRosario and Russo before. Among other things, the Italians helped bankroll *Anh hai*'s massage parlor at 300 Canal Street. In return, Thai had cut the Italians in on the proceeds of numerous BTK robberies in and around Chinatown and Little Italy. He'd been about to cut them in on their biggest bounty yet, the inventory of a thriving watch warehouse owned and operated by a fellow Vietnamese immigrant.

Now that the surveillance had been burned, Kumor and the others had to decide what to do next. They were even pondering extending the investigation, until they put Tinh Ngo on the phone with David Thai later that evening.

"You know," *Anh hai* told Tinh, "I was thinking while I was coming to Brooklyn to pick you up, the police followed all the way."

"The police followed you?" asked Tinh, trying to give the question an appropriately startled reading.

"Yeah," answered *Anh hai*. "All the places we went, we were followed."

David Thai's comments were disturbing to Kumor and the other investigators. For the first time, Thai was attributing the bungled robbery to something more than just bad luck. Now that the specter of police surveillance had taken root in his imagination, Kumor feared it would be a relatively short distance to the realization that, for the police to be onto the gang, somebody on the inside must be feeding them information.

Early the following afternoon, Kumor beeped Tinh Ngo. Tinh stepped over numerous gang members watching TV in the front room of the Sunset Park safe house and walked down the street to the AK&Y Laundromat.

"Timmy," said Kumor. "We need to see you over here right away."

Sitting on the subway as it rumbled across the bridge into Manhattan, it dawned on Tinh that he'd heard something unusual in Kumor's voice, a gravity that he couldn't recall ever hearing before.

Once he arrived at the ATF building, Tinh made his way to the room on the tenth floor that served as the investigation's main headquarters. For a while, surrounded by the familiar charts, maps, and mugshot displays that had piled up over the course of the investigation, Tinh waited alone, wondering, *What next? What do Dan and Bill and Albert and the rest have in store for me now?*

Kumor and Oldham finally came into the room looking glum.

"Timmy, we've got some bad news," Kumor announced. "We hear from a source of ours that Blackeyes has put a contract out on your life. We hear he thinks you gave him up, so he wants to have you killed."

Tinh froze for a second, struck dumb by the idea that someone would put out a contract on his life. The way Kumor said it, the words alone sounded chilling.

"We're gonna have to take you off the street," Oldham added gravely. "You understand? We don't want anything bad to happen to you, so we're gonna have to hide you away for a while."

Tinh was still trying to swallow the information. "Oh. Okay" was all he could finally say.

Kumor grabbed a nearby telephone and handed it to Tinh. "We want you to put in a call to David Thai. Tell him you're going to have to hide out for a few days. Tell him about Blackeyes. Tell him Blackeyes ratted you out to the police. Tell him the police are out looking for you, and you have to stay away from Chinatown."

"What if he don't believe me?" Tinh asked.

"He'll believe," Kumor answered reassuringly.

To Tinh, something seemed strange. This business about Blackeyes taking out a contract on his life didn't ring true. Who were these sources Dan and Bill were talking about? Why hadn't Tinh heard anything about this out on the street?

"Go ahead, Tim," said Oldham, nodding toward the phone. "Beep David."

Tinh did as he was told. A few minutes later, David Thai called.

"Hello, who is this?" asked Thai.

"This is Tinh, *Anh hai.*"

"Oh, Tinh, where are you at?"

"I am in Chinatown today," answered Tinh, clearing his throat. "*Anh hai,* the police are looking for me. I think it's Blackeyes. I don't know what's up with him, but he thinks I reported him to the police to be arrested."

"What?" exclaimed Thai. "Why would he say such a weird thing?"

Tinh explained how there were many crimes he and Blackeyes had participated in together over the years. For some reason, Blackeyes

261

had come to believe that Tinh had betrayed him. So now Blackeyes had implicated him in criminal activities, maybe even the computer-chip robbery in Florida for which Blackeyes himself had been busted.

Thai was concerned. He told Tinh to stay away from Chinatown and get back to him if he heard anything new.

The next day, Kumor and Oldham spent the afternoon walking up and down Canal Street with a mug shot of Tinh Ngo. "You know this kid? You ever seen his face?" they asked merchants and gang members in the area, flashing Tinh's photo. Of course, everyone shook their heads no. In the most serious voices they could muster, the cops warned, "Well, this guy's wanted by the police. Here's my card. If you see him, give us a call right away."

Meanwhile, Tinh was stashed away high in a Manhattan hotel suite, with two ATF agents on guard around the clock. Late that evening, he spoke with David Thai on the phone. "Damn, *Anh hai*, the police are really looking for me," Tinh said, sounding more urgent by the minute.

"I know," answered Thai. "I heard about them. So stay cool. Don't appear anywhere foolishly."

Anh hai and Tinh cursed Blackeyes for a few minutes. Then the conversation turned to the best course of action for Tinh to take, now that he was wanted by the law.

"You know, Tim," said David. "I could bring you to Texas for a while."

"Texas?" asked Tinh. "Who is there?"

"Oh, there are people there to accept you. . . . It is just our own brothers over there, that's all. There are some brothers from here who went over there."

"Yeah?" asked Tinh. "But is living there comfortable?"

"Living there is not too hard. There is some suffering, like here, but there's enough to eat and drink. The main thing, you will feel some relief."

Tinh paused, as if he were giving the offer deep consideration. David Thai was once again fulfilling his role as *Anh hai*, and, frankly, Tinh was touched. He knew of no one else in his life who would see it as a duty to be concerned about his welfare now that he was supposedly wanted by the cops.

"Here," Thai interjected suddenly, "talk to Uncle Lan for a little bit." Tinh could hear a rustling sound as the receiver was handed over to Lan Tran.

"So, what is the decision now?" barked Lan, in his familiar rapid-fire delivery.

"Let me think about it," answered Tinh.

Uncle Lan echoed *Anh hai*'s concerns about Tinh's predicament, and offered reassurances about life in Texas. "There is a lot of money down there," said Lan, who had himself lived in Texas once while on the run. "Just go there and relax, and our brothers will show you around. Mention to them our name; then they don't dare bother you."

"Okay."

"You go there, then I will go there later."

"You and me go there?" Tinh asked excitedly, impressed at the idea of traveling together with the BTK's most revered gangster.

"You and me go there?" repeated Lan, gently mocking Tinh's question with a chuckle. "Hey, why you always demand for me to follow you? Let me take care of *Anh hai* also."

Tinh let out a hearty laugh. Talking with *Anh hai* and Uncle Lan like this reminded him of what had drawn him to the gang in the first place. This was the part that meant the most: brotherhood. Looking out for each other in the midst of a cruel, hostile world. Being able to count on one another. Before the killings had started and Tinh began to see his life as a hopeless trap, this was the part that meant more than anything else in the world.

Tinh asked Lan if there were any "jobs" he could do for *Anh hai* before leaving town.

Again, Lan chuckled. "Here we are trying to take care of you and you keep on wanting to do [robberies]."

Tinh laughed. "I just want to help, you know?"

"Ahhh, now that the law has appeared, the feeling between you and me is alive," noted Lan, his voice crackling with emotion. Lan was acknowledging a truism of the underworld: Kinship between outcasts grows stronger in the face of adversity.

For thirty minutes more, Uncle Lan rambled on, seeking to reassure Tinh of the unbreakable bond that existed between members of the Vietnamese underworld, whether in New York, Texas, or anywhere else in the United States. Eventually, the conversation came around to the subject of Blackeyes and Lan's voice lowered. "There is an evil guy," he hissed. "Remember, Tinh, if anyone should get killed, you have to leave his address so I can take revenge. You remember. If anything happens, then I won't let him live. I'll tell you that straight."

Lan handed the phone back to David Thai, who offered Tinh some closing words of reassurance. "Go down there [to Texas] and you can live for a while in peace. Whenever you want to go, let me know and I will buy the ticket for you."

"Do you want me to do anything, any job, before I go?" asked Tinh.

"Well, now," *Anh hai* advised paternalistically, "one thing is that I want you to stay in one place so I will have less to worry about, you see?"

"Yes, *Anh hai.*"

"Because deep down inside, it doesn't feel safe."

"Yes, *Anh hai.*"

"You take care. And don't go out there. I just called out there. They are still showing pictures and looking for you."

"Okay, *Anh hai.* Bye." Tinh hung up the phone.

After that, the investigators seemed chipper as hell. But Tinh was strangely depressed. After all this time, after numerous failed robberies and a long streak of bad fortune for the BTK, David Thai still had no idea that Tinh was a government informant. *Anh hai* still trusted him.

Cooped up in a hotel suite just a few blocks from the ATF building, Tinh knew damn well what Dan and Bill and all the others had up their sleeves. They were about to make their arrests. They were going to lock up David Thai, Lan Tran, and other members of the BTK.

When Tinh asked the agents about this, he got nothing. "Why should we tell you something you don't need to know?" they said, making it sound more like a statement than a question. Even Albert Trinh clammed up, assuming the role of dutiful federal agent over that of confidant and fellow Vietnamese.

The investigators were so wrapped up in their work that none of them noticed how much Tinh seethed with frustration. Being left in the dark like this reminded Tinh of all the times he'd gone on BTK robberies, not knowing what the hell was happening until he found himself standing in the middle of a jewelry store or a restaurant or a massage parlor with a bag in one hand and a gun in the other.

Yes, Dan and Bill and Albert were the good guys—Tinh had long since figured out that much. But when it came to dealing with them, sometimes their methods were not all that different from those of his former boss, Tho Hoang "David" Thai.

Chapter 16

Clad in a dark-blue windbreaker with ATF emblazoned across the back, Dan Kumor stood in a small flower bed at the side of David Thai's house and peeked around a corner toward the front door. Behind him, nine more similarly dressed agents and cops were pressed up against the house, waiting for his signal.

It was approximately 7:00 A.M., and the pleasant, suburban neighborhood of Melville, Long Island, was as peaceful as a graveyard. The only sign of movement was a sprinkler swaying gently back and forth on the front lawn of a house across the street. Occasionally, some unseen bird chirped a few bars of an early morning melody. If any of David Thai's neighbors had looked out their windows at that moment, they would have thought it was a typical summer morning—except, of course, for the heavily armed SWAT team in David's yard, bristling with handguns, rifles, battering rams, and ominous looking "bunkers," portable protective shields used most commonly during riots and prison uprisings.

Although the lawmen really weren't expecting armed resistance from the inhabitants of 12 Davis Street, you never knew what might happen. During previous surveillances, they'd established there were at least five occupants inside the house—David Thai, his wife, Lan Tran, LV Hong, and Number Ten. They knew there were guns inside, but they didn't know how many or where. Besides Kumor's crew, another team of ten agents and cops had been assigned to watch the perimeter of the house. But once the entry team burst through that front door, they were on their own.

As the designated "seizing agent," Kumor was the lead man on an entry team that included Agent Tisdale, Detectives Oldham and Sabo, and a number of the ATF agents who'd played an ancillary role in the investigation. Kumor glanced over his shoulder at the group and almost smiled.

The last five months had been some ride, culminating in the sudden decision to move in and make the arrests. Alan Vinegrad still wasn't ready to move for a RICO indictment, but even he agreed that the arrests had to be made. Given the dangers facing their confidential informant, they could wait no longer. Warrants were issued for violations under the Hobbs Act, a federal statute pertaining to the interstate sale and transfer of guns. The plan was to hold the BTK members in prison on these and various New York State charges until the RICO indictment could be secured.

Though it was easily the most exciting investigation of his career, Kumor could not say he was unhappy to see it finally come to a head. The personality conflicts between some of the investigators had never really gone away, creating a level of tension that generally fell to Kumor to sort out, making his role as case agent a thankless task. The nature of the investigation itself, with Tinh supplying a steady flow of information that often called for immediate action, put everyone in a constant state of anxiety.

Of course, given the matter at hand, all of that seemed amazingly insignificant. Right now, with their weapons drawn and sense of mortality heightened, the investigators had become one—a true testament to just how far a little righteous police action can go toward establishing a feeling of camaraderie.

"Danny, this is Rossero. Do you read me?"

Kumor had the volume on his two-way radio turned so low he almost missed the transmission from his group supervisor. John Rossero was stationed in a command car inconspicuously parked half a block away.

"Roger, John," he whispered into his radio. "We're set and ready to go."

"Okay," replied Rossero. "Security team in place?"

"Roger," came another voice over the radio.

"Prisoner transport in place?"

"Roger."

"Evidence transport?"

"Evidence transport is ready."

Rossero paused a few seconds for dramatic effect. Then, using the catchy title the investigators had devised for the occasion, he commanded, "All right then, commence Operation Thai-Up."

Kumor and his team immediately stormed around the corner of the house, across the front lawn, and up three cement steps to the door. Alex Sabo, the biggest member of the entry team, stepped to the forefront and drew back a hand-held battering ram. *BOOM!* The ram hit the wooden door and bounced off. Sabo drew the ram back again and slammed the door three more times in quick succession. *BOOM! BOOM! BOOM!*

The sound shattered the early morning calm, echoing down Davis Street and sending birds fluttering. The door flew open and the agents streamed into the front room of David Thai's house. With their weapons pointed skyward, they separated into smaller two- and three-man teams and rampaged through the house, past expensive stereo equipment and a huge freshwater fish tank.

It was not surprising, given the hour, that the occupants of the house were still in various stages of slumber. The only reason they were even partially awake was because of the ATF team's loud and rambunctious arrival.

LV Hong, who'd been sleeping on a couch in the living room, was the first to sit up, rub his eyes, and try to figure out what the hell was going on. Lan Tran and Number Ten were in a small bedroom in the back of the house, stumbling out of bed when the entry team burst in.

David Thai and his wife were in the master bedroom, across the hall from where Uncle Lan and Number Ten were sleeping.

Dan Kumor led the charge into David Thai's bedroom, with Old-ham and two additional agents behind him. Thai was standing beside his king-sized bed, wearing nothing but a pair of magenta boxer shorts. Before Thai even had a chance to open his mouth, one of the agents had a set of handcuffs on him and was reading him his rights.

Thai, his wife, and the other occupants of the house were assembled in the front room while a search team of five agents began systematically combing the place. Underneath the bed where Lan Tran had been sleeping, they found a .38-caliber Rohm revolver with six rounds of ammunition. In David Thai's bedroom, underneath his mattress, they found a 9mm, loaded with fourteen rounds. In his closet, they found another loaded 9mm, this one with a silencer attached. There were numerous loaded magazines of ammunition in the closet as well, along with a bag containing what looked to be precious stones, and another bag containing around $2,000 in cash.

Down the hall, in a small workroom, another team uncovered a modest bomb-making factory. The agents found pipe insulation and steel wool, tacks and nails, glass jars, duct tape, and miscellaneous other items Thai used to construct his homemade explosives.

Within an hour, the arresting team had thoroughly searched every room, including a small attic and a garage attached to the house. During the search, David Thai and the other gang members scowled but never said a word. Eventually, they were all led away in handcuffs.

A few hours later and many miles away, a similar raid was conducted at the BTK's safe house in Sunset Park, Brooklyn. In the crowded three-room apartment, a team of ATF agents found eleven young males and assorted girlfriends, including Eddie Tran, Shadow Boy, Teardrop, and other gang members. They were all placed under arrest and taken to ATF headquarters for processing.

When everyone from the two raids was finally rounded up together, the tenth-floor headquarters at 90 Church Street looked like an airplane hangar during the evacuation of Saigon. A total of eighteen people had been taken into custody, with warrants still out on three or four more. They were herded together into a large, drab waiting room where they

269

huddled in the corners, tousled and disheveled in whatever they'd been able to put on before being thrown into the back of a paddy wagon.

David Thai, Lan Tran, and the other gangsters took a special interest in the young Vietnamese-American agent who was wearing an ATF jacket. During the raid on Thai's house, Albert Trinh had initially stayed in the command car with the group supervisor. After the BTK members were in custody in the living room, Albert was brought into the house, where, if the gangsters spoke in Vietnamese among themselves, he might overhear some incriminating dialogue.

Thai and the others had noticed Albert Trinh at the house and kept their mouths shut. But here at ATF headquarters, their curiosity got the better of them.

"Are you the same guy who was at the house?" David Thai eventually asked Albert.

Albert looked *Anh hai* straight in the face. "Yes," he stated coldly.

Thai smirked and looked at the other gang members, whose faces also bore varying levels of disdain.

Later, Thai and the gang members came face-to-face with Albert again, in a holding cell in the basement of the federal courthouse where they were waiting to be arraigned on charges. The detainees were being asked to give their "pedigree"—place and date of birth, height, weight, and immigration number. As Thai was giving an ATF agent the necessary details, he was looking past the agent at Albert Trinh, who was writing down the information on a clipboard.

"Can I ask you something?" David finally asked Albert, ignoring the ATF agent in front of him.

Albert looked up from his clipboard. "What is it?"

In Vietnamese, Thai asked, "Don't you have any compassion for your fellow Vietnamese?"

Albert didn't miss a beat. In English, he shot back, "No. 'Cause I'm not Vietnamese."

Agent Trinh's answer hit David Thai like a sharp slap across the face. Thai and the other gang members had heard Albert speak fluent Vietnamese—they knew he was a brother. Was this cop denying his own ethnicity? *Anh hai* stared dumbfounded at Albert, then returned his attention to the agent taking his pedigree.

In a way, even Albert was surprised by his response. The words had sprung forth almost of their own volition. Later, after he gave it some thought, Albert realized that the arrest of David Thai and the BTK gangsters had been a more emotional experience than he anticipated. Afterward, he could feel Thai and the others watching and evaluating his every move, making judgments about his loyalty and worth as a fellow Vietnamese.

Albert resented being judged by them. For the past five weeks, he'd listened to the voice of *Anh hai* as he sweet-talked, challenged, and manipulated Tinh Ngo and other so-called brothers. Tellingly, David Thai never took the risks and did the deeds. He'd used his ethnicity to coerce untold numbers of young Vietnamese males into throwing their lives away. In time, Albert became disgusted by the sound of Thai's voice, disgusted with the way Thai had poisoned the lives of so many while claiming he cared for them as fellow Vietnamese.

Why should he feel "compassion" for Thai and his gang of BTK hoodlums? Thai was trying to make him feel guilty—a cheap, reprehensible trick as far as Albert was concerned. Though perhaps poorly worded, his response to Thai was Albert's way of letting him know that he could not be manipulated. He was saying to David Thai, Maybe that shit works with a young, terrified refugee who doesn't know any better. Maybe it works with a kid who is so desperate for a sense of belonging and love that he will do almost anything.

But it sure as hell wasn't going to work with Albert Trinh.

271

The arrests of David Thai and his followers may have been the culmination of months' worth of investigation, but for Kumor, Oldham, and the rest of the investigative team, the real work, in many ways, had only begun. So much time had been spent frantically trying to prevent BTK crimes from happening that the actual nuts and bolts of the case—lining up witnesses, gathering physical evidence, getting the necessary documents together—had been largely neglected. For about two days, Kumor and his crew were able to savor the emotional satisfaction of bursting in on David Thai and rounding up the gang. Then it was time to get back to work.

Three weeks after the arrests, in early September 1991, the investigation's headquarters shifted from the ATF building in downtown

Manhattan to downtown Brooklyn, where Alan Vinegrad had an office at One Pierpont Plaza.

If the investigators hadn't realized it before, they soon discovered that the young federal prosecutor for whom they were now working was a difficult taskmaster. Vinegrad's scrupulous and sometimes humorless approach added yet more spice to an investigative stew already brimming with conflicting personalities. The various lawmen divided up the work, tried to stay out of one another's way, and focused on building a comprehensive, airtight federal case against the BTK.

With Tinh Ngo as their star witness, the investigators had surprisingly little trouble getting other gang members to "flip." One of the first to fall in line was Kenny Vu, who'd left the gang a few months earlier and was living with relatives far out on Long Island. Kenny was an important piece of the puzzle, since he'd known Tinh Ngo from the beginning and could corroborate much of his testimony. Rather than face conviction on RICO charges, Kenny reluctantly agreed to testify.

Another who quickly flipped was Eddie Tran. Like Kenny Vu, Tran had been with the gang from the beginning. But he had grown disenchanted with the way he was treated by David Thai, and with the way he was being coerced into taking part in robberies.

Along with Kenny Vu and Eddie, the investigators were able to secure the cooperation of Little Cobra, whose testimony would provide valuable corroboration on the BTK's out-of-state crimes in Connecticut, Georgia, and Tennessee. Eventually, Nigel Jagmohan, the East Indian-Trinidadian gang member who had been beaten senseless by LV Hong and David Thai, also signed a cooperation agreement.

With five accomplice witnesses lined up, the investigators turned to what they knew was the real heart and soul of the case. There was no way they could successfully prosecute the BTK without cooperation from the people of Chinatown. The basis of any RICO case is the alleged existence of an "ongoing criminal conspiracy." With the BTK—or, for that matter, any Chinatown gang—that meant the constant extortions, robberies, and terror tactics perpetrated by the gang on merchants and average citizens. The challenge to the investigators was to get those victims to step forward and testify.

Given Chinatown's history—a history so vividly reiterated with the murder of Sen Van Ta—the merchants on Canal Street were predictably reluctant to cooperate with the authorities. They may have had universally negative feelings toward the BTK, but those feelings were counterbalanced by a decided lack of faith in the NYPD. Convincing these merchants that cooperating with the United States Attorney's office might be a benefit to themselves and the people of Chinatown was a slow, agonizing cross-cultural waltz.

Throughout the fall of 1991, the investigative team went again and again to Canal Street, trying to elicit the cooperation of restaurant and produce-store workers, jewelry-store owners, street peddlers, proprietors of leather warehouses and electronics outlets. Their efforts were aided considerably by Detective Sergeant Doug Lee, the Chinese-American officer who had followed David Thai to Queens the day he purchased two dozen bulletproof vests. The vests were never put to use. More recently, Lee was transferred from the Jade Squad to Major Case to help prepare the BTK case for trial.

With his gentle demeanor and command of all the Chinatown dialects, Lee was persuasive in a way the Caucasian cops and agents never could have been. He was particularly helpful in securing the cooperation of Vinh Tran, Sen Van Ta's twelve-year-old nephew, the only eyewitness to the cold-blooded murder of his uncle. Vinh Tran was able to identify Lan Tran as the shooter that day, a claim ultimately corroborated by the testimony of Kenny Vu, who had accompanied Uncle Lan into Chinatown on the day of the killing.

Among other obstacles, Lee and the investigators found themselves fighting the persistent influence of David Thai. Even though the BTK leader was safely behind bars at the Manhattan Correctional Center (MCC) in lower Manhattan, he had a way of making his presence felt.

In October 1991, two months after David Thai's arrest, a strange pamphlet began to appear in Vietnamese restaurants, at newsstands, and in video arcades around Chinatown and in Sunset Park, Brooklyn. The pamphlet consisted of a collection of poems written by David Thai, along with some twenty-five pages of advertising from local Asian merchants. The ads gave the impression that Thai's efforts were being endorsed by the Asian business community; in fact, they'd been photocopied from phone books and newspapers and used without the knowledge of the merchants.

Taking a page from Uncle Lan, the unofficial bard of the BTK,

273

Thai's writings betrayed a wistful romanticism. Composed in florid Vietnamese script and gathered under the heading "Immortal Love Poems," *Anh hai*'s writings were an attempt to explain and justify his current predicament, both to himself and the people of Chinatown. In one poem, titled "Carrying the Vietnamese Blood," he wrote:

Leaving my country, I swore to build a new life. . . . /to create my own soul, my own identity./Even if my body shall be destroyed,/my blood scattered to every corner of the world,/or jailed in a dark room,/my heart shall not fail to remain free. . . . /How I remember the grudges/which I hold forever inside my heart./But having Vietnamese blood in my veins,/I learn to smile without shedding a tear.

Later, feeling slightly less magnanimous, Thai wrote:

Life is still being dark and deceiving, I find./Companions, disciples, close friends, I had plenty./Who would think of that today. . . . /Looking at the past, I have but myself to blame./Giving everything away instead of looking after myself./Where are the close friends? Where are the disciples?

274

Thai did not limit his public relations onslaught to a handful of turgid poems. In early October, for the first time ever, he granted an interview to a member of the mainstream, English-language press.

The interview was conducted by Peg Tyre, the reporter who had covered the rise of the BTK for *Newsday*, the Long Island–based newspaper whose main offices are located in Melville, just a few miles from where Thai had been arrested. Tyre wrote two articles: a long piece on the joint ATF/NYPD investigation, and a slightly shorter piece devoted exclusively to David Thai, titled "Suspected Gang Leader Denies Link to BTK."

Seated in an interview room at the MCC, dressed in a bright-orange prison jumpsuit, Thai presented himself to his American interviewer as a man who had been horribly wronged. Federal agents, he claimed, had misinterpreted his humanitarian concern for Vietnamese refugees. "They say I'm the head of the BTK gang, but that is not so," Thai was quoted as saying. "There is no such gang, it is just kids who have no family."

Thai claimed to have been out of the country when many of the crimes listed in the indictment were committed. For the last three years, he said, he had lived mostly in Philadelphia, where he supposedly worked restoring cars.

At one point during the interview, Thai's eyes welled with tears as he described how his love for his Vietnamese brothers ruined his first marriage. But it was worth it, he said, because there was nothing more important to him than the welfare of his troubled, wayward boys. "I tried to help them, and I tried to get the Vietnamese community to help them. . . . I see their misery and I know that. I know their misery because I too have lived the same life."

Despite the flagrant falsehoods about his involvement in specific BTK crimes, Thai's emotional defense was one that he and most other gang members held near and dear to their hearts. Thai had always presented himself publicly as a kindly benefactor. He even deluded himself into believing that he was the only powerful person in Chinatown who truly cared about the welfare of his young Vietnamese brothers—and he had successfully instilled this perception into the minds of dozens of youths. Never mind that behind closed doors Thai was venal and brutal. Never mind that many gang members were now dead, in prison, or on the run for the rest of their lives. "A model example of a young Vietnamese man"—that was how Uncle Lan had described *Anh hai* in his journal. And that was the version most gang members and Thai himself would cling to as their world crumbled all around them.

Of course, one gang member had seen the lie for what it was and chosen a different fate—Tinh Ngo. Although the identity of the government's star witness had not yet been publicly revealed, one gang member was conspicuous by his absence.

When asked by the *Newsday* reporter about the government's confidential informant, Thai dabbed the moisture from his eyes with the

275

back of his hand and shook his head sadly. "I fed him, gave him a place to stay, tried to send him to school, and he robbed me. I would say that he is troubled, extremely troubled."

Then Thai sighed wearily. Even in prison, he still thought of himself as the BTK's overburdened, underappreciated Big Brother.

The trial of *United States of America* v. *David Thai et al.* began in early January 1992 before Judge Carol Amon in a windowless courtroom at the federal courthouse on Cadman Plaza East, in downtown Brooklyn. Under harsh, antiseptic light, Alan Vinegrad delivered an opening statement framing the conspiracy he intended to prove in the nearly three months of testimony that would follow. The main motivation of Born to Kill, he explained to a jury of twelve citizens, was monetary. The members of the gang "shared at least two key characteristics: their Vietnamese heritage, and their willingness to join together to make money through crimes of violence."

The defendants sat in the courtroom next to their attorneys, listening quietly as the government prosecutor detailed a numbing litany of crimes. Considering that the BTK comprised as many as one hundred members at its zenith, the number on trial was a small sampling. Of the twenty-two gang members named in the government's thirty-eight-page RICO indictment, many had already pleaded guilty, hoping for a lighter sentence. Others were testifying for the government. That left eight who had chosen to go to trial—David Thai, Lan Tran, LV Hong, David "Hawaii Dat" Nguyen, Hoang "Jungle Man" Ngo, Jimmy "Hong" Nguyen, Minh Do, and Quang Van Nguyen.

Because the BTK was such a broad, sprawling conspiracy, the government had chosen to focus on an unusually busy one-year period, from August 1990 to August 1991. With twelve armed robberies, three murders and attempted murders, numerous extortions, and assorted other charges, it was enough to put most of the defendants away for life if convicted.

As the government's evidence unfolded over the weeks and months that followed, it became apparent that its case was not only strong, but overwhelming. Vinegrad and the small team of investigators had rounded up virtually everything they needed: phone logs, circumstantial evidence from crime scenes, Tinh Ngo's taped conversations of robberies in the planning stages, videotapes of extortions on Canal Street. During the arrests at David Thai's Long Island home, they had unearthed stolen jewelry, weapons, and incriminating personal correspondence between *Anh hai* and other gang members. Among the items confiscated were color photographs showing the gang marching through Chinatown holding aloft a BTK banner, and standing in the cemetery beside Amigo's grave just minutes before a fusillade of gunfire exploded from out of nowhere.

Even more impressive was the stunning array of government witnesses, more than sixty in all. Odum Lim and his wife and daughter were flown up from Doraville to testify. Crime victims from Tennessee and Bridgeport also made an appearance. And New York City's Chinatown was ultimately represented by the most comprehensive collection of its citizens ever to testify at a criminal proceeding, a group that included everyone from Ying Jing Gan to numerous Canal Street merchants, people whose daily lives were most directly affected by the existence of the dreaded BTK.

The most devastating single witness was Tinh Ngo. Over the course of two and a half weeks, Tinh described his budding involvement in the gang, his growing disenchantment, and his cooperation with Dan Kumor and Bill Oldham. Tinh had been well prepared by Vinegrad, who told him time and time again in the weeks leading up to the trial, "Use the truth as your anchor, Timmy. The lawyers will try to confuse you. They will call you a liar to your face. Just stick to the truth and everything will be okay."

For a nineteen-year-old refugee from South Vietnam—a high school dropout speaking in a difficult foreign language—Tinh showed a remarkable ability to hold his ground during the long hours of sometimes brutal cross-examination, revealing something deep inside that perhaps even he had not known existed.

Over the months, Tinh's cooperation with the United States government had been a slowly evolving affair. Had he known from the beginning that he would be forced to wear a recorder while circulating among his fellow gang members, then testify against them in court, he might never have agreed to cooperate. At each stage, he had undertaken these endeavors with a great deal of ambivalence, his willingness to go

277

along with the program fueled by a combination of guilt and skillful coercion on the part of his law enforcement handlers. In the end, talking on the phone with *Anh hai* and Uncle Lan just before they were arrested, he'd even felt that maybe he had made a terrible mistake by betraying the only people who seemed to care about his welfare.

But once he was seated on the witness stand, in stark, imposing, unfamiliar surroundings, Tinh arrived at an inner truth. The ambivalence washed away as lawyer after lawyer tried to portray him as a wanton crack addict and even a killer. When one of the defense attorneys asked him for the umpteenth time to describe the shooting of Odum Lim—the event that had traumatized Tinh and turned him against the gang—his voice remained steady. "I heard a gunshot, so I take a look around and I heard Tung Lai say, 'Uncle Lan, help me, help me, he have the gun! The owner have the gun!' Then I see Lan from the owner's side go over with the gun and put it against the owner's head and pull the trigger."

"Isn't it a fact," asked the defense attorney, "that you, Tinh Ngo, had the gun and you shot the owner in the head?"

"No," Tinh answered firmly. "That is not true."

The more the lawyers badgered and cajoled Tinh, the stronger his resolve became. The more they tried to portray him as an unconscionable criminal bent only on saving his own skin, the more it became apparent that Tinh was being driven to testify by an unshakable moral imperative instilled a long time ago, before the gang, before the refugee camps, when, as a small child in Hau Giang Province, he first learned the difference between right and wrong.

Sitting in the courtroom each day, David Thai, Lan Tran, and the other defendants looked as if they didn't know what hit them. Although they all spoke varying degrees of passable English, most of them chose to listen to the proceedings on headphones, translated into Vietnamese by an interpreter seated near the defense table. At first, they had taken Tinh's testimony lightly, sneering and giggling every time he was forced to admit he smoked marijuana and crack. But even they recognized the cumulative effect of Tinh's testimony and the other evidence that began to pile up. Soon they turned glum and then uncomprehending as they struggled to make sense of the government's portrait of the gang as a sophisticated criminal organization.

278

Their confusion was partly understandable. To establish the BTK as an enterprise worthy of conviction under the RICO statutes, Vinegrad often reminded the jury that the gang's primary reason for existence was financial. The government predicated its case on showing that the ranks of the BTK had banded together for one reason: to make money. The fact that they had been successful in doing so was further proof of their motives.

For most gang members, this was a grandiose concept. Yes, the end result of their actions was money. But "survival" was a better word to describe why most had joined the gang. Maybe David Thai lived the life of an underworld prince. Maybe he had an expendable income. But for most rank-and-file gang members the payoff was far less bankable.

Near the end of the twelve-week trial, almost as an afterthought, Vinegrad read into the record a revealing piece of correspondence seized in the raid on David Thai's house. The letter had been sent by Tommy Vu, Kenny Vu's brother, who had once accompanied Tinh to the tattoo parlor on Delancey Street, where Tinh received his tattoo and was initiated into the BTK. Tommy Vu was writing to David Thai from prison, where he was serving a seven-year sentence on robbery charges. In a letter dated July 29, 1991, two weeks before the arrest of David Thai and the others, Tommy wrote:

279

Dear *Anh hai:* Hi, how are you? I hope everything is fine with you. How is everything in New York? I sometimes worry about the problems that go on around you. Please be careful and take care of yourself, *Anh hai.* I will be coming home soon. *Anh hai*, when I come home I will be coming back to Born to Kill. I will try with all my power to take care of anything and everything that happens around Born to Kill. That's my word, *Anh hai.* I really want to keep in touch with you, so please stay in touch with me and let me know what's going on always, because, like I said, I will be coming home soon and want to look after you. . . . For now, *Anh hai*, I say good-bye. . . . Take care of yourself, and I love you with all my heart. . . .

Underneath his signature on the letter, Tommy wrote, "I love you, brother, forever." Near the bottom of the page, with little space left, he wrote in smaller and smaller lettering, "Say hello to everyone. I love all brothers." And finally, in a tiny, childlike scrawl along the bottom of the page: "BORN TO KILL FOREVER."

Tommy Vu's letter was an accurate reflection of the feelings of most BTK gang members—even Tinh Ngo before he became disenchanted with his shallow, confining life as a gangster. The letter may have been a minor piece of evidence in the case against the BTK, but it had everything to do with the emotional undercurrents that created the gang in the first place.

The level of affection suggested by Tommy Vu's letter was part of a thread that, if carried to its furthest extension, would stretch back through failed foster-care situations, terrifying experiences on boats and in refugee camps, to a time when bombs and napalm and Agent Orange ruled the night and displaced an entire generation. Eleven and a half weeks of testimony had convincingly established the culpability of David Thai and his minions on a broad array of charges, but little light was shed on these most troubling issues.

The question of who or what was responsible for creating the circumstances that gave birth to the BTK was a tricky one, shrouded in emotionalism and the whims of historical interpretation. Among themselves, BTK gang members rarely spoke of the war, a historical reality only a few of them experienced firsthand. Nonetheless, there was little doubt that the war's legacy of violence, inhumanity, and abandonment had played a formative role in shaping the lives and actions of these young gangsters. It was written on their faces. It was all too evident in their actions. And it was tellingly reflected in the chillingly appropriate moniker they had chosen for themselves.

U.S. District Court may have been the place where the guilt or innocence of the individual was determined beyond the shadow of a doubt, but in terms of condemning or even identifying the forces that created those individuals, it might as well have been an empty chamber. Common law courtrooms, of course, were never meant to serve as forums for a broader discussion of the human condition, and the case against the BTK would be no exception. After nearly three years of murder and mayhem on the part of the gang, months of dangerous and diligent work by Tinh Ngo and the team of investigators, and an airtight prosecution by Vinegrad, the circumstances that transported a legacy of violence from the jungles of Southeast Asia to the streets of America twenty years later would remain unexamined.

It was a neat, impervious *American* trial.

A trial at which the war in Vietnam was never even mentioned.

On April Fool's Day, 1992, Tinh Ngo picked up the phone and dialed ATF headquarters.

"Is Dan Kumor there?" he asked.

Tinh was calling long distance; he could barely hear the voice on the other end of the line. "Kumor's not in right now," it said faintly.

"Oh. This is Timmy calling. Tinh Ngo."

"Oh," the voice piped up excitedly, "Timmy. We got great news."

"Yes."

"They were nailed to the wall. Day before yesterday. All except Dat Nguyen, he got off. Everybody else was convicted on pretty much all of the charges. David Thai, Lan Tran, the whole lot of them."

Tinh said thank you and hung up the phone. Thinking about his convicted gang brothers, his mind wandered. He thought back to when he had first heard about the arrests of David Thai, Lan Tran, and the others.

At the time, Tinh was holed up in a lower Manhattan hotel. The only time his handlers let him out was to drive him the few blocks to the ATF building on Church Street.

On the evening of the arrests, after all the gang members had been processed and carted off to jail, Tinh was at the ATF offices when a news report about the gang came on television. The various cops and agents who were watching slapped each other on the back and seemed overjoyed at the sight of the BTK gangsters being herded off to jail in handcuffs.

Tinh felt a different emotion. No matter how hard he tried, he could not completely shake the feeling that he had somehow engaged in an act of betrayal. Seeing *Anh hai* and the others being arrested made him feel depressed.

"You think maybe I can go somewhere, anywhere?" Tinh asked an ATF agent. "Get a sandwich, a soda or something?"

Two ATF agents took Tinh to a nearby cop bar, where they figured he would be safe. Inside the bar, Tinh sat quietly while the American lawmen drank, laughed, and told each other stories. At one point, Tinh looked up at a television mounted above the bar. There, again, was the same report he'd seen an hour earlier—*Anh hai,* Uncle Lan, and all the others with their heads hanging down, being led off to jail.

Man! Tinh thought to himself. *When will it all end? When will I stop feeling so bad?*

Now, after getting the news about the guilty verdicts, Tinh was not so much depressed as relieved. Maybe he could finally begin to put his years as a gang member and a federal informant behind him. Maybe now he could live a normal life.

Tinh knew it wasn't going be easy. The most recent turn of events in his relatively brief life had landed him many thousands of miles away from New York City. He had a job washing dishes in the kitchen of an Italian restaurant. He'd changed his name and was renting a room in a house with a large Vietnamese family, trying to make it on his own.

Dan Kumor had offered Tinh the cover of the Witness Security Program (WITSEC), the U.S. government's vaunted relocation program for people whose lives were endangered because of their cooperation with the authorities. In WITSEC, a person was given a new identity, some money, and relocated to a different part of the country, hopefully beyond the grasp of those he'd helped put away.

Tinh considered the offer. It sounded okay to him, under one condition. He wanted to be relocated to Seattle. In the months leading up to the trial, he had been stashed in Seattle by the government. Tinh had stayed in a small apartment in a part of the city known as the University District, where he'd found a job in a Chinese restaurant and even a girlfriend. Not an Asian girl, either. A Caucasian girl. For the first time in his life, Tinh could imagine a world beyond the limits heretofore defined by war, his refugee status, his ethnicity.

When Tinh told Kumor and the others he wanted to be relocated in Seattle, they told him it wasn't a good idea. He would have to live somewhere else. Furthermore, he would have no say in the matter. He would live wherever they felt was best.

"In that case," Tinh said, "I think maybe I better off on my own, making my own decisions."

Tinh's response startled his government handlers. They tried to talk him out of it. We know what's best for you, they said. We feel responsible. Besides, there were too many risks.

The way Tinh saw it, life was full of risks, no matter what you did. He would honor their wishes by not returning to Seattle. But he did not want the U.S. government telling him where he could or could not live.

It was not an easy decision, but Tinh felt good about it. All his life, he had been controlled by a higher authority—the dictates of fate, *Anh hai*, the cops and agents who eventually brought down the BTK. His life had been a tumultuous, disorienting affair, an adventure worthy of *The Tale of Kieu*.

Along the way, Tinh had learned some valuable lessons. He had learned there is sometimes a wide gulf between what a person says and the true motivations buried deep inside. He learned the difference between good and evil, yin and yang. And he had learned that for Tinh Ngo to truly become the controller of his own destiny, he must stand on his own two feet. He must learn, by himself, what it means to be an American.

He must learn what it means to be free.

To the people of Chinatown, the successful prosecution of David Thai and his BTK brothers was a startling, momentous event. Unlike similar prosecutions in the mid-1980s involving influential tong-associated gangs like the Ghost Shadows and the United Bamboo, the BTK trial received extensive coverage in all of the local Chinese-language newspapers. It was as if the community's traditional powers were gloating over the demise of the renegade Vietnamese gang, reasserting their cultural and territorial imperative over a group of gangsters who had shown so little respect for the area's deeply ingrained underworld rules.

The mainstream media, on the other hand, was not nearly as interested in the fall of the BTK as they had been in the gang's volatile, highly sensational rise to power. At the time of the arrests there had been some newspaper and television reports, culminating with *Newsday*'s jailhouse interview with David Thai. But scant follow-up coverage was given to the court-room testimony of Tinh Ngo, Odum Lim, Ying Jing

Gan, and others whose lives had been so inexorably affected by their encounters with the BTK. In part, the media's lack of concern was an extension of a long-standing negligence when it came to issues relating to the Asian community. Mostly, it was because of a more "newsworthy" event that was taking place elsewhere in the same courthouse, one that dominated media coverage not only in New York City but throughout most of the United States.

There was no denying that the prosecution of Mafia boss John Gotti was an important story. The demise of Gotti, the leader of the largest *Cosa Nostra* family in New York, symbolized the further erosion of a once-proud criminal tradition. Although the federal government had been successfully chipping away at the Mafia for at least the last decade, two previous attempts to prosecute Gotti ended in acquittal. Each trial brought a higher level of media attention, with this latest proceeding attracting hordes of reporters, not to mention Hollywood celebrities like Anthony Quinn, Mickey Rourke, and others whose careers revealed an enduring professional fascination with "the Mob."

On journalistic grounds, the story of Gotti's fall was historic, but the real secret of its appeal with the media and the public at large was its familiarity. The Dapper Don was the latest in a long line of New York gangsters whose exploits had been lionized in countless movies and books. The mystique of the Mob—established during the years of Prohibition, embellished in the decades that followed—had long since become central to the American identity. By now, the public had come to feel a nostalgic, almost sentimental attachment to these Old World mobsters, who hark back to a time when the underworld was ruled mostly by Caucasian men of European extraction.

Asian gangsters in America have never been embraced in quite the same way. Aside from an occasional lurid melodrama like *Year of the Dragon*, Hollywood has largely avoided the subject, although Chinese organized crime has been around at least as long as the Mafia. When written about in newspapers and magazines—usually in connection with the latest gang shooting or robbery—the word most often used to describe Chinese or Vietnamese gangsters is "vicious," as if the wholesale plundering of labor unions, violent intimidation, and brutal gangland rubouts of yesteryear represented a more honorable form of criminal behavior.

The fact that hordes of reporters trudged daily to the Gotti court-room while, two floors away, the BTK trial unfolded in virtual anonymity was indicative of more than just a cultural bias. During the months of the BTK trial, four floors below Judge Amon's courtroom, the case against the Green Dragons was also unfolding, making the Eastern District courthouse perhaps the hottest crime beat in the United States. The argument could be made that, taken together, the Born to Kill and Green Dragons proceedings were more relevant to an understanding of crime in the 1990s than was the Gotti trial. The two trials were the end result of investigations that involved over forty gang members—a representative sampling of an entire generation of young Asian males. The charges against the nineteen defendants who chose to go to trial included eleven murders, numerous attempted murders, over a dozen robberies, numerous kidnappings, and countless extortionate acts, all of which took place during an intensely violent three-year period. Additionally, the victims of these crimes were not other gangsters, as they were in most traditional mob cases like Gotti's. The BTK and Green Dragons preyed mostly on innocent citizens whose only crime was that they were Asian and therefore susceptible to a group of gangsters who had always seemed to be beyond the reach of American law enforcement.

Not only that, but the BTK and Green Dragons were part of a larger criminal conspiracy currently in its prime—a complex, multilayered underworld with pockets of influence throughout the United States and much of the world. Domestically, they represented an aspect of contemporary organized crime that the media and the public have yet to fully acknowledge.

As the ethnic makeup of the country has changed, so has the face of organized crime. A new generation of immigrants has been following patterns of criminal activity remarkably similar to those first established by Irish, Italian, and Jewish immigrants. For an earlier generation of gangsters, bootleg liquor was the elixir that made it all possible. Today, it's illegal narcotics, though the country's vast, regionalized criminal marketplace has made it possible for organized crime groups to thrive in a number of ways, including the constant armed robberies, home invasions, violent extortions, and assorted other crimes from which most Vietnamese gangs derive their income.

287

The BTK trial and, to a lesser extent, the case against the Green Dragons, provided a rare opportunity for the media and the public to gain insights into the changing face of organized crime. Instead, the media clung exclusively and affectionately to a story that evoked a by-gone era—a time when the world, presumably, was a much simpler place.

Twelve months after the conviction of David Thai and his BTK brothers, the lack of attention paid to the Asian underworld was dramatically underscored once again. Early on the morning of June 7, 1993, a huge freighter ran aground off Rockaway Beach, in the outer reaches of New York City. Over the days and weeks that followed, the public was to find out about a massive, thriving criminal racket believed to be at least as profitable as wholesale cocaine and heroin smuggling.

More than three hundred illegal immigrants transported all the way from China were packed onto the freighter, known as the *Golden Venture*. After the ship accidentally buried its bow in a sandbar, many on board panicked. One hundred and twenty people jumped overboard into freezing, choppy waters. Ten met their death by drowning or later expired from hypothermia. Sixty more were plucked from the sea by helicopters and U.S. Coast Guard vessels. Throughout the day, a small army of city, state, and federal rescue personnel took the rest of the ship's massive human cargo into custody.

With dead bodies washing ashore and hundreds of starving, shivering travelers lining the beach, the story of the ill-fated *Golden Venture* was a tabloid editor's dream come true. Local and national media organizations assigned teams of reporters and photographers to cover the event. The media noted that the ship was actually one of dozens like it that had brought thousands of undocumented East Asians to the United States. The passengers aboard these ships paid on the average $30,000—sometimes as much as $50,000—to be smuggled into the country. Their passage halfway around the world was arranged and overseen by a vast criminal network, with the primary operatives being the Fuk Ching gang, based in New York City's Chinatown.

Esteemed media outlets like *The New York Times* and CNN presented their findings as if people-smuggling were a brand-new phenomenon, a criminal racket that had only now reached its apex with the terrible tragedy in the waters off Rockaway Beach. In fact, the trafficking of human cargo by Chinese gangsters had been flourishing for the last five or six years. In New York, untold thousands of immigrants had been smuggled into the city, most by circuitous routes through South and Central America. Once in the New York area, many paid off their huge smuggling debts by working at paltry wages in restaurants, sweatshops, and massage parlors while living in tiny cubicles. The end result was a type of indentured servitude as pernicious as anything that existed in Chinatown a century ago.

Although aspects of this modern-day slave trade had been sporadically reported, it had never been deemed a major story. Nearly two years before the *Golden Venture* spilled its human cargo, Ying Chan, a journalist with the *Daily News*, wrote a two-part exposé on Asian people-smuggling. Few media outlets followed up on her disturbing revelations. An international criminal conspiracy continued to flourish largely unnoticed by the American press, until three hundred smuggled immigrants washed ashore in the country's largest city, making the story impossible to ignore.

The same mentality that treated an international smuggling conspiracy based on the exploitation of Asians as if it were less newsworthy than, say, a mob war between rival Mafia families in Brooklyn, has helped make it possible for Chinese and Vietnamese gangs to continually regenerate. When speaking frankly, most federal agents and cops admit that their mandate as lawmen is all too often determined by what the media and, by extension, the public designate as a priority. Only recently, with the discovery of massive shipments of heroin being transported into the United States by Chinese syndicates, has the issue of Asian organized crime been labeled a significant national problem.

One federal agent determined to keep the subject on the front burner is Dan Kumor, who made a number of valuable community contacts through his six-month-long immersion into the world of the BTK. In December 1993, Kumor made the most of his newfound expertise. After a long investigation, he and other members of a joint ATF-NYPD task force arrested fifteen members of a gang known as the Tung On. The most notable of those charged on a multitude of federal RICO violations was none other than Paul Lai, adviser-for-life of the Tsung Tsin Association, one of Chinatown's most influential tongs.

Three years earlier, Paul Lai was among those who gathered at police headquarters during the unprecedented meeting among City Hall, the police, and community leaders to discuss the gang problem in Chinatown. At the meeting, Lai had been the first business leader to speak up; he condemned the rash of gang crimes then being perpetrated by the BTK. Lai claimed he was motivated by a desire to protect the image of the community. If the indictment filed by the U.S. government was accurate, Lai's real motivation was to apply political and police pressure to eliminate a vexing rival: the BTK.

The case against Paul Lai and other members of the Tung On gang was unique. In the past, many Chinatown gang members had been prosecuted at the state and federal levels. Since the mid-1980s, dozens of young gangsters had paid the price for their involvement in the underworld. Never, however, had an attempt been made to clearly establish a criminal link between a powerful tong boss—a "reputable" community elder—and the day-to-day operations of a Chinatown street gang.

The indictment alleged that Lai "relied on the gang's use of violence to maintain the prestige of the Tung On and Tsung Tsin Associations vis-à-vis other Chinatown business and criminal groups. . . . Among other things, gang members slept and held their secret initiation ceremonies in the Tung On Association, regularly met in both Associations to plan murders, assaults, firebombings and extortions, and provided security for an illegal gambling operation housed in the basement of the Tsung Tsin Association."

Of course, neighborhood merchants, the cops, and citizens in the know were well aware that Paul Lai's relationship with the Tung On gang was not atypical. Traditionally, the primary function of youth gangs in Chinatown has always been to do the dirty work for an older, so-called legitimate stratum of the business community. But no one had ever tried to prove it in court. The prosecution of Paul Lai had the potential to rock Chinatown to its foundations, to significantly alter the area's criminal hierarchy for the first time ever, perhaps changing irrevocably the way the local underworld conducts business.

As for Vietnamese gangsters in Chinatown and beyond, there was little doubt that the prosecution of David Thai and his minions had dealt a devastating blow to the single most notorious gang in their midst. Seven months after their conviction, the BTK gang members received the ultimate adjudication. Thai and his right-hand man, Lan Ngoc Tran, were given multiple life sentences without the possibility of parole. The others received slightly less harsh sentences ranging from twelve to sixty years.

In the end, perhaps the most significant result of the government's successful prosecution of the BTK was that David Thai had been stopped before he was able to fulfill his most ambitious schemes. *Anh hai* would never be able to further cultivate his relationship with "the Italians," as he had planned. And he would never again forge ties with the country's larger Vietnamese underworld, with the hope of one day establishing himself as the leader of a vast multistate network of young, wayward criminals.

That network, however—the less savory representatives of a lost generation of Vietnamese youth—remained relatively unaffected by the conviction of eighteen BTK gang members, who either copped a plea or were found guilty in court. The circumstances surrounding the creation of this underworld still exist as a gaping wound on the body politic, both in the United States and half a world away in the Republic of Vietnam. Despite improving diplomatic relations between the United States and its former arch-enemy, shell-shocked refugees continue to flee the Land of the Ascending Dragon. Once in America, they drift aimlessly, with few points of entry into a society that, historically, has rarely been receptive to "their kind."

Into the early months of 1994, merchants and citizens were still being victimized by young Vietnamese-born gangsters at an alarming rate. The International Association of Asian Crime Investigators bimonthly newsletter still contained information about criminal activity and violent fugitives from California, Texas, Virginia, Massachusetts, and other states. There is no way of knowing exactly how many gang members there are spread throughout the United States, but the IAACI estimates thousands—maybe tens of thousands.

For Dan Kumor and other lawmen who received a crash course in Asian organized crime through the first successful investigation of a major Vietnamese gang, the results were a wake-up call. In New York City and beyond, the parameters of a substantial new criminal phenomenon had been defined more clearly than ever before, and the results were sobering.

For those in law enforcement and elsewhere who cared to notice, the successful prosecution of the Born to Kill gang was not the end.

It was only the beginning.

Sources

The following is a partial list of books that contained information and insights that were helpful, if not instrumental, in the writing of *Born to Kill*.

Of the dozens of books published on the subject of the Vietnam War, Stanley Karnow's *Vietnam: A History* (New York: Viking Press, 1983) is still the most comprehensive. Neil Sheehan's *A Bright Shining Lie* (New York: Random House, 1988) provides unparalleled insights into the American military mind-set that created and sustained the war. Also helpful was *The Vietnam Wars: 1945–1990* (New York: HarperCollins, 1991) by Marilyn B. Young.

On the subject of life in Southeast Asia during the tumultuous years of the war, there are few testaments more moving than Haing Ngor's *A Cambodian Odyssey* (New York: Macmillan, 1987), which details the author's experiences in Cambodia during the horrendous reign of the Khmer Rouge. Le Ly Hayslip's *When Heaven and Earth Changed Place* (New York: Doubleday, 1989) is the autobiographical account of a woman's coming-of-age in Vietnam during some of the worst years of the war. John Balaban's *Remembering Heaven's Face* (New York: Poseidon Press, 1991) is a different kind of memoir, written by a poet and conscientious objector who lived in Saigon in the late 1960s and early 1970s.

On the subject of Vietnam in the years after the U.S. evacuation, two very different books were helpful: Duong Thu Huong's *Paradise of the Blind* (New York: William Morrow, 1993), a novel that beautifully evokes the colors, sounds, and textures of Vietnamese culture, and Neil Sheehan's *After the War Was Over* (New York: Random House, 1992), a telling examination of, among other things, the political failures of Vietnam's postwar government.

Not much has been published in the United States on the subject of the refugee camps, although *Ban Vinai: The Refugee Camp* (New York: Columbia University Press, 1993), by Lynellyn D. Long, is an excellent source of information, particularly on the camps in Thailand.

The Asian experience in America has been the subject of numerous books, including a poignant memoir by Nguyen Qui Duc titled *Where the Ashes Are: The Odyssey of a Vietnamese Family* (New York: Addison-Wesley, 1994). Ronald Takaki's *Strangers from a Different Shore: A History of Asian Americans* (New York: Little, Brown, 1989) provides an informative overview of Asian immigration. Le Ly Hayslip's *Child of War, Woman of Peace* (New York: Doubleday, 1993) continues where her first book left off by recounting the author's years as a Vietnamese refugee trying to adjust to life in America.

Two works of fiction by Robert Olen Butler were especially inspiring, both for their insights into the Vietnamese experience in America and the exquisite quality of the writing: *A Good Scent from a Strange Mountain* (New York: Henry Holt, 1992), a collection of short stories, each narrated in the voice of a different Vietnamese refugee living in the United States, and *The Deuce* (New York: Henry Holt, 1989), a fictional account of an Amerasian teenager living on the streets of New York City.

Considering that the Chinatowns of America have been around for more than a century, not many books have been published on the subject. However, two recent books—*The New Chinatown* (New York: Noonday Press, 1987), by Peter Kwong, and *Chinatown: Portrait of a Closed Society* (New York: HarperCollins, 1992), by Gwen Kinkead—

examine the social and historical forces that have shaped the "Gilded Ghetto."

The subject of Asian organized crime is one that will no doubt be receiving more attention in the years ahead. Of the books already published, Herbert Asbury's venerable *The Gangs of New York* (New York: Alfred A. Knopf, 1927) contains a chapter on Chinatown's early tong wars. Gerald Posner's *Warlords of Crime* (New York: McGraw-Hill, 1988) gives a broad overview of Asian organized crime, focusing mostly on the heroin trade. *Nightmare: Vietnamese Home Invasion Robberies* (Falls Church, Va.: International Association of Asian Crime Investigators, 1992), by Phil Hannum, is a case-by-case look at an especially brutal form of criminal activity. *Chinese Subculture and Criminality* (Westport, Conn.: Greenwood Press, 1990), by Kolin Chin, is a small gem—the most detailed study to date on the sprawling subject of triads, tongs, and Asian gang culture in the United States.

Index

298

ALSO BY T. J. ENGLISH

HAVANA NOCTURNE
How the Mob Owned Cuba . . .
and Then Lost It to the Revolution

ISBN 978-0-06-171274-6 (paperback)

Havana Nocturne takes readers back to Cuba in the years when it was a veritable devil's playground for mob leaders. English deftly weaves the parallel stories of the Havana Mob and Castro's 26th of July Movement in a riveting, up-close look at how the Mob nearly attained its biggest dream in Havana—and how Fidel Castro trumped it all with the Cuban Revolution.

"A whiz-bang account of the Mafia's short-lived romp through 1950s Cuba." —*New York Times Book Review*

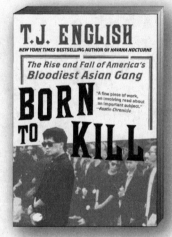

BORN TO KILL
The Rise and Fall of America's Bloodiest Asian Gang

ISBN 978-0-06-178238-1 (paperback)

T.J. English chronicles Vietnam war refugees who laid the foundation for a terrifying underworld of violence and power in 1980s New York City.

"A must for anyone interested in the emerging multiethnic face of organized crime in the United States."
—*Washington Post Book World*

PADDY WHACKED
The Untold Story of the Irish American Gangster

ISBN 978-0-06-059003-1 (paperback)

Bestselling author and organized crime expert T. J. English brings to life nearly two centuries of Irish American gangsterism. Stretching from the earliest New York and New Orleans street wars through decades of bootlegging scams, union strikes, gang wars, and FBI investigations, *Paddy Whacked* is a riveting tour de force that restores the Irish American gangster to his rightful preeminent place in our criminal history—and penetrates to the heart of the American experience.